Turning Points
IN WORLD HISTORY

The Rise of Communism

Robert J. Sims Jr., *Book Editor*

Daniel Leone, *President*
Bonnie Szumski, *Publisher*
Scott Barbour, *Managing Editor*
David M. Haugen, *Series Editor*

GREENHAVEN
PRESS®

THOMSON
™
GALE

San Diego • Detroit • New York • San Francisco • Cleveland
New Haven, Conn. • Waterville, Maine • London • Munich

THOMSON

GALE

LIBRARY OF CONGRESS CATALOGING-IN-PUBLICATION DATA

The rise of communism / Robert J. Sims Jr., book editor.
   p. cm. — (Turning points in world history)
Includes bibliographical references and index.
ISBN 0-7377-1295-3 (pbk. : alk. paper) — ISBN 0-7377-1294-5 (lib. : alk. paper)
   1. Communism—History—20th century. I. Sims, Robert (Robert J.), Jr. II. Turning points in world history (Greenhaven Press)
HX40.R547 2004
335.43—dc21
                                            2003055272

Contents

and brought a fractured Communist movement together by uniting nationalists and Communists.

Foreword

Certain past events stand out as pivotal, as having effects and outcomes that change the course of history. These events are often referred to as turning points. Historian Louis L. Snyder provides this useful definition:

> A turning point in history is an event, happening, or stage which thrusts the course of historical development into a different direction. By definition a turning point is a great event, but it is even more—a great event with the explosive impact of altering the trend of man's life on the planet.

History's turning points have taken many forms. Some were single, brief, and shattering events with immediate and obvious impact. The invasion of Britain by William the Conqueror in 1066, for example, swiftly transformed that land's political and social institutions and paved the way for the rise of the modern English nation. By contrast, other single events were deemed of minor significance when they occurred, only later recognized as turning points. The assassination of a little-known European nobleman, Archduke Franz Ferdinand, on June 28, 1914, in the Bosnian town of Sarajevo was such an event; only after it touched off a chain reaction of political-military crises that escalated into the global conflict known as World War I did the murder's true significance become evident.

Other crucial turning points occurred not in terms of a few hours, days, months, or even years, but instead as evolutionary developments spanning decades or even centuries. One of the most pivotal turning points in human history, for instance—the development of agriculture, which replaced nomadic hunter-gatherer societies with more permanent settlements—occurred over the course of many generations. Still other great turning points were neither events nor developments, but rather revolutionary new inventions and innovations that significantly altered social customs and ideas, military tactics, home life, the spread of knowledge, and the human condition in general. The developments of writing, gunpowder, the printing press, antibiotics, the electric light, atomic energy, television, and the computer, the last two of which have recently ushered in the world-altering information age, represent only some of these innovative turning points.

Each anthology in the Greenhaven Turning Points in World History series presents a group of essays chosen for their accessibility. The anthology's structure also enhances this accessibility. First, an introductory essay provides a general overview of the principal events and figures involved, placing the topic in its historical context. The essays that follow explore various aspects in more detail, some targeting political trends and consequences, others social, literary, cultural, and/or technological ramifications, and still others pivotal leaders and other influential figures. To aid the reader in choosing the material of immediate interest or need, each essay is introduced by a concise summary of the contributing writer's main themes and insights.

In addition, each volume contains extensive research tools, including a collection of excerpts from primary source documents pertaining to the historical events and figures under discussion. In the anthology on the French Revolution, for example, readers can examine the works of Rousseau, Voltaire, and other writers and thinkers whose championing of human rights helped fuel the French people's growing desire for liberty; the French *Declaration of the Rights of Man and Citizen*, presented to King Louis XVI by the French National Assembly on October 2, 1789; and eyewitness accounts of the attack on the royal palace and the horrors of the Reign of Terror. To guide students interested in pursuing further research on the subject, each volume features an extensive bibliography, which for easy access has been divided into separate sections by topic. Finally, a comprehensive index allows readers to scan and locate content efficiently. Each of the anthologies in the Greenhaven Turning Points in World History series provides students with a complete, detailed, and enlightening examination of a crucial historical watershed.

Introduction: The Rise and Spread of Communism

Communism is a political philosophy that advocates state control of the means of production and the equal distribution of wealth among the people. It is a philosophy that is meant to stand in stark contrast to the free-market capitalism of the West, in which the fortunes of nations are seemingly guided by those with the greatest wealth.

Communism is more than a political philosophy, it is a dogma, an ideology that comes near to a religion.

Loyal, steadfast Communists adhere to the faith put forth by Karl Marx, which is that the worldwide Communist revolution is inevitable. To Communists, political structure is just an extension of human evolution, and therefore as society evolves, so too will political interests abandon outdated capitalism in favor of the more advanced communism.

Marx's Communism

Karl Marx, one of the founders of communism, was a German economist and Socialist writer from England. Marx and Friedrich Engels, his colleague, collaborated to produce *The Communist Manifesto* that was published in 1848. The *Manifesto* calls for the workers of the world to unite and overthrow the capitalist system that had entrusted power to the hands of the wealthy and tied workers to a life of subservience.

Marx was not alone in his critique of capitalism. As the Industrial Revolution took off in Western Europe, a wide gap began to develop between the rich and the poor in the 1800s. Many reform-minded citizens began to search for new and progressive ways to structure society and more evenly distribute the wealth achieved by industrialization. Many of these people were labeled "socialists" because they believed that the means of production should be owned by the people who toiled in the factories and mines, not by those who simply had the initial capital to start the industries.

Karl Marx was one of the concerned socialist thinkers. He was disturbed with both the poverty and the social injustice which were visible all around him. His radical ideas were sparked by the Industrial Revolution's impact on England in the mid-1800s. To Marx, the rapid growth threw British society into chaos and confusion. It produced a society of haves and have nots. Laborers worked for low wages in mines and factories, while the owners (who did not share in the physical toil) reaped the tremendous profits of production. And with an ever-expanding labor pool, the owners had no need to increase wages or attend to worker complaints.

Factory workers labored for excessive hours under harsh and squalid conditions. Many families were forced to put their children to work and forego education. As a young journalist, Marx viewed the plight and misery of the industrial worker firsthand. He recognized that with no voice to counter the decisions of the capitalists, the workers were doomed to perpetual servitude, and the state was fated to be built upon economic inequality.

Marx saw the capitalist as the source of social and economic injustice. He urged the workers to rise up and throw away the chains of oppression. To succeed, the workers would need to overthrow the system, take the reigns of government, and appropriate the means of production. He believed that the working class, or the proletariat, could, if united, achieve vicinity and stop capitalism in its tracks. For although the capitalists had various means of persuasion from wages to brute force to keep workers at their jobs, the industrialists did depend on the service of the workers. Without the proletariat, the capitalist machine would stall.

The Worldwide Revolution

Karl Marx's revolutionary philosophy was not simply a cry to the English proletariat to seize the means of production and establish a workers paradise for themselves. It was much more extensive. Marx understood society and politics as an evolutionary process, of which capitalism was an intermediary stage and communism its ultimate perfection. He predicted that the success of communism in one nation would eventually lead to worldwide revolution. This would not happen all at once. Instead, for Marx, communism would spread throughout the world slowly.

Its origin would be the industrial powers of Western Europe (France, Germany, England); the revolution would then move through the less-developed nations of Europe and Asia, until at last communism was globally dominant.

Marx expected that capitalism would unravel, that it would crumble under its own weight because the pillars of capitalism were unstable. Marx believed that the outmoded system would suffer from a string of economic downturns or depressions. He predicted that as the wealth of society became concentrated in fewer and fewer hands, the huge mass of workers would rise up against these plutocrats and uproot the system of profit and capital. The capitalist system would be replaced with a proletarian dictatorship, whereby "the State" would eventually fade away and communism would reign supreme.

Marx was known as an energetic man who was full of conviction. He argued vigorously with his more moderate contemporaries such as the Social Democrats. The Social Democrats wanted to establish a more egalitarian society within the framework of the capitalist system. They believed that they could turn the capitalist state from a tool of class oppression to an economic force that worked for the people and provided needed social services.

Marx on the other hand, was quite adamant that the state in the capitalist system was nothing more than a coercive political entity that only served the purposes of the ruling class. He saw the destruction of the present conception of "the State" as the only way to achieve a classless society.

The Revolution Begins in Russia

Marx's prediction that the proletariat revolution would emerge from the industrial powers of Western Europe would prove inaccurate. Instead, toward the end of the nineteenth century, Marxist thought was gaining momentum in imperial Russia, a primarily agrarian nation.

In Russia, Marxist rumblings were a reaction to the oppressive czarist regime which catered to the propertied classes. At the turn of the century Russia was an unstable nation. The autocratic regime ignored the wishes of the working people in favor of the ruling class. The result was an alienated and exploited working class. This led to strikes, demonstrations, and worker uprisings in 1905, and constitutional reform in 1906.

These reforms did little to stem discontent. Radical peasant and worker organizations had already blossomed, and to the disaffected, any reforms were viewed as ineffectual and highly suspect. A workers movement had already been established and it could not be placated.

Forming the First Socialist State

Russia was ripe for revolution at the turn of the century, but progressives were often split on how the revolution should be carried out. The Russian Social Democrats were split ideologically between Vladimir Lenin and his followers, the Bolsheviks (majority), who called for direct action against the government and all power to the Soviets (workers councils); and the Mensheviks (minority), who accepted more gradual changes such as wage increases and shortened working hours.

Lenin and the War

Vladimir Lenin was a dedicated disciple of Marx. He took Marx's philosophy and turned it into a program for political action. He believed that the working classes would never rise up and overthrow the autocratic regime on their own. Unlike Marx, Lenin believed that the working classes needed a vanguard of professional revolutionaries to lead the revolution.

By the advent of World War I in 1914, the Bolsheviks and Mensheviks were divided on which stand they should take in relation to the war against Germany and its Central Powers allies. Lenin opposed the war. He believed the war was a capitalist venture started by the European upper class but fought by the poor and powerless. Lenin and his followers were indifferent as to who won the international war, as it would not change the conditions for European workers.

The Russian Revolution

The radical Socialist groups, however, were united in their hatred of the czarist regime, headed by Nicholas II. During the war, the balance of power in Russia was shifting in favor of the proletariat, but Czar Nicholas still controlled the army, and the unarmed workers could not hope to rise up against that kind of force. But the czar's power weakened over time. More people began to lose their patience in the cold and harsh winter of 1917, and the capital of Petrograd quickly slipped into chaos as famine spread.

Workers were marching and demonstrating in the streets, the Russian women were forced to wait in long lines for bread, and the soldiers (many formerly peasants) were sympathetic to the people and the hardships they were facing. Nicholas II was assured by his generals that everything was under control, but food shortages in Petrograd fomented riots, and the military could not contain the populace for long. The possibility of a popular revolt loomed on the horizon.

The February uprising was a popular revolution which started from the bottom up. It was a peoples uprising assisted by a soldier mutiny. The popular revolution began on February 26, as the starving citizens of Petrograd crowded Znamenskii Square for a political rally in opposition to the Czarist regime. A regiment of Russian troops fired upon the crowd of demonstrators, killing close to sixty people and injuring many more. The Petrograd garrison abhorred the killing, and one by one the units of soldiers turned their backs to the government and joined the civilian population in their rioting. With the majority of the military garrison in mutiny, the czar could not contain the crowds.

In the end, it was not the people who forced Czar Nicholas to step down but his own generals and the ruling elite. They felt that placating the rioters would be the best route in which to regain control of Russia. It was a severe miscalculation. When the czar was forced to abdicate on March 15, 1917, three hundred years of Romanov rule ended, and the empire collapsed right along with it. The revolutionaries had taken the capital, and the Duma (Russian parliament) took emergency steps to form a provisional government, still made up of landowners and other nobility, to fill the power vacuum. The workers parties also sponsored their own governmental office, the Petrograd Soviet, to see that workers' complaints were addressed.

Red October

The provisional government attempted to pacify the growing discontent among the Russian people, while continuing to cater to the propertied classes. The workers and peasants quickly lost faith that this ruling body could deliver on the hopes and promises of the revolution. The provisional government, for example, failed to establish needed land reform and the economy continued to falter. The Petrograd Soviet, torn by conflicting ideology within its Socialist parties, was powerless. Most of its moderate members, in fact, had thrown their lot in with the provisional government in hopes of achieving some type of reform.

As Russia was moving into chaos and the workers and peasants refused to listen to authority, the Russian people were ready for a political will which would deliver on the reforms that were promised them.

Lenin had hurried home from exile in Zurich, Switzerland, where he had been writing letters demanding that the Petrograd Soviet bring down the provisional government. Bolshevik leader Leon Trotsky joined him soon after, arriving from New York. Lenin and the Bolsheviks promised land, peace, and bread, which was exactly what the people were looking for.

The Bolsheviks, once a small Socialist organization, were gaining momentum with their clear and concise vision. The Mensheviks and Social Revolutionaries had lost all credibility after their dealings with the provisional government. The people turned to the Bolsheviks for a solution to the crisis.

Lenin planned and executed an armed uprising against the provisional government and took control of all state institutions. Once he was in power, Lenin immediately called for land reform, moved the capital from Petrograd to Moscow, and made a treaty with the Central Powers that withdrew Russia from the war.

The First Socialist State

The bold maneuvering of the Bolsheviks helped establish the first Socialist state in the history of the world. It would be Russia that would start the worldwide Socialist revolution. Great challenges lay ahead for the neophyte Socialist state. In the wake of the Bolshevik takeover, civil war had commenced between the Red Army (Communists) and the White Army (a counterrevolutionary movement supported by outside Allied forces) in December 1917. The Red Army won the civil war under the leadership of Trotsky, but the nation now found itself in a series of crises. Industry was nonexistent, disease spread quickly, and starvation had settled into the countryside.

The Communists looked to jump-start the nation through a rigid program of increasing industrial output and developing large farming collectives among the peasantry. The Comintern (Third International) was started in 1919. Founded in Moscow, the Comintern was designed as an international organization whose goal was to set the course for the world revolution and spread communism across Soviet borders.

Soviet Dominion

Lenin suffered a series of debilitating strokes and died in 1924. Joseph Stalin ousted Trotsky as his main competition for power and took over as the new Soviet leader. He managed to advance Russia both economically and industrially. His totalitarian regime converted rural backward Russia into an international industrial superpower. The price of progress was great, as many Russians suffered through forced collectivization and labor camps. Although Russia advanced meteorically, millions died in state servitude or due to Stalin's purges of dissidents.

The Soviet Union suffered through and emerged from World War II as a powerful and industrially advanced nation. By war's end in August 1945, Soviet dictator Joseph Stalin began a campaign to establish Soviet dominion over most, if not all, of Europe. The Soviet Red Army, which had pushed Nazi German forces out of most of Eastern Europe, set up puppet governments in the nations it overwhelmed. The Soviets established Communist systems in Hungary, Romania, Bulgaria, Albania, Poland, Czechoslovakia, and East Germany.

The Soviets liberated these nations from fascism, but at the same time these Communist revolutions were choreographed from the top down. The new Communist regimes did not derive from the people of these Eastern European nations but from Moscow. These liberated nations, now fully occupied by the Red Army, became buffer zones between the West and the Soviet homeland.

Communist Deviation

The Soviet satellite nations followed the hard-line Soviet policy under Moscow's directive and Stalin's iron fist. According to Soviet leadership, this was in line with the Marxist-Leninist prediction of a worldwide Socialist revolution. But the conquered were not always adherent to the worldwide revolution. Certain nations in Eastern Europe, such as Yugoslavia and Czechoslovakia, deviated from the Soviet plan. Czechoslovakia had a history of liberal and democratic institutions, and its people did not welcome a new regime. It became a democratic nation with Communist officials in office. Czechoslovakia operated as a model of democratic socialism up until 1948. A fear that they were losing popularity among the Czech people forced the Czech Communists to stage a coup in a desperate attempt to hold onto their power. The nation slipped into a totalitarian regime and fell squarely under the Soviet curtain.

The Communist Party in Yugoslavia had grown significantly at the close of World War II, and Tito (Josip Broz) became its leader. Tito had established his own brand of communism in Yugoslavia, much to the chagrin of Soviet leader Joseph Stalin. The division which formed between Tito and Stalin began in 1947, when Tito participated in meetings discussing the formation of a Balkan federation, a union of Balkan nations that would be free of Soviet influence.

Stalin saw this as a renegade maneuver. The Soviet leader accused Tito of everything from being too independent to following the Soviet model too closely. The reality was that Yugoslavia was a well-respected Socialist nation among the international community. It was a workers state without the oppressive and totalitarian abuses that were characteristic of the Soviet Union. The Yugoslavian people resisted any gravitational forces attempting to carry them into the sphere of Soviet domination. The Yugoslav people were fiercely nationalistic. Although they looked to Russia as a leader in the master plan for worldwide socialism, they did not want to be trapped under the economic constraints of Moscow. In 1948 Stalin expelled Yugoslavia from the international Socialist movement.

Nationalism, Communism, and Anticolonialism

While Eastern Europe was gobbled up by the Soviet Union after World War II, communism spread to Asia without the aid of Soviet military. Asian nations such as China, Korea, and Vietnam suffered under Japanese occupation during the war, so liberation had invited thought of rebuilding and beginning anew. Yet many of the smaller Southeast Asian nations were under colonial control by major European powers. Some of these colonized nations believed that their assistance to the Allied war effort would prompt the Europeans to grant independence. It was not to be, so many Southeast Asian leaders turned to Communism—and Soviet assistance—to combat the imperialism of the West.

The Sino-Soviet Pact

China was not one of the many European colonies, but its wartime government had fairly strong ties to the West. Up until 1924, the Nationalist government had been run by Sun Yat-sen, the leader of the Kuomintang. Sun lacked the power to control China, however. He did not have the support of the army, and the people owed allegiance to local warlords, not some distant central government. Sun looked to the Soviet Union for help. The Soviets lent assistance, and soon the Nationalist fervor of the Kuomintang gained a great following. Although various warlords still held power. The Chinese people turned their frustrations upon foreign influences and imperialist culture of the West.

The deaths of Sun Yat-sen and Lenin in 1924 broke the Sino-Soviet alliance in half. Military leader Chiang Kai-shek staged a coup, took China for himself, and broke off relations with Moscow. He redrafted the Nationalist cause to oust the Communists who had gained a foothold in government.

Moscow ordered the Communists in China to spark a workers revolt in the major port cities. Moscow figured that Chiang would be so busy fighting warlords en route to dominating all of China that he would ignore a workers' uprising. The Soviets were mistaken. They failed to realize the workers' loyalty to the Nationalist Kuomintang movement. The Communist forces were badly defeated and forced to scatter.

The Rise of Mao

The Chinese Communist Central Committee looked to a young and dedicated revolutionary named Mao Tse-tung for leadership. Mao was the son of a moderately wealthy peasant from the Hunan province of China. He worked his way through teaching college, served a tour of duty with the revolutionary army, and ended up in Peking as a librarian's assistant.

Mao gladly offered assistance to the Central Committee. He had committed himself to organizing the peasantry in the Hunan province around 1926. He saw potential in the peasantry to set off a Communist revolution without the assistance of the proletariat, which made up a minute portion of the Chinese population.

His theory conflicted with the hard-line Marxist-Leninist dogma, which stipulated that the revolution must be carried out by the industrial workers. Mao's faith in the peasantry was unorthodox and in turn set him apart from the rest. He was initially ignored by both Moscow and the Chinese Central Committee alike. That is, until Chiang routed the Communist forces, and new leadership was needed.

Mao built up an impressive guerrilla force which took refuge in the mountains of Hunan. Chiang launched a major offensive against Mao, whose forces continued to grow rapidly, to eliminate the Communists once and for all. This offensive sent Mao and his guerrilla army on an epic retreat across the vast and rugged countryside. Mao lost many soldiers in what is now known as the "Long March." Although

Mao's loyal cadre diminished, the hardships formed a tight bond between those who remained.

While Chiang enjoyed dominance of China in the 1930s, the coming of World War II would change things. The Japanese invaded much of China, and Chiang was sent into exile. The nationalists fought the Japanese with Allied aid, but by the end of the war, anti-imperialist feelings ran high. Chiang, who had come to rely on the West, watched as the Kuomintang lost power. The Communists, who had been slowly gathering strength during the war, brushed aside the remnants of the nationalists and forced Chiang's government to relocate to Taiwan. On October 1, 1949, Mao Tse-tung and the Chinese Communists declared victory over the Kuomintang army. The People's Republic of China was born and Mao accepted the mantle of leadership.

The Korean Communist Movement

Unlike the Chinese Communists, other Asian Socialist organizations had to throw off the yoke of colonialism before battling anti-Communist sentiment among their own people. In 1919 U.S. president Woodrow Wilson made a speech in Versailles, France, espousing the right of self-determination for all nations. His speech was directed toward Western Europe, but many Korean and Vietnamese nationalists such as Yi Tong-hwi and Ho Chi Minh found inspiration in the speech in their fight for independence from Japanese imperialism and Western exploitation.

A famine and the Japanese annexation of Korea in 1910 sparked a mass exodus of Koreans to Russia and China. In Russia, the Koreans witnessed the Russian Revolution first-hand. Although many of the exiles remained neutral when the Bolsheviks seized power in 1917, some like Yi Tong-hwi, a former Korean military officer, sided with the Bolshevik cause. In turn the Bolsheviks were more than happy to give Yi economic and moral support if he chose to export the Bolshevik ideology to Korea. Yi agreed.

Yi was able to capitalize on the strong nationalistic and anticolonial atmosphere among the Korean exiles, but Yi faced strong resistance from rival Korean Communist factions in

Russia who were battling for Comintern funds. In a protracted struggle, Yi won out and brought communism back to Korea. There, he used it as a tool to solidify nationalist feeling against Japanese occupation. Still, many Korean nationalists wanted nothing to do with communism, and even those who did could not overthrow the Japanese. When World War II brought Western support to the nation, the definition of nationalism was tested and the people divided. North Korea came to be dominated by the Communists and South Korea embraced democracy. A young Korean militant named Kim Il Sung (formerly Kim Song-ju) who had served in the Soviet Red Army and had close ties to Moscow and the Soviet Union, became head of the North Korean Communist Party in 1946. Kim then managed to shed his opposition and become the prime minister of the Korean People's Democratic Republic in 1948. He ruled Korea with an iron fist, and turned himself into a cult hero through Soviet-style propaganda and brute terror.

Communism in Vietnam

Vietnam also suffered from Japanese aggression and French occupation during the colonial period. Ho Chi Minh, a fierce patriot and disciple of Lenin, brought many young nationalist Vietnamese to China to be indoctrinated in Communist ideology. These young nationalists were asked to renounce their parties and unite under the Communist banner. Those who did remained in China, and those who did not, were promptly arrested by the French upon their return as suspected Communist sympathizers. Ho Chi Minh organized his loyal cadre into the Young Revolutionary Youth League (Thanh Nien) in 1925. The Thanh Nien was to be the spark that would eventually ignite Communist revolution in Vietnam. But the organization, made up of adherents to several brands of socialist thought, was not yet an effectual and united force.

Ho Chi Minh was born in 1890 in a rural province of northern Vietnam. He rubbed shoulders with nationalists while growing up and was determined to gain independence for Vietnam. In 1917 he journeyed to France. While there, he gained the attention of many left-wing Socialists and became deeply influenced by Lenin's philosophy and his critique of colonialism.

Ho was deeply impressed by Lenin's passion for Russia and his patriotic spirit. Ho Chi Minh spent some years studying Marxist-Leninist principles in Moscow before ending up in Canton, China, where he gained a loyal following of Vietnamese exiles.

The Comintern directed Ho to unite the Vietnamese Communists into a tight and disciplined organization. Ho Chi Minh unified the fractured Thanh Nien at a Hong Kong sports arena in 1929. The Thanh Nien then became the Vietnamese Communist Party, which infiltrated Vietnam and fought two successful wars against the French and then the United States.

Western Frontier

The influence of the Soviet Union and communism during the first half of the twentieth century was limited to Eastern Europe and Asia. The Communists had tried to gain a foothold in Latin America for many years, but they suffered from division and strife. Some progressive groups looked to follow the lead of the Bolsheviks and follow the line of the Comintern, while others refused to accept Soviet-style communism because it was not attuned with the political situation in Central and South America.

Communists also continued to teeter-totter in their popularity all along the South American continent. During World War II, the Communists were extremely unpopular when they supported fascist Germany, and then they fell back in favor when they joined the Allied cause. After the war, the Socialists fell back out of favor when the Soviets espoused rigid anti-Americanism as part of Communist doctrine.

The Cuban Insurrection

Cuba was the first Communist government established in the West. The Communist regime was founded without Soviet assistance, but the leaders of the revolution were influenced by Marx and Lenin.

Cuba had long been one of the most prosperous nations

in Latin America, both economically and socially. That had all changed by the late 1950s, as Cuba's overdependence on its sugar industry combined with Fulgencio Batista's oppressive regime contributed to Cuba's downfall and eventual overthrow by the Communists.

The insurrection was led by a young and bold revolutionary named Fidel Castro. Castro was a young lawyer who became disillusioned with the political system and responded by launching an attack on a set of military barracks in 1953. The coup was a failure, Castro ended up in jail until 1955 and was then exiled to Mexico. Still, the Communists fought a guerrilla war against Batista and kept Cuba in a state of civil war.

The Mythical Voyage

In November 1956 Fidel Castro and a small group of Castro's disciples set off from Mexico on a small boat named the *Granma* and landed in Cuba. The radical cadre suffered debilitating losses against Batista's army. Castro and those who survived retreated into the Sierra Maestra. There, Castro and his men soon gained a strong peasant following, and Castro pushed his men to achieve their full fighting potential. It was the will, morale, and Castro's charisma that allowed the guerrilla forces to overthrow Batista and his dictatorial regime.

Castro came to power in 1959, and he set off to establish radical and broad reforms in order to make good on the promises he made to the peasantry. Castro's charisma allowed him to win the hearts of the Cuban people and his daring and boldness instilled fear in the hearts of his enemies. He nationalized most of the industry on the island, including the sugar industry, and proceeded to confiscate American holdings. Castro moved ever closer to Marxist ideology and established close ties with the Soviet Union.

From that point onward, the United States, long the archrival of communism, had an ideological enemy within fifty miles of its shoreline. The United States and the rest of the world had witnessed the success of communism. As the Soviet Union and its allies squared off against America and the West, only time would tell if Marx's prediction of a worldwide revolution would come true.

Chapter 1

The Founders of Communism

Turning | Points
IN WORLD HISTORY

Karl Marx Viewed the State as a Tool of the Ruling Class

George Douglas Howard Cole

Socialist theorist Karl Marx viewed the "state" (the political, military, and economic forces that regulated the lives
of a nation's citizens) as a coercive political entity that only
served the purposes of the ruling class. He rejected the
view of his more moderate contemporaries, such as the
Social Democrats, who believed that Socialist ideals could
be achieved through evolutionary means, by shaping the
progress of the state from a tool of class coercion to a
provider of social services without destroying its capitalist
base. This moderate agenda that hoped to salvage the economic fruits of capitalism was put forth, for example, by
the German Socialists in their Gotha Programme of 1875.

In the following viewpoint, George Douglas Howard
Cole (1888–1959), an English economist, restates Marx's
argument that a Socialist state can only be achieved
through a Communist program that would demolish the
capitalist state. Marx envisioned a complete overhaul of
the major social institutions, such as the legislature, the
police, the judiciary, and the military force. A new state
would emerge in the image of the proletariat, which
would then serve the needs of the working class.

One of Marx's most famous phrases is his characterisation of
the modern State. "The executive of the modern State," he
and [Friedrich] Engels wrote in the *Communist Manifesto*, "is
but a committee for managing the common affairs of the
bourgeoisie [middle-class property owners] as a whole." In
these words Marx characterised the modern State as essen-

George Douglas Howard Cole, *What Marx Really Meant*. Westport, CT: Greenwood Press, 1970. Copyright © 1934 by Alfred A. Knopf, Inc. Renewed 1962 by
Margaret Isabel Cole. Reproduced by permission of the publisher.

tially an organ of class-dictatorship.

Later on in the *Communist Manifesto*, Marx and Engels set out to define the policy of the proletariat [laboring class] towards the *bourgeois* State. "The first step in the working-class revolution," they wrote, "is to raise the proletariat to the position of ruling class, to win the battle of democracy." They add that "the proletariat will use its political supremacy to wrest, by degrees, all capital from the *bourgeoisie*, and to centralise all instruments of production in the hands of the State, i.e. of the proletariat organised as the ruling class."

Much later, in 1875, Marx wrote in his criticism of the Gotha Programme[1] of the German Socialists a passage which further clarifies his meaning. "Between Capitalist and communist society lies a period of revolutionary transformation from the one to the other. To this also corresponds a political period of transition during which the State can be nothing else than the revolutionary dictatorship of the proletariat."

There are two important points to notice in these passages. First, in the contrast which they draw between the two types of State, *bourgeois* and proletarian, each is regarded as embodying the rule, or dictatorship, of a particular class which is the holder of political power. There is not, in Marx's idea, any such thing as a classless State, or any State which is not the embodiment of the ruling authority of a particular class. This is made abundantly plain in Marx's criticism of the Gotha Programme. . . .

Marx Envisioned the Overthrow of the State

Secondly, Marx clearly envisages a period of transition from Capitalism to Socialism or Communism, during which there will exist a new form of State, based on the authority of the proletariat. This State will be, not the *bourgeois* State simply "captured" by the proletariat and applied to the ends of the proletarian Revolution, but an essentially new State made by the proletariat to serve its own revolutionary purpose. But

---

1. At the Gotha Congress in May 1875, two of Germany's worker parties united to form the Socialist Labor Party of Germany [Social Democrats]. Their political agenda involved the gradual evolution of the State toward Socialism without the destruction of its capitalist base.

the proletarian State will not be lasting; for the object of the proletarian Revolution is to abolish classes and institute a classless Society. When this has been done there can be no room for any State at all. The State, which is by Marx's definition an organ of class-domination, obviously cannot remain in being in a Society wherein all class-distinctions have ceased to exist. In such a Society there will be no need or room for a State, in Marx's sense of the word. For no organ will be needed to keep one class in subjection to another. Government will endure no longer: there will be left only the problem of administration. In a familiar phrase, "the government of men will give place to the administration of things."

It is, of course, above all on this part of Marxist doctrine that modern Communism has been built up. Lenin's *The State and Revolution* is in essence a simple amplification of this view. At this point the divergence between the Social Democratic and Communist interpretations of Marxism is widest; and round it centred the bitter controversy between Lenin and [moderate socialist thinker and editor Karl Johann] Kautsky as the outstanding theorists of the rival schools. In this controversy, there can be not the smallest doubt which side can rightly claim to be "orthodox," in the sense of basing itself firmly upon the writings of the master. Marx's conception of the State and of the transition is utterly plain and unequivocal. There is not the smallest question about his own view. Lenin, and not Kautsky, says what Marx said. Kautsky was only continuing to say what the German Social Democrats so angered Marx by saying in the Gotha Programme of 1875. For Kautsky, and the Social Democrats as a party, had come to think in terms of the capture and democratisation of the capitalist State and not, like Marx, in terms of its overthrow and destruction.

This, of course, does not settle the question whether Marx was right or wrong; for we are not accepting the view that anything Marx said or held must of necessity be right. But it is well to be clear before we approach the discussion of the merits of the case that, despite all the casuistry [excessively subtle reasoning] that has been used in trying to represent Marx as holding a different view, there is no uncertainty at all about his own words, either in 1848 or, much later, in 1875. On this issue, Marx was unquestionably a Communist, and not a Social Democrat. . . .

Government Is an Instrument of the Ruling Class

Whereas other thinkers dwell mainly upon the existence of representative institutions, the extent of the franchise, the growth of the modern State as an instrument for the provision of common services, the Marxists think of it chiefly as a set of institutions for the maintenance of the capitalist system of property-holding, the punishment of subverters of the established order, and the coercion of the proletariat to labour in the service of the capitalist class. The law courts, the police, and the armed forces loom as large as the legislative body in this conception of the State; and the legislative body itself—King, Lords and Commons, or whatever it may be—is thought of less as an authority for the passing of fresh legislation than as the authority under whose auspices the existing body of legislation has been enacted, to serve as the instrument of the existing dominant class. Emphasis is therefore laid rather on those features of the legislative machine which check or prevent radical legislation—the powers of the Second Chamber [the parliamentary house made up of the Lords], and the Royal Prerogative [the King's veto power]—than on those which make possible the introduction of changes into the existing system of law.

This does not mean that Marx or his followers deny the possibility of securing progressive legislation from the capitalist State. On the contrary, Marx was well aware of the growth of such legislation; and all the programmes of the bodies which he led or inspired were full of demands for more. He believed it to be entirely possible to bring pressure to bear upon the capitalist State, and to secure social legislation by this method, at any rate at the stage of a Capitalism still advancing in wealth and prosperity. He believed, further, that the struggle for such measures of social amelioration formed, at that stage, a vital part of the training of the proletariat in solidarity and class-consciousness. But he did not believe that the cumulative effect of measures of this sort could be a change of system, or that such methods could be employed for the attainment of Socialism, or to any extent inconsistent with the maintenance of Capitalism as a working system. For such ends as the establishment of a new social order he believed an utterly different method to be required.

Revolution Through Proletarian Dictatorship

This method was revolution, involving the complete destruction of the capitalist State, and the substitution for it of a quite different type of State made by the workers in the image of their own needs, as the instrument of a proletarian dictatorship. The establishment of this new State would involve not only the setting up of a totally new legislative authority, resting directly on the organised economic power of the working class, but also the establishment of a new proletarian judiciary and code of law, a new proletarian police and military force, a new proletarian Civil Service, both national and local—all under the authority of a proletarian party organised as a new governing class. It was equally inconceivable to Marx that the Socialists should attempt to govern, after their victory, through a Parliament of the *bourgeois* type, and that they should leave the old judiciary in possession, or the armed forces and the police under their old leaders. He envisaged, at the very out-set of the Revolution, the complete smashing and putting out of action of all the coercive machinery of the capitalist State, and the setting up in its place of a wholly new organisation, conceived throughout in accordance with the needs and interests of the proletariat organised as a ruling class. . . .

The Social Democrats, for their part, were looking at the State in a quite different way. They thought they saw it in process of being transformed gradually from an engine of class-coercion into an institution for social service—a grand Cooperative Society of all its citizens. They thought of the widening of the franchise, up to the final establishment of universal suffrage, as making the State an essentially democratic body, within which the anti-democratic powers of Crown and Second Chamber would not be able to stand out long against the popular will, and law courts, police, and armed forces would become, by a process of evolution, the loyal servants of a triumphant democracy. The first step was to give the people the vote; the second was to educate the people to use the vote aright; the third was to institute Socialism by a series of evolutionary changes under the sanction of the popular will.

Marx utterly rejected this conception. To his mind, there was, and could be under Capitalism, no such thing as "the people," which he regarded as a mere figment of the *petit bourgeois* imagination. There were classes, contending for power, exploiting and exploited; but there could be no "people," because social solidarity could not exist within the framework of a capitalist society. If the Socialists came to believe in the figment of "the people," and to base their electoral policy on an appeal to "the people," that would be the end of their chance of getting Socialism; for it would cause them to dilute their programme in order to win this mythical "people" to their side, instead of coming out plainly in support of a revolutionary attempt to substitute working class for capitalist dictatorship. It would cause them to try to use the capitalist State as an instrument of Socialist construction, instead of setting out to smash it and build on its ruins a new proletarian State of their own. . . .

There have been many followers of Marx who, admitting that this was Marx's opinion, have argued that he would not have held to it if he had lived on into the age of Social Democracy's parliamentary advance. The master, they have said, formulated his essential doctrines before the modern democratic State had come into being, or even into view, before the great growth of social legislation and re-distribution of wealth through taxation, and before the advent of manhood or universal suffrage and popular education had created the possibility of a truly democratic electorate. They contend that, if he had lived on, he would have changed his views, and realised that the State was merely a piece of machinery capable of being used for the most diverse purposes, according to the ideas and class-affiliations of the persons placed in command of it by a democratic vote. Surely, they say, it is undeniably possible to convert a majority of the electorate to support the Socialist Party, and for a Government thus returned to power to make what use it pleases of the machinery of State, so as to effect the Socialist Revolution by strictly constitutional means, and avoid all the dislocations and dangers which are involved in revolution and the smashing of the existing State. What waste, to smash a perfecty good instrument, which has gone wrong only because it has been hitherto controlled by the wrong people! . . .

This evolutionary conception is always defended by stressing the parliamentary nature of the State as a representative institution capable of becoming completely democratised. It is assumed that, in the existing state, the representative and democratic elements are in process of triumphing over the other elements, and will be strong enough, with the popular will behind them, to complete the extermination or subjection of these other elements—to destroy or democratise the Crown, the Second Chamber, and the judiciary and magistracy, and to exact in the name of democracy loyal obedience from the armed forces and the police. This, however, is precisely what Marx believed to be out of the question. He held that these other institutions of the capitalist State would be strong enough to resist the process of democratisation, and at need to destroy the democratic elements, as they had done in the course of the counter-revolutions which followed the "Year of Revolutions," 1848.

Class Consciousness Is Vital to Revolution

Morover, Marx held that, if the Socialists attempted to conduct their political action on the basis of an appeal to the "people," rather than to the working class, and of an evolutionary instead of a revolutionary programme, they would inevitably fail to create among the proletariat the will and driving force requisite for the winning of Socialism. For Marx, though he has often been wrongly accused of preaching a fatalist doctrine, laid in fact overwhelming stress on the need for creating among the workers a vigorous revolutionary consciousness, and believed profoundly in the educative influence of the day-to-day class-struggle in bringing this consciousness to maturity. A policy of social peace seemed to him to stand in open contradiction to the revolutionary aim of Socialism, and to be therefore inadmissible as a Socialist technique. It might be necessary at times to step back, and it might be exceedingly foolish to promote a revolutionary outbreak that could, in the circumstances, be nothing more than an abortive *émeute* [riot], because it lacked the support of the working class as a whole; but Marx held as firmly as he held any of his doctrines that the basic policy of Socialists must be to develop the class-consciousness of the workers into a revolutionary opposition to the capitalist State, and to make no compromise with the forces of Capitalism or with the *petite bourgeoisie* that might stand in the way of this consciousness. . . .

When, however, a Socialist party definitely devotes itself to an attempt to make Capitalism prosperous, in order to increase the bargaining strength of its own supporters, it is hard for it to avoid placing itself in the power of the capitalist class. For the conditions requisite for the restoration of capitalist prosperity are likely to be quite irreconcilable with the simultaneous pursuit of a constructive Socialist policy. This contradiction arises chiefly because capitalist prosperity is largely a matter of capitalist "confidence"—confidence, that is, in the prospect of sustained profit-making. But a Socialist Government, if it pursues a Socialist policy, is committed to destroying as soon as it can the very foundations on which the opportunities for capitalist profit-making rest. It can therefore only secure capitalist confidence to the extent to which it is prepared to forswear Socialism, and can only press on with Socialist measures to the extent to which it is prepared to forswear capitalist confidence.

In this dilemma a Socialist party which is trying to rest on a wide basis of "popular" support rather than on a determined working-class following is readily driven to prefer the confidence of the capitalists to an attempt to advance towards Socialism in the teeth of their opposition, and at the cost of a depression resulting from their lack of confidence in its measures. It hopes by this method not only to reassure the more timid of its supporters among the middle classes, but also to command the assent of the Trade Union leaders by improving the conditions under which collective bargaining has to be carried on.

Where the circumstances are favourable to a revival of capitalist prosperity, there is no reason why a professedly Socialist Government which follows this policy should not govern a capitalist country quite as successfully in the capitalist interest as a capitalist Government could; for the less degree of confidence it is likely to inspire among the more stupid capitalists will be offset by its greater success in keeping the working class in order. But when the conditions are not favourable to a capitalist revival, a Government of this sort is bound to find itself in an impossible position. It cannot create capitalist confidence in the absence of favourable objective conditions: it dare not attempt Socialist measures for fear of provoking a crisis and estranging its own more timid followers: it cannot create favourable conditions for Trade Union bargaining, and so expiate its failure to make a constructive advance towards Socialism. It can, in effect, only dither as the German Social Democrats dithered after the war [World War I]. . . .

Such a Government is lucky if it does nothing worse than dither. For, if the economic circumstances are sufficiently adverse, it is likely to be faced by a revolt among its own working-class followers, and to be compelled to choose, in the last resort, between acting as the policeman of Capitalism against its own adherents, and convicting itself of a sheer failure to govern—unless, indeed, it is able and willing to revise its entire strategy and come out boldly with a constructive Socialist programme. Even in that event its lot is likely to be hard. For it will be certain to forfeit a proportion of the "popular" support with the aid of which it rose to power; and it will not have prepared the workers for becking it up in an attempt to maintain its authority on a definitely proletarian basis. It is, in fact, unlikely to make the attempt: it is far more likely to break up in the course of an internal quarrel about the right course to pursue, and to be compelled ignominiously to resign and hand over the task of bolstering up Capitalism to more appropriate defenders of the capitalist regime.

Marx on Capitalism and the Alienation of the Worker

Bertell Ollman

In this essay, Bertell Ollman explains the tenets of Marxist theory on the alienation of the worker and class struggle. According to Marxist theory, the system of capitalism has produced a society where the workers are alienated from the very products that they produce. They are also alienated from the capitalists who employ them and their fellow workers through a system of capitalist control and competition for survival. In addition, Ollman describes Karl Marx's materialist theory of history. As society moved from a feudal system to a capitalist system based on profit, a class struggle emerged. The class struggle is a constant battle between the workers and the capitalists who have conflicting interests. The capitalists control the state and major institutions, giving them a distinct advantage over the workers. Marx believed that the contradictions of capitalism would yield its overthrow and the establishment of a socialist society. Bertell Ollman is a professor at New York University.

Marx's specific theories are best understood as answers to his pointed questions about the nature and development of capitalism. How do the ways in which people earn their living affect their bodies, minds and daily lives? In the theory of alienation, Marx gives us his answer to this question. Workers in capitalist society do not own the means—machines, raw materials, factories—which they use in their work. These are owned by the capitalists to whom the workers must sell their "labor power", or ability to do work, in return for a wage.

This system of labor displays four relations that lie at the core of Marx's theory of alienation: 1) The worker is alienated (or cut off) from his or her productive activity, playing no part in deciding what to do or how to do it. Someone else, the capitalist, also sets the conditions and speed of work and even decides if the worker is to be allowed to work or not, i.e. hires and fires him. 2) The worker is alienated from the product of that activity, having no control over what is made or what happens to it, often not even knowing what happens to it once it has left his hands. 3) The worker is alienated from other human beings, with competition and mutual indifference replacing most forms of cooperation. This applies not only to relations with the capitalists, who use their control over the worker's activity and product to further their own profit maximizing interests, but also to relations between individuals inside each class as everyone tries to survive as best he can. 4) Finally, the worker is alienated from the distinctive potential for creativity and community we all share just because we are human beings. Through labor which alienates them from their activity, product and other people, workers gradually lose their ability to develop the finer qualities which belong to them as members of the human species.

Alienation of the Worker

The cutting of these relationships in half leaves on one side a seriously diminished individual physically weakened, mentally confused and mystified, isolated and virtually powerless. On the other side of this separation are the products and ties with other people, outside the control and lost to the understanding of the worker. Submitted to the mystification of the marketplace, the worker's products pass from one hand to another, changing form and names along the way—"value", "commodity", "capital", "interest", "rent", "wage"—depending chiefly on who has them and how they are used. Eventually, these same products—though no longer seen as such—reenter the worker's daily life as the landlord's house, the grocer's food, the banker's loan, the boss's factory, and the various laws and customs that prescribe his relations with other people.

Unknowingly, the worker has constructed the necessary conditions for reproducing his own alienation. The world that the worker has made and lost in alienated labor reappears as someone else's private property which he only has access to by selling his labor power and engaging in more alienated labor. Though Marx's main examples of alienation are drawn from the life of workers, other classes are also alienated to the degree that they share or are directly effected by these relations, and that includes the capitalists. . . .

Class Warfare

How did capitalism originate, and where is it leading? Marx's materialist conception of history answers the first part of this question with an account of the transformation of feudalism into capitalism. He stresses the contradictions that arose through the growth of towns, population, technology and trade, which at a certain point burst asunder the feudal social and political forms in which production had been organized. Relations of lord to serf based on feudal rights and obligations had become a hindrance to the further development of these productive forces; over an extended period and after a series of political battles, they were replaced by the contractual relation of capitalists to workers. With capitalists free to pursue profits wherever they might take them and workers equally "free" to sell their labor power to the capitalists however they might use it, the productive potential inherent in the new forces of production, especially in technology and science, grew to unmeasured proportions.

However, if maximizing profits leads to rapid growth when rapid growth results in large profits, then growth is restricted as soon as it becomes unprofitable. The periodic crises which have plagued capitalism from about 1830 on are clear evidence of this. Since that time, the new forces of production which have come into being in capitalism, their growth and potential for producing wealth, have come increasingly into contradiction with the capitalist social relations in which production is organized. The capitalists put the factories, machines, raw materials, and labor power all of which they own into motion to produce goods only if they feel they can make a profit, no matter what the availability of these "factors of production", and no matter what the need of consumers for their products. The cost to society in wealth that is never produced (and in wealth which is produced but in forms that are anti-social in their character) continues to grow and with it the need for another, more efficient, more humane way of organizing production.

Within this framework the actual course of history is determined by class struggle. According to Marx, each class is defined chiefly by its relation to the productive process and has objective interests rooted in that relation. The capitalists' interests lie in securing their power and expanding profits. Workers, on the other hand, have interests in higher wages, safe working conditions, shorter hours, job security, and—because it is required to realize other interests—a new distribution of power. The class struggle involves everything that these two major classes do to promote their incompatible interests at each other's expense. In this battle, which rages throughout society, the capitalists are aided by their wealth, their control of the state, and their domination over other institutions—schools, media, churches—that guide and distort people's thinking. On the workers' side are their sheer numbers, their experience of cooperation—however alienated—while at work, trade unions, working class political parties (where they exist), and the contradictions within capitalism that make present conditions increasingly irrational.

Capitalist Ideology

In capitalism, the state is an instrument in the hands of the capitalists that is used to repress dangerous dissent and to help expand surplus value. This is done mainly by passing and enforcing anti-working class laws and by providing the capitalists with various economic subsidies ("capitalist welfare"). Marx also views the state as a set of political structures interlocked with the economic structures of capitalism whose requirements—chiefly for accumulating capital (means of production used to produce value)—it must satisfy, if the whole system is not to go into a tailspin. And, finally, the state is an arena for class struggle where class and class factions contend for political advantage in an unfair fight that finds the capitalists holding all the most powerful weapons. An adequate understanding of the role of the capitalist state as a complex social relation requires that it be approached from each of these three angles: as an instrument of the capitalist class, as a structure of political offices and processes, and as an arena of class struggle.

In order to supplement the institutions of force, capitalism has given rise to an ideology, or way of thinking, which gets people to accept the status quo or, at least, confuses them as to the possibility of replacing it with something better. For the most part, the ideas and concepts which make up this ideology work by getting people to focus on the observable aspects of any event or institution, neglecting its history and potential for change as well as the broader context in which it resides. The result is a collection of partial, static, distorted, one-sided notions that reveal only what the capitalists would like everyone to think. For example, in capitalist ideology, consumers are considered sovereign, as if consumers actually determine what gets produced through the choices they make in the supermarket; and no effort is made to analyze how they develop their preferences (history) or who determines the range of available choices (larger system). Placing an event in its real historical and social context, which is to say—studying it "dialectically", often leads (as in the case of "consumer sovereignty") to conclusions that are the direct opposite of those based on the narrow observations favored by ideological thinking. As the attempted separation of what cannot be separated without distortion, capitalist ideology reflects in thought the fractured lives of alienated people, while at the same time making it increasingly difficult for them to grasp their alienation.

As the contradictions of capitalism become greater, more intense, and less amenable to disguise, neither the state nor ideology can restrain the mass of the workers, white and blue collar, from recognizing their interests (becoming "class conscious") and acting upon them. The overthrow of capitalism, when it comes, Marx believed, would proceed as quickly and democratically as the nature of capitalist opposition allowed. Out of the revolution would emerge a socialist society which would fully utilize and develop much further the productive potential inherited from capitalism. Through democratic planning, production would now be directed to serving social needs instead of maximizing private profit. The final goal, toward which socialist society would constantly build, is the human one of abolishing alienation. Marx called the attainment of this goal "communism".

Marx's Flawed View of Capitalism

Louis O. Kelso

The Industrial Revolution in Europe produced a chaotic and disorganized society in the mid-nineteenth century. Most of the economic wealth was concentrated in the hands of a small minority. Workers, who gained very little from the profits of their labor, toiled for excessive hours in inhumane conditions to serve the industrial capitalists. It was this social and economic injustice that inspired Karl Marx to search for a new economic system.

In the following article from the *American Bar Association Journal*, Louis O. Kelso does not question the sincerity in Marx's quest for social justice. Instead, Kelso provides a fascinating insight into the fundamental errors in Marxist theory. According to the author, Marx underestimated or rejected the value of capital instruments (that is, the factories and machines) in creating wealth for society. Marx also failed to realize that the socialist agenda of disbanding the private ownership of industry allowed the state to hoard both economic and political power. Both of these flawed beliefs stem from Marx's view that economic disparity results from the state's failure to distribute the wealth. Kelso, however, believes the disparity arose from a small percentage of citizens who monopolized capitalism. Kelso postulates that had Marx understood the basic properties of capitalism, he might have embraced capitalism instead of socialism and thus changed the course of history.

England of the mid-nineteenth century, in the throes of the industrial revolution, was not a pleasant place to work. Any-

Louis O. Kelso, "Karl Marx: The Almost Capitalist," *American Bar Association Journal*, March 1957.

one who entertains the contrary idea need merely consult the writings of the economists of that period, or its historians, or even its novelists, such as [Charles] Dickens.

It was against a background of the disintegration of the agricultural economy of England, and the human chaos incident to the industrialization of production that Karl Marx set himself the task of improving the lot of the factory worker.

Beginnning slowly during the first seventy-five years of the eighteenth century and reaching a crescendo during the last quarter of that century and the first half of the nineteenth century, incalculable changes took place in the lives of laboring people. The transformation was initiated first by the intensification of the division of labor and later by the crowding of workers into hand or hand-and-machine factories. This phase was, in factory after factory, followed by the mechanization of progressively more of the manual tasks, shifting to animal power, then water power and wind power, and then to steam for basic motive power.

Changes Brought on by Industrialization

The resulting disorganization in the lives of the people affected was stupendous and frightful. Only the few who were quick to adapt themselves to the era of the machine were able to avoid the destruction—frequently successive destructions—of their means of livelihood through the radical changes resulting from rapid technical obsolescence of the methods of production. The impact of these swift transformations was more than could be safely digested and absorbed by the farm populations which began to turn to the industrial cities for their means of living.

The division and subdivision of tasks once calling for the most highly developed skills until the tasks could be performed in many instances by women and children provided the opportunity, and the indigence [poverty] entailed in the shifting from an agricultural life to dependence upon the fluctuating employment in factories provided the inducement: thousands of parents exploited their children by forcing them into the factories. Wives neglected their families to become factory employees. The full fury of competition between man and machine, between merchants, between manufacturers and between nations was unleashed among people who had not the faintest idea of its implications. Methods by which producers could become reasonably informed about markets were almost wholly lacking. Laws against adulteration of products had not yet been enacted. Industrial safety codes and means of compensating the dependents of injured workmen were unknown. The sanitary conditions of factories in general were incredibly bad. An employer who worked the men, women and children in his factories only twelve hours a day was something of a public-spirited paternalist. Foreign trade brought the local supplier into competition with foreign producers he had never seen or heard of.

Newly born industrial enterprises and the people whose fortunes were tied to them, learned the nature of industrial production primarily by successive bitter experiences. Businesses ran through constantly recurring cycles of expansion, boom, over-production, liquidation and depression. Superimposed upon this disorganizing parade of booms and slumps were the disrupting effects of primitive money and credit systems providing mediums of exchange containing built-in erratic gyrations of their own. The money system of Great Britain, like that of other countries experiencing the industrial revolution, suffered not merely from irresponsible banking, inadequate knowledge, poorly designed regulatory laws and rampant exploitation of the opportunities for financial fraud, but also from the results of heavy importations of gold and silver—the monetary metals—from the New World.

Without analyzing here the causes, we need merely note that the problems of the workers fell upon deaf political ears in Britain and elsewhere as the industrial revolution progressed, until agonized suffering reached the notoriety of an unsuppressible public scandal. Even then, the factory owners, who could point proudly to the fact that for the first time in history, *per capita* increase in the output of goods and services was beginning to race ahead, had no basis in experience for knowing whether they could at once be humane in their labor relations and still maintain their positions in the unprecedented hurly burly of competition.

Marx Pushes for Economic Reform

Against this background, in which the mere outlines of industrial production under free enterprise were vaguely taking shape, Marx set himself the task of finding the cause of economic injustice. His masterpiece, *Capital*, draws and documents the picture of the industrial revolution from the standpoint of the industrial worker. He was the one primarily responsible for having attached the name "capitalism" to the theretofore unclassified economic system of Great Britain. . . .

Because of the dire suffering of the industrial workers, Marx, who knew the facts and knew how to describe them, made a powerful emotional case for economic reforms to improve the lot of the worker. Since the actual operation of the system, which he called "capitalistic" was as enormously beneficial to the segment—less than 10 per cent—of the population who owned the factories as it was destructively detrimental to most of the 90 per cent who worked in them, Marx could have led a revolt against the established order by pointing to this disparity alone. But he did not choose to do so. He made the most painstaking and ponderous effort to seek out the cause of the injustice.

At length, Marx rendered his verdict. The malefactor, the cause of all this limitless human misery, was the capitalist. His crime, felonious by all canons of human decency and fairness, was the unrecompensed piracy from the defenseless industrial workers of most of the wealth which *they alone* created. No plunder in history, said Marx, could compare with the enormity of the offense of the capitalist who, without working himself, appropriated the products of the worker, leaving the worker with only the minimum amount paid as "slave-wages" to keep him alive and to enable him to produce.

The root of all of the evil Marx surveyed was, he concluded, the private ownership of the means of production. The emotional case which he built in favor of a revolution to improve the position of the industrial worker was mountainous. The method of carrying out the revolution, he advocated, was for the workers to seize the government by force and then to use the state to expropriate the ownership of capital. Unfortunately, the moral truth of the massive case which Marx marshaled for improvement of the lot of the industrial worker was dwarfed by the magnitude of his error in assigning as the cause of the maldistribution of wealth, *the private ownership of capital.*

In the course of his investigation, Marx actually saw, but was prevented by this error from comprehending, the underlying principles of capitalism. Since there can be no doubt about Marx's honest effort and fierce desire to find the key to a workable industrial economy, we are justified in venturing the speculation that had Marx understood the implications of the principles of capitalistic distribution which presented themselves to him as "appearances" only, *he might have become a revolutionary capitalist* instead of a revolutionary socialist.

Karl Marx, as he reflected upon the causes of economic injustice in the first century of capitalism, came to a conclusion as momentous as it was mistaken. The world was to suffer as much from the critical error of the decision as it had suffered to provoke Marx to make it. Had he not been blinded by a borrowed myth, Marx might well have proclaimed "People of the world, unite! Extend the benefits of capitalism to all mankind." Instead, he exhorted the workers of the world to unite and "throw off the chains" of capitalism.

Had Marx chosen the capitalistic alternative rather than the socialistic one, the world would be a vastly different place in which to live today. Without the false and seductive promises of socialism, Russia, the nation built on Marxism, would be without the principal rhetorical weapon which it uses to seduce the minds of men.

Yet it is a fact that Marx actually considered the problems which should have led him to discover capitalism. But for three basic errors in reasoning, Marx might have been looked upon today as the apostle of capitalism rather than its detractor and tormentor.

Three Mistakes

The three mistakes that turned Marx away from capitalism rather than towards it, have made Marx the false prophet of the industrial worker. Together with the socialist writers who have followed in his footsteps, Marx deprived generations of workers from realizing that in capitalism—not in socialism—lies their hope for economic well-being, the good life, and political freedom.

The three errors which Marx made were these:

(1) His adoption of the labor theory of value which had previously been advanced by [English economist] David Ricardo.

(2) His failure to understand that the private ownership of property, including capital instruments, is indispensable to political freedom; in short, his failure to understand the menace to human freedom of the ownership of the means of production by the state.

(3) His mistaking the wealth produced *by capital* for "surplus value", *i.e.*, value which he thought was created by labor and stolen from the laborer by the capitalist.

Let us examine each of these mistakes. In the course of doing this, we shall see in each case how closely Marx came to acknowledging the actual principles of capitalism. Yet in every case, having grasped the principles, he also rejected them because of his fundemental errors.

Except for the few wants which men can satisfy directly by things adequately supplied by nature, human labor, for untold ages, had been the primary source of the creation of wealth. Man, with his hands and his brain, has given value to raw materials found in nature by imparting to them qualities which render them able to satisfy his wants. Similarly, man has performed personal services for himself or for others which have also satisfied needs. Nothing is more obvious than that man must wrest his living from nature through the cleverness of his mind, the strength of his muscles and the skill of his body. Since, at the outset, then, man was the only acting force, the idea that all changes in nature's raw materials were wrought by man alone was both obvious and indisputable. The labor theory of value—the idea that labor is the only agency capable of creating wealth, *i.e.*, adding "value" to raw materials and performing services—must have been approximately correct in primitive times and, to a lesser degree, in preindustrial economies.

But once men applied their intelligence to constructing tools and machines which were able to produce wealth, or at least to co-operate with human labor in the production of wealth, a basic change occurred, the significance of which was not at once fully appreciated. The fact that all economic value was not created by labor, but rather by labor and capital together, was obscured by the fact that, in the early stages of machine production, machines were usually "operated" by their owners. As a result, the services of the machine were indistinguishably commingled with those of the machine-owner and so there was yet no occasion for recognizing the separate economic functions of each.

The significance of the labor theory of value is more than academic. *If labor is the source of all value created in the productive process, then labor has a valid moral claim to all wealth created through production.* Then the only moral claim of the owner of capital is to have his capital restored to him, *i.e.*, to get back the value of his capital with compensation for the effects of wear, tear and obsolescence. Honestly to reach his conclusion that the capitalist was thieving from the laborer, Marx had only to believe that labor did in fact create all economic value (*i.e.*, the values added to raw materials found in nature).

But confronted with the fact that capital instruments were actually performing more and more of the functions which added value to raw materials and were even beginning to compete with labor in the performance of purely service activities, Marx could not *prove* the proposition that labor was the sole creator of value and *he did not try.* He merely asserted, again and again, that the proposition was *historically true* and that its truth was of very recent discovery. All commodities, including capital instruments, said Marx, "are only definite masses of congealed labour time" *(Capital).* . . .

At this point Marx actually saw one of the basic principles of capitalism: *that capital instruments do create wealth, just as labor does.* But he rejected the idea as an "appearance" only and held doggedly to his belief that only labor *could* create wealth. By denying the obvious, that in an ever-increasing number of instances, the performance of particular production tasks may be carried out alternatively either by labor or capital instruments; and by asserting that regardless which method was used, the capital instruments owned by a "capitalist", were in fact, "labour instruments"; and by concluding that whichever method was used, labor in fact created all the value, Marx put the capitalist in the unethical role of getting something for nothing.

Today we are not merely familiar with the phenomenon of machines to make machines, we are also acquainted with the trend to make automated machines with automated machines. Nevertheless, tracing the process backwards through several technological generations sooner or later brings one to the point where the predecessor of a particular machine was made by hand labor. Since Marx regarded human labor not only as an ingredient in an economic product, but as the *only* ingredient other than raw materials provided by nature, the problem of machines made largely by machines was a disconcerting one for him.

The value of a product, he said, is determined by the amount of labor time it contains. After a few technological generations of producing machines primarily by machines, what could be said of the machine which, although it contained almost no "value" in terms of man-hours and required very little assistance from labor in the form of an operator's man-hours, turned out a vast quantity of products, all of which sold for very good prices?

Marx actually considered this problem. How could he square the labor theory of value with a machine containing very little "value" (in terms of man-hours of labor) which at the same time is operated with very few man-hours of labor, yet which produces a great amount of wealth? Confronted with this problem, Marx might have announced another of the basic principles of capitalism: that the productiveness, the "productivity", of capital instruments, *in comparison with that of labor* (other than the top echelon of labor consisting of management and technical workers) *is steadily rising*. But here again Marx rejected the clearly discernible truth and supplemented it with a corollary to the labor theory of value.

In this case, he said, the machine, after yielding up what little "value" it contains, *works gratuitously*, just as the sun works ripening the corn in the field. Marx here came within a hair's breadth of recognizing the increasing productivity of capital instruments in comparison with that of labor. Had he allowed himself to see the point, it is safe to assume that a man of Marx's sincerity would have cried, "If capital instruments are the source of the increasing production of wealth in an industrial economy, the owners of capital instruments are rightly the persons who should receive the proceeds of the wealth so produced. Let us then set as our goal the greatest possible accumulation and perfection of capital instruments for the greater production of wealth. And let us so regulate our economy as to extend the opportunity of engaging in production *through the ownership of capital instruments* to an ever increasing proportion of the population."

Marx missed this critical point. Faced with the spectacle of the production of vast wealth through a large contributory effort by capital instruments and a negligible contribution by labor, Marx could merely say: "In modern industry man succeeded for the first time in making the product of his past labour work on a large scale *gratuitously, like the forces of nature.*" *(Capital)* Thus did Marx substitute for objective analysis the dogma he had borrowed from Ricardo.

The Political Significance of Property

Before examining Marx's second critical error, it may be helpful to take note of what the concept "property" means in law and economics. It is an aggregate of the rights, powers and privileges, recognized by the laws of the nation, which an individual may possess with respect to various objects. Property is not the object owned, but the sum total of the "rights" which an individual may "own" in such an object. These in general include the rights of (1) possessing, (2) excluding others, (3) disposing or transferring, (4) using, (5) enjoying the fruits, profits, product or increase, and (6) of destroying or injuring, if the owner so desires. In a civilized society, these rights are only as effective as the laws which provide for their enforcement. The English common law, adopted into the fabric of American law, recognizes that the rights of property are subject to the limitations that

(1) things owned may not be so used as to injure others or the property of others, and

(2) that they may not be used in ways contrary to the gen-

eral welfare of the people as a whole. From this definition of private property, a purely functional and practical understanding of the nature of property becomes clear.

Property in everyday life, is the fight of *control*. . . .

Marx did not err in his understanding of the dependence of capitalism upon private property. In fact, the Communists, following Marx, appreciate this absolute dependence more than do non-Communists, many of whom, influenced by the conviction that Marx is full of errors, have falsely entertained the idea that this is one of them.

Marx, however mistaken he was in his program for achieving the economic changes he thought were needed, cannot be charged with having intended to worsen the economic and political condition of modern man. The facts of his life and character permit us little doubt that his intention was to eliminate suffering by substituting a fairer distribution of economic goods and services, and through this, a more equitable distribution of leisure and the opportunity to lead a good life. Marx was rightly, if also vehemently, critical of the exploitation of the many by the few.

Had Marx seen that the socialization of capital (*i.e.*, its ownership by the state) would *of necessity* place the control of capital in the hands of those currently wielding political power, thereby unifying economic and political power, the two basic sources of social power, we can assume that Marx would not have advocated the destruction of private property in capital instruments. If the factory owners of the nineteenth century, having political influence but not unlimited political power, were in a position to exploit the workers, the bureaucrats of the twentieth century in a socialized state, possessing not only unlimited political power, but also unlimited economic power through ownership (*i.e.*, control) of the instruments of production, are infinitely better equipped to exploit workers and other non-bureaucrats. What better proof of this than Russia and the Russian satellites? . . .

Focusing on Distribution, Not Production

Each of the three critical mistakes which Marx made in his study of capitalism arose from the fact that he began his analysis with a study of distribution *rather than with a study of production*. At the distributive end, something less than a tenth of the population, for the most part owners of land and capital, were faring infinitely better—receiving a proportionately greater share—than were the other nine tenths, whose only participation in economic activity was as workers or as recipients of public charity under the poor laws. The pattern of distribution was bad from whatever standpoint it might be judged. Those who were receiving the great share were the capitalists, the owners of the expanding industrial and commercial enterprises.

For Marx, capitalism was simply what he observed in the European world around him, and primarily in Great Britain. Since the distributive pattern was unsatisfactory, capitalists and capitalism, he concluded, must be at fault. Labor had "historically" been the source of all production of wealth, and the workers were now receiving a progressively smaller proportion of the proceeds of production. Down with capitalism!

Had Marx started with an objective analysis of production and a deeper insight into the property-freedom relation, he might well have concluded with a declaration of war against capitalists *for hoarding capitalism*.

Let us now examine once more the principles of capitalistic production that Marx might and should have used as a starting point. In an exchange economy, and particularly in an economy of freely competitive markets, each service and each commodity is valued for its peculiar ability to satisfy a certain desire of the consumer. Whether the service of commodity is produced by labor alone or by capital alone or by the co-operation of these two, is unimportant to the potential purchaser except as the method of production implants specific characteristics in the thing marketed. It is the finished product which is demanded by the purchaser, not the knowledge that it is produced in one way or another—a mere means by which the product was brought forth. Contrary to what some sentimentalists think, there is nothing sacred about the products of labor that is not equally sacred about the products of capital or those produced jointly by capital and labor.

To effect any change in the nature or position of material goods or to perform any kind of a service, material goods must be acted upon. Marx recognized this; but, because of his obsession with the labor theory of value, he contended that only labor could be credited with the value of material goods produced or services performed. "Useful labor" he said, "is an eternal necessity imposed by Nature without which there can be no material exchanged between man and Nature, and therefore no life." *(Capital)* To effect such changes in matter, or to perform such services, purely physical, *i.e.*, mechanical means, must be used. With rare exceptions, pure thought is not economically compensable. Speech, writings, mechanical action—all these things performed by man, are capable of entering into economic transactions. The thought behind such speech, writings, mechanical action, is not *by itself* capable of entering into ordinary commerce. . . .

Marx recognized that machines and men are competitors in the sense that scientists and and managers, in carrying out their function to produce goods and services in a competitive market, strive to eliminate labor costs and to improve upon hand methods of production. "The instrument of labour [meaning, of course, machines, *the instruments of the capitalist*] when it takes the form of a machine, immediately becomes a competitor of the workman himself." *(Capital)* In speaking of this competition, Marx comes as near as possible to recognizing that capital instruments are active forces in the production of wealth, performing an economic function of the same sort as labor, and frequently performing functions which can interchangeably be performed by either. . . .

But for the basic and demonstrable errors in his theory of capitalism—the three errors discussed above—Marx would have reversed his views about capitalism and socialism. His writings leave no doubt that he was making an honest search for the truth about capitalism and the causes of maldistribution of wealth under capitalism. But it is also true that his writings leave no doubt that, had he caught and prevented himself from falling into his three foundational errors, he would have become as defiant in his espousal of capitalism.

Lenin Viewed the Worldwide Revolution as Inevitable

Fernando Claudin

As history unfolded, Karl Marx and Friedrich Engels shifted their focus away from western Europe and turned to Russia as the harbinger of a worldwide socialist revolution. Their disciple, Nikolai Vladimir Lenin viewed the Russian Revolution of 1917 as a prelude to international socialism. Lenin believed that the revolution would consume Russia and then spread west into the more advanced industrial nations. He recognized, though, that the revolution would be a long and evolving process, not a decisive event. Even though Russia acted as a prelude to a theoretical worldwide revolution, Lenin still believed that the fate of the revolution hinged on western Europe.

Fernando Claudin was a political philosopher and socialist. He was expelled from the Spanish Communist Party in 1964 for what was termed revisionist heresy. In the following excerpt, Claudin argues that Lenin's assurance of a worldwide revolution began to fall apart at the seams as socialist movements in the west, such as Germany, were either crushed or began to fade away. For many staunch Communists the dream of a worldwide Marxist movement would have to be postponed, though not forsaken.

For Lenin, as for Marx and Engels, the socialist revolution was essentially a *world* revolution, even if it was not possible for the working class to take power simultaneously in every country, or even, except in unusual circumstances, in several countries at once. This world-wide nature of the socialist revolution followed, for Marx, from the very nature of mod-

Fernando Claudin, *The Communist Movement: From Comintern to Cominform*, translated by Brian Pierce. New York: Monthly Review Press, 1975. Copyright © 1975 by Brian Pierce. Reproduced by permission.

ern productive forces, which makes capitalism a world system, an economic system that tends towards the integration of human society on the planetary scale. *A fortiori* [all the more], socialism, being the product, in the last analysis, of a transition of the productive forces to a still higher level, cannot really exist otherwise than as a world system. Hence the necessity for the revolution to win through in the *advanced* countries 'when a great social revolution shall have mastered the results of the bourgeois epoch, the market of the world and the modern powers of production, and subjected them to the common control of the most advanced peoples, then only', Marx emphasized, 'will human progress cease to resemble that hideous pagan idol, who would not drink the nectar but from the skulls of the slain.'

The version according to which Lenin revised Marx on this point, by establishing theoretically that it was possible to build socialism in one country taken separately, does not correspond to historical truth: it was manufactured by [Soviet dictator Josef] Stalin in order to furnish the support of authoritative arguments to his own theses on the question. [Subsequent] Soviet leaders have 'developed' these theses so far as to proclaim the possibility of building *Communism* in the USSR even if capitalism continues to dominate a considerable proportion of the world's productive forces.

Stalin's manipulation of Lenin's ideas on this subject was facilitated by the very widespread confusion between two concepts which are commonly formulated in the same terms: the concept of the socialist revolution as a *social* revolution, as the socialist transformation of economic and social structures and of political and cultural superstructures; and the concept of the socialist revolution as a *political* revolution, marked with the distinctive feature of the capture of power by the working class. The first content of the concept 'socialist revolution' *wholly* includes the second: every social revolution, whether socialist or bourgeois, includes as a necessary stage a political revolution, the taking of power by a new class. The second content, however, includes the first only *partly*: every political revolution—unless it is merely a *coup d'état* [swift overthrow] that transfers power from one group to another within the same ruling stratum—has a more or less developed social content; and this is all the more so when the political revolution in question is the one implied by the capture of power by the working class. But this politico-social content is only the first stone of a building the construction of which is subject to laws and conditions different from those that made it possible to lay that first stone. In order to distinguish between the two contents of the concept 'revolution', Lenin brought in the expressions 'revolution in the broad sense' and 'revolution in the narrow sense', and these I shall make use of from now on.

Prelude to World Revolution

The difference of content between the socialist revolution in the broad sense and the socialist revolution in the narrow sense includes, among other fundamental aspects, a difference of space and time. In the first case, the space is world-wide and the time covers an entire epoch of history; in the second, the space is national (or, more precisely, country-wide) and the time is reduced to a brief period of history. When Marx and Engels speak of the possibility of a victory of the socialist revolution in some particular country, taken separately, they are employing the concept in its narrow sense. They do not contemplate the hypothesis that this victory may remain isolated, within a nationally confined space, for a long period. This problem was thrown up by practice itself, when the proletarian [laboring class] revolution was crushed everywhere except in Russia, in the years following the war of 1914–18, while Soviet power became consolidated. The failure of Marxists, from Marx to Lenin, to consider this eventuality was due to the fact that their theoretical conception of the socialist revolution as necessarily a world revolution caused them to rule out any such possibility.

Starting from this conception of theirs, the assumption made by Marx and Engels about how the socialist revolution would develop concretely went as follows. This revolution would cover a whole period of history and would be a long process, not an act—a process in which structural transformations affecting politics, culture and so on would follow one another and overlap on a world-wide scale; but the *beginning* of this process the essential condition for it to start, was a victory of the revolution (in its narrow sense) in the economically most advanced countries. And although Marx and Engels never supposed that this victory could occur *simultaneously* in all those countries, the nevertheless saw it as a succession of socialist political revolutions following each other closely and being closely dependent on each other. As we shall see Lenin did not depart in essentials from this overall conception.

Owing to the changes that took place in the situation in Europe in the 1840s and in the second half of the nineteenth century, Marx and Engels put forward a series of more precise prognostications [predictions] regarding the way the revolutionary process would begin. While keeping to their central thesis, namely that the *socialist* revolution would begin in the most advanced countries, they considered the possibility that *other* types of revolution—bourgeois-democratic, national-liberation, etc.—which might break out in the backward countries of Europe could serve as a prelude to the socialist revolutions in the advanced countries, eventually becoming merged with these in a single revolutionary process. In the 1840s they thought that the German revolution might play this role; in the last quarter of the nineteenth century they transferred their hopes on to Russia. Echoing Marx, [moderate socialist thinker and editor Karl Johann] Kautsky wrote in 1902 that 'the centre of evolutionary thought and revolutionary action is shifting more and more to the Slavs', and he saw in the Russian revolution, the warning-signs of which were already undeniably visible, 'the storm that will break the ice of reaction and irresistibly bring with it a new and happy spring for the nations'.

The Stages of Revolution

During the revolution of 1905–7 Lenin reflected upon the dialectical interdependence between the Russian revolution and the socialist revolution which, as he saw it, in common with Kautsky and other 'orthodox' theoreticians of the Second International [a congress of socialist groups formed in

1889], had matured in Europe. The way in which Lenin understood this interdependence is of capital importance for appreciating the attitudes he took up in 1917 and after October. Not only did he consider that 'the Russian political revolution' would be made 'the prelude to the socialist revolution in Europe', he also thought that the fate of the Russian revolution depended on its nature as a 'prelude', that is, on its being followed by a socialist revolution in the West. This was the conclusion to which Lenin was led from his starting-point in an analysis of the revolutionary process in Russia. As this process went deeper, he thought in 1905, the liberal bourgeoisie and the well-to-do peasants, and even a section of the middle peasants, would go over to counter-revolutionary positions. A new crisis would break out, in which the proletariat, while defending the democratic gains won in the first phase of the revolution, would now put forward the socialist revolution as its immediate aim. In this new phase, had it come to that, wrote Lenin, defeat would have 'been as inevitable as the defeat of the German revolutionary party in 1849–50, or the French proletariat in 1871, *had the European socialist proletariat* not come to the assistance of the Russian proletariat'. Given this aid, however, 'the Russian proletariat can win a second victory. The cause is no longer hopeless. The second victory will be the *socialist revolution in Europe*. The European workers will show us "how to do it" and then together with them we shall bring about the socialist revolution.' In order to be able to see with such assurance this prospect before the Russian revolution, Lenin *needed* to have confidence in the revolutionary maturity of the proletariat in the West. This predisposition on his part accounts, perhaps, for the optimism characteristic of the views he expressed in this period: 'The *masses* of workers in Germany, as well as in other countries, are becoming welded ever more strongly into *an army of revolution*, and this army will deploy its forces in the not far distant future—for the revolution is gaining momentum both in Germany and in other countries.' Or: 'Only the blind can fail to see that socialism is now growing apace among the working class in Britain, that socialism is *once again* becoming a mass movement in that coun-

try, that social revolution is approaching in Great Britain.' Or
again: 'This figure [the circulation of the weekly *Appeal to
Reason*] . . . shows more clearly than long arguments the kind
of revolution that is approaching in America.'. . .

The Russian revolution was no longer the 'prelude' to the
revolution in the West alone but also to the revolution in the
East.

Lenin, as a revolutionary leader in what was 'in very many
and very essential respects . . . undoubtedly an Asian country and, what is more one of the most benighted, medieval
and shamefully backward of Asian countries', understood
better than the Marxists of advanced capitalist Europe the
meaning and the implications of the 'awakening of Asia'
though without getting free of the 'Eurocentrist' standpoint
that was as typical of the Second International as it had been
of Marx and Engels. . . .

Regarding as 'altogether reactionary' the dream accord-

Trotsky's Success

*Leon Trotsky is credited with planning and organizing the October
Revolution as well as establishing the Red Army. His accomplishments
allowed the Bolshevik regime to survive. Author Michael Lynch
points out that despite Trotsky's success, it was Joseph Stalin, not Trotsky, who succeeded Lenin as supreme leader of the Soviet Union.*

Trotsky's single greatest practical achievement remains his organisation of the October rising. Without him the Bolshevik
Revolution would not have followed the course it did. Lenin was
the great inspiration behind the Bolshevik coup but the actual
planning of the event was the work of Trotsky. As he himself put
it, "If neither Lenin nor I had been present in Petersburg [cap-
ital of tsarist Russia], there would have been no October Revolution." Ironically, Stalin was still more generous in his estima-
tion of Trotsky's role in 1917: "The entire work of the practical
organisation of the uprising was carried out under the immediate direction of the chairman of the Petrograd Soviet [formerly
St. Petersburg]. One may state without hesitation that the party
was indebted first and foremost to Comrade Trotsky."

ing to which 'capitalism can be "prevented" in China and that a "social revolution" there will be made easier by the country's backwardness, and so on', Lenin compares [Chinese revolutionary leader] Sun Yat-sen's programme to that of Russia's Narodniks. The Chinese revolution, in Lenin's view, will be bourgeoisagrarian in type, and a long period will have to elapse before the question of abolishing bourgeois production-relations arises.

Success Rests on the Proletariat

Thus, before the war of 1914, Lenin had determined the essential elements of his strategic schema of the world revolution, in which the Russian revolution constituted the prelude and the link between the socialist revolution in the West and the bourgeois-democratic revolution in the East. This theoretical construct of his linked together *three* types of revolution: directly socialist revolutions in the advanced capitalist

Trotsky's other major success was the creation of the Red Army, whose military victory over the Whites [counterrevolutionary military] guaranteed the survival of the Bolshevik regime and enabled it to consolidate its hold over Russia. These were outstanding accomplishments. But they did not bring Trotsky power. It was Stalin, not he, who succeeded Lenin as Soviet leader. Trotskyism survived only in exile as a set of ideas in opposition to Stalinism. Since Trotsky was in government for only four of his forty-two years as a politician, Trotskyists are thrown back on to the inspirational quality of his political ideas as the rationale for their belief in him. Yet here, too, his record is very limited. Trotskyism as a political movement has been very much a minority, fringe, activity. The Fourth International [world Communist organization] for which Trotsky had high hopes won supporters in thirty countries but then broke up into competing factions. In historical terms it is merely a curiosity.

Michael Lynch, "Angel of Enlightenment or Frustrated Dictator," *History Review*, March 1999.

countries (Western Europe and the USA); the Russian bourgeois-democratic revolution, which, taking place in a situation where a relatively large and concentrated proletariat was present, could proceed without any interruption, given the help of the victorious proletariat of Europe, to develop into the socialist revolution; and the revolutions in the East, where, as there was practically no proletariat, a protracted phase of capitalism *sui generis* [unique to itself] would be necessary. The essential agent in the grand combination of revolutionary forces foreseen by Lenin continued to be the proletariat of the advanced capitalist countries. It was they who would have to show the others 'how to do it'. On them it depended whether the Russian revolution would be able to unfold fully, to the end, and whether the Oriental revolutions, once the proletariat had developed in those countries, would in their turn be able to go forward to socialism. And, as we have already seen, Lenin had no doubt that the Western proletariat possessed this revolutionary capacity. His conception of the *world* revolution thus remained in essentials that of Marx and Engels, though perceived from the angle of the Russian revolution.

Until he wrote his famous 'April Theses', Lenin did not think that the Russian working-class could take power before the working-class of the West. The change of outlook he then revealed was supported by [revolutionary orator Leon] Trotsky but resisted by some well-known Bolshevik leaders who clung to the party's traditional line, according to which conditions in Russia did not permit the proletarian revolution to start there before it had begun in capitalist Europe. Lenin's new attitude was not inspired solely by the unprecedented situation of 'dual power' created after the February revolution; it was also based on conviction that revolution was imminent on the European and the world scale, and that the taking of power by the Russian proletariat would merely be the first act in this European and worldwide revolution. Lenin maintained, in defiance of his adversaries: 'The Russian revolution of February–March 1917 was the beginning of the transformation of the imperialist war into civil war. This revolution took the *first step* towards ending the war; but it requires a *second* step, namely, the transfer of state power to the proletariat, to make the end of the war a *certainty*. This will be the beginning of a "break-through" on a world-wide scale, a break-through in the front of capitalist interests.' And he asserted that 'the proletariat, as represented by its class-conscious vanguard, stands *for* . . . the development of a world workers' revolution, a revolution which is clearly developing also in Germany and *for* terminating the war by means of *such* a revolution. . . . The world situation is growing more and more involved. The *only way out* is a world workers' revolution . . .' When, on 23 October 1917, the Bolshevik Central Committee met and took the historic decision to prepare for armed insurrection, the resolution which explained why the moment was opportune stressed that the socialist revolution was growing throughout Europe and there was danger of a separate peace being signed between the imperialist powers with the aim of crushing the Russian revolution before the European socialist revolution could come into play.

Lenin's Theories Manifest

Lenin's confidence regarding the imminence of the world revolution was organically connected with the analysis of imperialism that he had made in 1915–16, basing himself on the researches of [other political and economic philosophers]. His conclusion, so far as the connection between imperialism and the revolution is concerned, can be summed up in these expressions he uses: 'imperialism is the eve of the socialist revolution', it is 'moribund capitalism'. Today, after fifty years of capitalism's 'death-agony', some Soviet theoreticians—inspired, apparently, by the pious desire to safeguard Lenin's infallibility—claim that by 'moribund' [dying], Lenin only meant to say that imperialism was capitalism 'in transition'. But all Lenin's writings of this period show that he was using this expression in its strictest and most ordinary sense.

The October victory looked like the first great confirmation of Lenin's schema: the world front had been broken through, and broken through where the 'April Theses' had foreseen that this would happen. Moreover, the terrible situation in which the Russian revolution found itself in 1918, compelled to accept the Treaty of Brest-Litovsk, seemed to confirm another forecast of Lenin's: the Russian revolution was doomed unless it spread to the West. In November of the same year the German revolution (which, at first sight, presented a pattern suggestively similar to the Russian revolution of February 1917: overthrow of the monarchy, workers' councils, reformist hegemony [political domination] in the government, opposition down below) came on the scene to provide brilliant final confirmation, apparently, of Lenin's assumptions. The real world seemed to be conforming to the world-as-thought with [exacting] rigour.

As soon as he received the first news of the German crisis, Lenin sent orders to Sverdlov, chairman of the Executive Committee of the Soviets. 'The international revolution,' he wrote, 'has come so close in *one week* that it has to be reckoned with as an event of the *next few days*,' and he urged Sverdlov to organize aid for the German workers, including 'military aid'. 'We must have *by the spring* an army of three millions to help the international workers' revolution.' Lenin was more than ever convinced that the hour of the 'final struggle' had sounded; but there was a cloud darkening this horizon: 'Europe's greatest misfortune and danger is that it has *no* revolutionary party.' And without a revolutionary party the revolution could not win.

This attitude of Lenin's may seem incongruous if we look at it in the light of a version of his thought that [owes less to Marx than to other socialist thinkers]. If the revolution is the work of a conscious minority, organized and determined—which was Lenin's theory, according to this version—how could Lenin see the revolution taking place while at the same time noting the absence of a revolutionary party? Who, then, had 'orgarnized' this revolution? Actually, Lenin's conception of the revolution does not differ from that of Marx and *Engels*, for whom the social phenomenon called revolution is comparable to natural phenomena, in so far as it does not depend on the will, taken in isolation, of individuals, classes and parties; revolution is the independent *result* of all of these separate wills, the product of their contradictory interaction, of the extremely complex articulation of economic, political, social, cultural and other factors, even if, 'in the last analysis', the determining, element in this diachronic–synchronic totality is the dialectic of the economic structures. This is perhaps why all revolutions up to the present have begun for apparently fortuitous reasons and why the development of each of them has displayed very original features as compared with its predecessors. Freely exaggerating the similarity between revolution and natural phenomena, Engels wrote in a letter to Marx on 13 February 1851 (*after*, that is, Marx's conception of revolution had reached the mature stage expressed in the *Manifesto*, and had undergone the test of 1848): 'A revolution is a pure natural phenomenon which takes place more under the influence of physical laws than under that of the laws which govern the development of society in normal times. Or, more precisely, these laws acquire in times of revolution a much more physical character: the material force of necessity is manifested more intensely. And inasmuch as one comes forward as the representative of a party one will be swept into this maelstrom of natural inevitability.' In 1918 Lenin considered that the 'maelstrom' was present there and then, drawing the entire world into itself, and that all that was needed was a party capable of inserting itself into this maelstrom as the conscious representative of 'natural inevitability'.

Lenin's vision of the march of the world revolution at the time of the German revolution of November 1918 can be summarized like this:

(1) The contradictions of the imperialist system have brought about—through their outcome, the world war—the complete maturing of the objective premises (on the plane of economic structures and of social forces alike) for the international socialist revolution;

(2) The revolution has begun where the concentration of these contradictions involves the biggest explosive charge (where oppression by the Tsarist autocracy is combined with the contradictions between capitalist and pre-capitalist structures, with the ruin caused by the war, the oppression of the non-Russian nationalities, and so on) and where, at the

same time, a political agent exists which has been trained and prepared on the theoretical, political and organizational planes, namely, the Bolshevik party;

(3) In inevitable obedience to the international character of the contradictions that have engendered it, the revolution is beginning to spread into the advanced capitalist countries of Europe. Victory on *this* terrain will be decisive for the world revolution. The Russian revolution will be reinforced, the proletariat of North America will follow Europe's example, and the liberation movement that has begun in the colonies will see its triumph assured;

(4) In Europe, however, the conscious and organized agent, the revolutionary party of the Bolshevik type, is missing. Unless such a party is created, the fate of the world revolution is in danger.

The operational conclusion that emerges from this schema is obvious. The revolutionary party must at all costs be created, on the European and the world scale; and this must be done before the favourable objective situation changes. The Bolshevik leaders were engaged in a dramatic race against time. At a not very representative gathering, and ignoring the contrary opinion expressed by the Spartacists (the revolutionary group of greatest importance after the Bolsheviks, at that time), the Communist International [Comintern], the 'world party of revolution', was founded in March 1919.

The Dream Is Deferred

In closing this First Congress of the Comintern Lenin said: 'The victory of the proletarian revolution on a world scale is assured. The founding of an international Soviet republic is on the way.' And, the same day, at a meeting of the foreign delegates with leaders of the Bolshevik party, he assured those present that they would live to see world-wide victory: 'The comrades present in this hall saw the founding of the first Soviet republic; now they see the founding of the Third, Communist International, and they will all see the founding of the World Federative Republic of Soviets.' A year and a half later, when the Second Congress of the Comintern met, Lenin's forecasts had been sadly rebuffed by reality, but it was still possible to suppose that the world revolution was 'there'. True, the Hungarian Soviet revolution had been crushed, together with the ephemeral Workers' Republic in Bavaria, and the German revolution had moved on to the rails of the very bourgeois-democratic Weimar Constitution. Nevertheless, the situation continued to be highly unstable in Germany and throughout Central Europe, as also in the Balkans, Italy and Spain—and, above all, the Red Army was at the gates of Warsaw. These last hopes were to collapse very soon. When the Third Congress of the Comintern met, in the summer of 1921, it had begun very clearly to appear that the 'final struggle' would have to be postponed. The real world was separating itself from the world-as-thought. Something had cracked in Lenin's theoretical schema, and this 'something' could not but have serious consequences for the tool that had been created precisely to serve this schems, namely, the Communist International.

Chapter 2

The Rise of Soviet Russia

Turning|Points

IN WORLD HISTORY

Lenin's Early Bid for a Socialist Revolution

G.F. Hudson

Leader Vladimir Ilyich Lenin rallied against watered-down socialism and short-sighted economic goals for the industrial worker. He believed that these objectives would not significantly alter the economic system in czarist Russia. Lenin professed that a socialist revolution was only possible if it was led by a small cadre of professional revolutionaries. He didn't trust the proletariat (working-class) population to accomplish revolution on their own. Lenin wanted socialism realized in his lifetime.

According to author G.F. Hudson, at the dawn of the twentieth century, socialism was an immediate political goal for Lenin. But Lenin's lack of patience did not sit well with the Russian Social Democratic Party. His radical political beliefs, in fact, eventually split the party into the radical Bolsheviks and the more moderate Mensheviks. Meanwhile, the czarist government was under revolutionary attack, and Lenin saw opportunity in the chaos. Lenin believed that a political void would be created if the czar was ousted, and that his highly trained Bolshevik cadre could take over. In 1905, however, the czar appeased middle-class dissidents with the approval of a new national constitution and the creation of a parliament. Lenin's dream of socialism in Russia was temporarily thwarted.

The writings of [Karl] Marx were known in Russia by legal publication from the year 1872, when the first volume of *Das Kapital* appeared in a Russian translation. It got past the Russian censorship because it was classified as a treatise on economics and could not therefore be politically dangerous as

G.F. Hudson, *Fifty Years of Communism, Theory and Practice, 1917–1967*. New York: Basic Books, 1968. Copyright © 1968 by G.F. Hudson. Reproduced by permission.

were the works of [British political philosopher] John Stuart Mill and other exponents of democratic thought.

Even before 1872 Russian revolutionary theorists had been acquainted with Marxism and had been influenced by it, but it appeared to be inapplicable in so essentially an agrarian country as Russia was until after 1880. The Populists were . . . the main element in the Russian revolutionary movement between 1872 and 1881, but they lost ground rapidly after the assassination of the Tsar Alexander II in the latter year, and by the year 1887 when Vladimir Ulyanov, later to be known as Lenin, became a student in the University of Kazan, Marxism had already begun to sway the minds of the *avant-garde* of the Russian intelligentsia.

Lenin was born in 1870 at Simbirsk on the Volga in eastern Russia of a curiously mixed ancestry. His paternal grandfather was a Russian tailor in Astrakhan who married a Kalmuk [Mongol tribe] woman—whence came probably his markedly "mongoloid" features; his maternal grandmother was German and his maternal grandfather, who bore the name of Blank, was according to one version a converted Jew from Odessa—though this has been strongly denied. It seems to have been Blank at any rate who established the fortune of the Ulyanov family, for having made money through the practice of medicine, he purchased a country estate at Kokushkino, and this later passed to his son-in-law Ilya Ulyanov, who in 1863 married his daughter, Maria Alexandrovna, the mother of Lenin. Even before making his financially advantageous marriage Ilya had come up in the world; having acquired a university education, he became a teacher of science and mathematics, and in 1869 he received an official appointment as Inspector of Schools for the province of Simbirsk. Lenin spent the early years of his life at Simbirsk in the circumstances of a well-to-do Russian home with occasional excursions to the estate at Kokushkino, where his grandfather had once owned the peasants as serfs.

Influential Events

Before his death in 1886 Ilya had been so successful in his official career that he received an appointment as State Councillor, which conferred on him a rank of nobility. As far as is known, he never had the idea of demolishing the social and political system under which he had prospered so well. But his son Alexander, by four years the elder brother of the future Lenin, was drawn into the revolutionary movement as a student in the University of St. Petersburg and took part in a plot to assassinate the Tsar Alexander III in 1887. The plot was discovered and Alexander Ulyanov and his fellow conspirators were arrested; he was sentenced to death and hanged at the age of twenty-one.

Alexander was still a Narodnik [early Russian revolutionary], but had already before his death been attracted towards Marxism. There is no evidence that Vladimir had yet any definite political views at the time of his brother's execution. But that event made him emotionally a revolutionary even though without any clear doctrinal commitment. Within a year of Alexander's death he was involved in a student demonstration in Kazan which caused him to be both arrested by the police and expelled from the University. He was soon released from prison, but condemned to a period of enforced residence on the family estate at Kokushkino. Later the family moved to Samara, where for four years Vladimir privately studied law and then applied for official permission to take law examinations without being a member of a university. The concession was granted to "Nobleman Vladimir Ulyanov" and he qualified professionally as a lawyer. In 1893 he went to live in St. Petersburg.

He had already begun to study Marxist literature in Samara and in St. Petersburg he at once joined a circle of enthusiastic adherents of the new doctrine. In this circle he soon made an impression by his combination of great theoretical erudition with skill and vigour in debate. According to a memoir by someone who knew him at that time he was noted for "his undeviating and uncompromising attitude toward principles amounting to, as we soon began to say, 'stone-hardness'", but also "relatively very flexible on questions of day-to-day tactics".

In 1893 there was not yet any regularly organized Social Democratic Party in Russia, but there were a number of more or less secret study circles inside the country which maintained tenuous communications with a group of Russian exiles in France and Switzerland headed by the Marxist writer Plekhanov. The exiles were of course free to express and discuss their political ideas in a way which was impossible inside Russia, but they could only exert influence in Russia to the extent that they were able to smuggle their writings across the Russian frontier. The practical problem that confronted the Marxists under conditions of Russian censorship and police repression was that of creating an organization which would both coordinate the various centres inside Russia and facilitate the introduction of propaganda literature from abroad. The first effort was made from within Russia and took the form of a congress held secretly in Minsk in 1898 to found an "All-Russian Social Democratic Labour Party". Most of the delegates were, however, arrested by the police soon afterwards, and no effective organization was set up. This situation left the way open for the exiles to try their hand at organizing the movement, and this was undertaken in 1900, when a newspaper called *Iskra* "The Spark" was started in [the German city of] Munich; it was intended both to provide ideological direction and to give organizational unity to the groups inside Russia, for the agents who would distribute the paper inside Russia would form an underground network through which a central control could be exercised over all true believers.

This idea was specially Lenin's, though at first he was only one of six persons who formed the editorial board of *Iskra*. He had only recently arrived in Western Europe after a period of imprisonment and exile in Siberia. He had been arrested for illegal political activities in December 1895. In prison he wrote part of a book on the development of capitalism in Russia; in Siberia, where he lived in a village within sight of the Sayan mountains on what was then the frontier of the Chinese empire, he lived comfortably, married Nadezhda Krupskaya, a school-teacher who had also been exiled to Siberia for subversive activities, and carried on a correspondence with Marxist leaders both in Russia and in Europe. After Lenin had himself become the ruler of Russia, political prisoners were not to have such an easy time of it, but at the end of the nineteenth century, although the Russian government was still an unqualified autocracy, the rigour of state repression of dissent had been considerably softened, at least for persons of high education and social rank.

The Need for Professional Revolutionaries

Lenin left Russia after his term of banishment to Siberia had expired and now devoted himself to a campaign against a trend which he regarded as most dangerous for the Social Democratic movement in Russia. This was the heresy of "economism", the idea that Marxists should encourage the industrial workers to concentrate their energies on immediate economic goals—higher wages and better conditions of work—leaving political aims to be pursued as a consequence of this activity. For Lenin this meant in effect an abandonment of the objective of socialism in favour of piecemeal improvements which would never alter the fundamental character of the economic system. In his attack on "economism" Lenin expressed his disbelief in the capacity of the proletariat to originate a genuinely revolutionary action by itself alone. "The history of all countries", he declared, "bears witness that the working class by virtue of its own powers alone is capable solely of developing a trade union consciousness, that is the conviction of the necessity of uniting in trade unions, carrying on a struggle against employers, or putting pressure on the government to pass this or that law to the advantage of the workers." But the political class consciousness which would drive on the workers to make a real social revolution could only be brought to them from outside, that is to say, from an *élite* of ideologically qualified revolutionaries. In this attitude the Marxist conception of the destiny of the proletariat as the revolutionary class is combined with the élitism of the Narodniks; the industrial workers may be more promising material than the peasants for the construction of a socialist order, but they also need to be guided and directed; if left to themselves and leaders whom they may freely choose, they will get nowhere. . . .

Lenin expressed his view of what the Party ought to be

like in his book entitled *What is to be done?* published in Geneva in 1902. In this he argued that "no revolutionary movement can be durable without a stable organization of leaders which preserves continuity"; that "the broader the mass which is spontaneously drawn into the struggle . . . the more urgent is the necessity for such an organization"; and that "such an organization must consist mainly of people who are professionally engaged in revolutionary activities".

Life of a Professional Revolutionary

The "professional revolutionaries" of whom Lenin wrote were no mere products of his imagination; they already existed as a type in Russia. They did not earn a living apart from their political activities, partly because they gave their whole time to the cause, and partly also because they were usually on the move from place to place in order to escape from the attentions of the police. For their livelihood a few of them depended on their own property or allowances from their families—Lenin himself received money from his mother—but more often they relied on party funds which were raised by a variety of means, which might even include armed robberies. Cut off from all normal social life, living always in danger of arrest and pursued even abroad by police spies, and associating mainly with his own kind, the dedicated professional revolutionary became a distinct type of human being, austere and resolute, but secretive, suspicious and skilled in every sort of deceit and dissimulation, convinced that nothing in human life mattered compared with politics and that men must be saved or damned according to the exact definition of their political beliefs. This type had already emerged among the Narodniks; it now came to the fore in the Russian section of a movement which in Western Europe was moving further and further away from conspiratorial techniques towards mass party activity under conditions of political democracy. It could, of course, be claimed that the special situation in Russia, by 1902 the only European country except Turkey to be without any form of national parliamentary representation, required for the time being a type of party organization such as Lenin postulated.

But, although Lenin advocated the overthrow of the autocracy and the attainment of political liberty as an immediate political goal, it is clear from the pages of *What is to be done?* that he did not regard his organizational model as something that would be rendered superfluous by the advent of political democracy. On the contrary, he considered it would be even more necessary in a period when everyone would have a vote and be free to use it. If a majority of the industrial proletariat was liable to be led astray by "economism", with the proletariat itself only a small minority of the total population, the only prospect for socialism lay in a party of rigorously selected and highly disciplined membership which would know how to act in a crisis without regard to majorities either in the country at large or in even the ranks of the working class. If Russia had to wait until the proletariat was a majority of the population and had itself freely decided to give priority to the task of socialist transformation, Lenin did not see how socialism could come in his lifetime. But by temperament he was not inclined to work merely for a "far-off divine event"; he wanted socialist revolution and he wanted it soon. In his impatience he was out of line with most of the other leaders of the Russian Social Democrats at that time. . . .

The Bolsheviks Split from the Mensheviks

At the Second Congress of the Russian Social Democratic Party, which was convened in Brussels in July, 1903, Lenin tried to get the constitution of the Party framed in accordance with a draft which he had prepared, but he ran into serious opposition, and on an issue he regarded as crucial he was defeated by twenty-eight votes to twenty-three. But the opposing majority included the five delegates of the Jewish Socialist Party, known as the Bund, which claimed autonomy within the Russian Party, and two representatives of the "economists". When a majority vote denied the Bund the autonomy it sought, all seven delegates withdrew from the Congress, and Lenin was left with a majority of the votes that remained. In this way his faction came to be known as "the majority" or Bolsheviks, while his opponents were styled "the minority" or Mensheviks. The classification was by no means conclusive, for it is very doubtful whether Lenin could at any time between 1903 and 1917 have confirmed his claim to leadership by a counting of heads of Party members. The Mensheviks retained a strong following and were able to prevent Lenin from getting his own way altogether in the Party. But to get his own way was always what Lenin was determined to do, and if he could not convert the Mensheviks to his own way of thinking, he was prepared to split the Party so as to have an organization composed entirely of his own followers. The split did not come immediately; the two factions continued nominally to coexist for nine years as groups within a single party, and various attempts were made to reconcile them, but in 1912 the breach became final, and Bolsheviks and Mensheviks became to all intents and purposes separate parties. Both, however, continued to claim the title of Social Democrat until in 1919, after the capture of political power in Russia, the Bolsheviks renamed themselves the Communist Party; this was more than a mere matter of words, for by the change of title the Bolsheviks repudiated all connexion with the contemporary Social Democratic parties of Central Europe and proclaimed their historical continuity with the original League of Communists which had produced the *Communist Manifesto* in 1848.

Tsarist Government Begins to Crumble

In 1903, however, there were not yet any Communists; there were only quarrelling factions of Social Democrats. The quarrel did not then appear to be very relevant for practical politics, for there was nothing to suggest that a collapse of the Tsardom was imminent. But in 1904 Russia was at war with Japan and a succession of naval and military defeats deeply discredited the Tsarist government, resulting in a general demand for a parliamentary constitution in which bourgeois [middle-class property owners] liberals, Narodniks (now reorganized to form the Social Revolutionary Party) and Social Democrats could join forces for the time being. The slaughter in St. Petersburg on "Bloody Sunday" in January, 1905, when troops opened fire on a workers' demonstration, was followed by a revolutionary upheaval which shook the régime to its foundations. Everywhere in Russia there were strikes, demonstrations, riots and assassinations of officials; in the countryside there were peasant risings with pillage and burning of mansions of the nobility. On 13th September a council (soviet) of workers' delegates was set up in St. Petersburg and similar councils came into being in a number of other Russian cities. The first chairman of the St. Petersburg Soviet was arrested in November and was succeeded by a fiery revolutionary orator who went under the pseudonym of [Russian revolutionary leader and political orator Leon] Trotsky. Almost simultaneously Lenin returned to Russia and assumed the leadership of the Bolsheviks in the capital.

Trotsky was an admirer of Lenin, but not a follower; a man of highly original views and independent mind, he did not at this time consider himself either a Bolshevik or a Menshevik. . . .

Lenin Plans for the Future

In terms of revolutionary action Lenin did very little in 1905. The armed rising in Moscow which marked the climax of the revolutionary movement was led by Social Revolutionaries, not by Bolsheviks. Lenin's efforts were devoted to building up his own underground organization with a view to the future. Meanwhile the tide turned; by granting a constitution the Tsar appeased and detached the moderates in the revolutionary camp while the end of the war with Japan made available large military forces for repression of the extremists who wanted more than a Duma [Russian parliament]. As order was restored and police activity against subversion was intensified Lenin came to be increasingly in danger of arrest, and in November 1907 he again left Russia for Western Europe, not to return until after the fall of the Tsardom in 1917. He was not a coward, but he considered that he could lead his party more effectively from Paris or Geneva than from the inside of a Russian prison or a village in Siberia.

The Russia that confronted Lenin after 1905 was no longer the Russia of the beginning of the century; it now possessed a national parliament, even though executive authority remained in the hands of the Tsar and his ministers who were not responsible to the Duma. The censorship was relaxed and political parties now competed in the open for public support. Any further progress towards full political democracy could only accentuate the trend towards a state of affairs in which small conspiratorial groups would be replaced by mass parties seeking national electoral majorities. But in such a society what would be the prospects for socialism? The ever more numerous and wealthy middle classes would strive for the further development of capitalism; the peasants, still more than four-fifths of the total population, would demand agrarian reform but in order to own the land they tilled as their private property. Even among the industrial workers there was likely to be more effort for higher wages and social services than for state ownership of the means of production. In the end no doubt the growth of industry and the proletarianization of the masses would bring about a socialist revolution—no Marxist could but believe that—but the day would be far off, further off than in Western Europe, since capitalism in Russia was still so much less advanced.

Political Chaos Was the Road to Socialism

There was only one hope for a revolution of the kind willed be Lenin, and that was a breakdown of the existing régime in Russia which would produce not a free democracy; but political chaos. The upheaval of 1905 had provided glimpses of what was possible, particularly in the violent disorder of the peasant revolts. If the remaining power of the Tsardom with its army and police could be eliminated without a parliamentary democratic régime being able to consolidate its authority, then in that vacuum of government a small group of disciplined and determined men who knew what they wanted would have their hour of opportunity. Lenin did not candidly declare a desire for chaos, for that would be tactically inexpedient, but it was implicit in the formula he coined in 1905 to define his objective: "a revolutionary-democratic dictatorship of the proletariat and the peasantry". Such a phrase went far beyond anything Marxists had hitherto contemplated in the way of a political alliance with peasants; indeed it savoured of heresy. But Lenin was not forsaking Marxism; he did not really mean that the urban workers should share power with the peasantry, much less give them the decisive voice to which their superior numbers would entitle them. The role of the peasantry in Lenin's calculation, as he was to show in 1917, was to be a negative and destructive one; they were to wreck the old social and political order and make such a confusion in Russia that no liberal democratic republic could be set up. Lenin realized from his own observation of what happened in 1905 that the peasants were a force not to be ignored and that they were capable of furious violence. . . . But Lenin also saw that the peasants were too dispersed, unorganized, and incoherent to be able to create a new national authority in a period of political disintegration. The "democratic dictatorship of the workers and peasants" would in practice be one of the workers only, and it would, of course, be exercised by the workers' party, the Bolshevik Social Democrats obedient to the will of Lenin himself.

The Bolsheviks Seize Power

Graham Darby

The Russian Revolution began in February 1917. By then, the Russian people were losing their patience with the czarist government. Food shortages and a protracted war (World War I) incited revolt among the working class. It was a cold and unforgiving winter, but the streets of the capital, Petrograd, were alive with worker demonstrations and mass rioting. Czar Nicholas II ordered the military to break up the demonstrations by force if necessary. After a violent confrontation between the starving citizens and an army regiment, part of the Petrograd garrison mutinied and joined the protests. Without the solid backing of the military, the czar's generals and governmental elite forced Nicholas II to abdicate. Responding to the power vacuum, the Duma (Russian parliament) created a provisional government in an effort to pass emergency reforms and pacify the populace.

A great deal was expected from the provisional government. Still composed of landowners and military leaders, the provisional government had a difficult time fulfilling the wishes of the people. Occasionally, it was unresponsive to calls for reform—especially to land reform that would challenge the power of the landowners. Sensing the government was not moving fast enough, propertiless peasants took direct action in seizing land. Meanwhile, in the cities, the workers were taking over factories, and the military abandoned the government again. Without any support, the provisional government collapsed.

In the following viewpoint, Graham Darby, a contributing writer for *History Review*, argues that the Russian people turned to the radical Bolsheviks when the moderate

Graham Darby, "The October Revolution," *History Review*, September 1997, p. 33. Copyright © 1997 by History Today, Ltd. Reproduced by permission.

provisional government failed to live up to expectations. The Bolsheviks represented the majority at the Second Congress of the Russian Social Democratic Labor Party in 1903. They split from the Social Democratic Labor Party in 1912 to become a separate party due to philosophical differences with the Mensheviks (minority socialist faction). The people backed the Bolsheviks because the other socialist parties had cast their lots in cooperating with the provisional government. The peasants and workers looked to the Bolsheviks for immediate, effectual change. Unfortunately, the Bolshevik Revolution resulted in the creation of an oppressive Communist dictatorship.

With the eightieth anniversary of the Communist Revolution looming large on the horizon, it is probably an appropriate moment to consider once again how it was that the Bolsheviks were able to seize power in October 1917. Of course until 1991 the Revolution remained very much a part of living history, part of the Cold War—an event which, according to Soviet sources, was part of an unfolding grand design as predicted by Karl Marx, part of the inevitable process on the road to world socialism. In short, the Bolshevik Revolution was bound to happen. Admittedly this view never found much favour in the west, but now with the Soviet Union consigned to the 'dustbin of history' it should be ignored and our focus can turn back to the Provisional Government—for it was the failure of the Provisional Government (and the other socialist parties) that allowed the Bolsheviks to seize power and hijack what had become a largely popular revolution.

First of all it is important to remember that [Russia's Tsar] Nicholas II was not really swept away by a popular revolution. He was removed by his own class—by his generals to be precise. And their purpose was to prevent revolution. They mistakenly believed that by removing the Tsar, the unrest would subside and the people would be satisfied. How wrong they were! The very thing they sought to prevent, they actually made possible. The people's aspirations were given full rein. But there was perhaps never any real possibility of the people's aspirations being satisfied by the Duma [Russia's parliament] politicians. Like the generals, these were men of wealth and privilege, men of property and business—they were not revolutionaries; they too were there to prevent revolution. So from the very start, the objectives of the Provisional Government were very different from those of the ordinary people. It is hardly surprising that an impasse developed. Thus in order to make sense of what happened between February and October 1917 we need to look not only at the failings of the Provisional Government, but also at the aspirations of the ordinary people, and finally at how the Bolsheviks were able to exploit both of these.

A number of criticisms have been made of the Provisional Government. The liberal politicians had little understanding of the workings of government; they wasted time over legal niceties; they were too aware of their provisional nature; they were themselves bitterly divided; they were reluctant to use force to impose their will; they were unable to control the Soviets [workers' councils]; they could not manage the economy; they failed to distribute the land; they wished to continue the war [World War I]; they upheld the interest of the bourgeoisie [middle-class property owners]; they betrayed the masses; and they failed to call the Constituent Assembly [an electorate of voters chosen by universal ballot].

There is a great deal of truth in all these charges but they miss the point. The point is that too much was expected of the Provisional Government in too short a time. Soldiers wanted an end to the war; peasants wanted the land; workers wanted better conditions; the politically articulate wanted freedom of association, press etc.; different nationalities wanted self determination; the Allies [nations that fought against Germany, Austria, and Turkey in World War I] wanted an offensive against the Germans. Any government would have found all these aspirations difficult to fulfill in peacetime let alone during a difficult war. Moreover the government was only provisional (clearly the failure to call the Constituent Assembly was a major mistake) and its power was undermined by the Soviets. Thus it can be argued that it faced an impossible task.

From February onwards the central government was simply drained of power as ordinary people took matters into their own hands. The Tsarist system had held Russia together; with Tsar gone the power structure had collapsed. Traditional authority had been smashed beyond repair and a climate of disobedience took its place. The government had to comply with the wishes of the masses (and quickly); otherwise it was doomed. There was a honeymoon period perhaps until May, when the government could have acted, but by June it was over. For this reason the June offensive was meant to restore the government's prestige. Accordingly its failure had significant political implications. In particular it was a personal calamity for Kerensky whose self-confidence and judgement suffered as a result. The people increasingly ignored the Provisional Government and when in August [Provisional Government leader Aleksandr] Kerensky fell out with [Russian General] Kornilov (another major mistake—he feared the right and ignored the left) he succeeded in alienating the army. What little power the government had left, evaporated. However, the government not only failed to accede to the people's demands, it consciously tried to resist them. This was the policy of the Kadets, the most influential liberal group of politicians.

There is much truth in [revolutionary leader Nikolai] Lenin's oft-quoted parody of Provisional Government policy: 'Wait until the Constituent Assembly for land. Wait until the end of the war for the Constituent Assembly. Wait until total victory for the end of the war.' The Kadets did not want to distribute land until the Constituent Assembly was called and as peasant demands became more radical they sided with the landowners. The Kadets were opposed to the state regulation of the economy on philosophical grounds. The Kadets fully supported the war even after the failure of the summer offensive. The Kadets wished to halt the revolution and favoured a military coup to restore discipline and smash the soviets. And the Kadets deliberately postponed the calling of the Constituent Assembly because they knew they would be swamped by the socialist parties (this proved to be correct; in November they only polled 4.7%). Looked at in this light it is not surprising the Provisional Government failed. Given that the Kadets consciously wished to resist the aspirations of the ordinary people but lacked any power to resist them, it is remarkable that the Provisional Government lasted as long as it did.

The Peasantry Organize

Resistance to popular demands was impossible in the climate of 1917. In the absence of coercion the peasants, workers and soldiers could simply disobey landlords, managers and officers, thereby destroying the authority of the politicians in government. In short no one would do as they were told! But this was not simply blind obstinacy; the people had their own aspirations. And they did not need politicians—even socialist ones—to tell them what they wanted.

The peasantry believed the land should belong to those who worked it. The seizure of private land was usually planned and coordinated through the village commune. They also sought equitable justice, local government officials elected by the peasants themselves and free education. . . .

The peasant revolution began slowly and did not really get under way until the autumn. Initially the peasants organized themselves into committees, sought to bring unsown land back into productive use, withdrew their labour from landlords and intervened in the management of estates where landowners looked as though they were asset stripping. The government tried to steer a middle course between the landowners and peasants (which was impossible) and after July tried to take a firmer line against the latter. For instance on 8th July the government confirmed that land seizures were completely impermissible pending the decision of the Constituent Assembly. The subsequent decline in peasant 'incidents' in August was deceptive as the majority were working on the harvest. Although the position of Soviet historians has always been that all the peasants rose in revolt in September and October, in seems likely that this is an exaggeration. There were serious disturbances but these were largely confined to about a dozen provinces and carried out by a minority of the peasantry. Many peasants showed remarkable patience and were prepared to wait for a legal transfer of land but only because they were confident that there was a new environment in which their wishes would be fulfilled. However, the patience of others was running out and at the time of the October Revolution direct action was coming to the fore, and there was little the government could do about it. In short, the Provisional Government could not control events in the countryside.

Workers Panic

Most historical research has focused on the proletariat, the working class, though in truth the workers were not as important as the soldiery in terms of the collapse of government authority. In particular the phenomenon of the Soviets has generated much attention. There were 300 of these within three months, 600 by August and 900 by October, but in reality they were controlled by an elite of activists and, for many workers, the unions and factory committees were the organs through which their demands were made and met. What did the workers want? They wanted better conditions: improved wages, a shorter working day, an end to the authoritarian factory structure, and an end to the humiliating treatment meted out by management. In the aftermath of the February Revolution many of these demands were met and unpopular managers were 'purged'.

Initially Factory Committees were quite moderate in their requests. However, the improvement in working conditions did not bring an improvement in the economy; it continued to deteriorate and as it did so worker demands became more extreme as workers moved from their own agenda to a reactive one. Rising prices, shortages of raw materials and problems of food supply led to an increasing number of strikes from May onwards (peaking in September). However, strikes did not keep the factories open and after the July Days [worker demonstrations] the workers in Petrograd [former name of Leningrad, a seaport on the Gulf of Finland] faced mass redundancies and the possibility of counter revolution. 1917 then was not a glorious episode for the proletariat; it was a growing nightmare. Seen in this light the increasing radicalization of worker demands takes on a different hue and the takeover of factories (workers' control) should be interpreted as a last ditch act of desperation to save jobs, rather than a manifestation of some radical agenda. Motives remained economic though politicization went on apace. However, workers were true to issues rather than parties and they were prepared to support anyone who could restore the economy. Thus they had little time for the Provisional Government and if their leadership in the Soviet failed they were prepared to support new leaders here too. It is in this context that Bolshevik success should be seen.

Where did all this leave the Provisional Government? Well, quite clearly it was powerless to resist initial worker demands and powerless to prevent their increasing radicalization. The responsibility for the collapsing economy must also rest with the government, though all the problems that we have mentioned were inherited. However, they got worse, rather than better. Clearly worker demands did not help the economy (working less hours and being paid more money cannot have helped company viability) but much of subsequent worker intransigence was, as we have seen, the result of economic collapse rather than its cause. The Provisional Government's failure to manage the economy lost it the support of the working class. As in the countryside, the Provisional Government had little control in the cities, and the main reason for this is because it did not control the soldiers either. Thus by far the most significant group, as far as government authority was concerned, were the soldiers. It was with them that the fate of the government rested.

The soldiers, who were largely peasants in uniform, naturally shared the wish for land reform but they also wanted to transform traditional military discipline. They wanted representative committees, the dismissal of unpopular officers and more humane treatment. These changes occurred almost instantaneously throughout the Empire and were reflected in the Petrograd Soviet's Orders No. 1 and No. 2 (which, though for the Petrograd garrison only, had widespread repercussions across Russia). Generally speaking the changes were "spontaneous, orderly and responsible", and symptomatic of a "massive, self-generating revolutionary movement from below".

Initially the government adopted a conciliatory attitude and proclaimed a limited Declaration of Soldier's Rights (May 11). The soldiers also wanted an early end to the war and did not want to conduct offensive operations. There was, however, an inherent contradiction in this position. The Germans were not simply going to go away! This attitude accounted for the failure of the June offensive and the rebellious garrison troops in early July. In the aftermath the government tried to tighten up discipline by reintroducing the death penalty (July 12) and reports from the front in mid-August indicated that the situation was quite stable, in fact the incidence of desertion (before October) has been much exaggerated and the soldiers were committed to stopping the German advance.

However, the Kornilov Affair[1] destroyed any trust that there might have been. The incident was interpreted as an attack on soldiers' rights. Now no one supported the government and relations between soldiers and officers sunk to an all time low. The soldiers were tired and hungry and had little faith in either the High Command or the possibility of victory. As with the peasantry this disaffection was generated by the soldiers themselves, not by outside political agitators. Hunger was more powerful than propaganda. By October the whole army was being swept by a "virtual tidal wave . . . of self-assertion by the soldier mass on behalf of peace regardless of consequences or conditions". Increasingly radical resolutions were passed by the soldiers and a refusal to obey orders became widespread. The Russian army was disintegrating and once again there was absolutely nothing the government could do about it. Moreover, without military force the government was impotent.

Of course the leading arbiter of national politics was the Petrograd garrison, and garrison troops tended to be more

---

1. In August 1917, General Kornilov left his post fighting German armies on the Russian border. He rode with an armed contingent toward Petrograd, perhaps attempting a coup against the Provisional Government. He was, however, stopped before reaching the city and stripped of his position.

radical than those in the front line. The soldiers would have supported any government which was prepared to carry out the policies they favoured (peace, land, democracy etc.), but the growing inability, or unwillingness, of the Provisional Government to carry out these policies meant that when the government was threatened the garrison did nothing to save it.

It would appear, then, that the increasingly radical challenge to traditional authority by the peasants, workers and soldiers dictated the course of the revolution and sealed the fate of the Provisional Government. Once it became clear that the government was not going to fulfill their wishes, the ordinary people took direct action through their committees. But there was a limit to what these committees could do: they could not end the war, restore the economy or ensure food supplies throughout Russia. The people needed a government of politicians who were prepared to carry out the people's policies. They needed a party with a programme that coincided with theirs. This is where the Bolsheviks come in.

The Bolsheviks Take Over

If we look at the state of the political parties in February 1917 we would have to say that the Bolsheviks were the least likely party to take control. The Kadets dominated the government but they were unable to attract mass support as there was an inherent contradiction in wanting universal suffrage and serving the interests of the propertied few. They suffered a precipitate decline. The Soviets were dominated by the Mensheviks [socialist party opposed to the Bolsheviks] and the Social Revolutionaries (SRs); the former had considerable support among the proletariat, the latter among peasantry, and both had support among the soldiers. The Bolsheviks were behind all these parties with a membership of 10,000; and things did not get much better for them. Lenin's return in April generated more interest and his position, 'no support to the Provisional Government', and no collaboration with other socialist parties, was unique and proved to be valuable later. However, up to the July Days the party had made little progress and their suppression after this episode seemed to herald their demise. Yet remarkably from this time on their political strength began to grow, as they came to be seen as the one party untainted by collaboration with the Provisional Government. This growth in support in August predated the Kornilov Affair but that event proved to be the real turning point. What had been a trickle became a flood in September as more and more people turned to the Bolsheviks as their next best hope. By October membership had ballooned to 300,000.

However there is an important point to be made here. People (and we are mainly taking about workers and some soldiers—the Bolsheviks were always weak amongst the peasantry) were turning to the Bolsheviks not because they were becoming committed to Bolshevism, but because they had become dissatisfied with the socialist parties which had worked with the Provisional Government and failed to deliver on the fundamental issues of peace, land and bread. The Mensheviks and the Social Revolutionaries were discredited by their collaboration and the Mensheviks in particular suffered a dramatic collapse. This was because they had in fact set themselves against popular opinion by refusing to create a soviet government. Many were hamstrung by their belief in the Marxist theory that a long bourgeois phase had to precede socialism. Theirs was a significant missed opportunity. So the Bolsheviks inherited the people's hopes somewhat by default. They did not hold out 'a new vision of the revolution', but rather 'a more speedy realisation of the original one.'

The fact that the Bolsheviks were able to absorb such a dramatic increase in membership and support belies the old view that they were ruthless, rigid, centralised, disciplined, streamlined machine. At this stage they were in fact a flexible, fluid organization, and while Lenin's prestige was immense he did not have the control Soviet historians used to have us believe. In addition the party's propaganda and policies did not educate and persuade the masses; rather, they evoked a response because they coincided with the masses' view. They did not create the people's programme: they merely articulated it.

What Lenin brought to the movement was a programme

distinct from the other parties and an unstoppable drive to seize power. Whether or not he was behind the July Days is a moot point; but in the autumn he saw a real opportunity and, although his timing was wrong in September, without him it is unlikely that the Bolsheviks would have taken power in October. It is still likely that the Provisional Government under Kerensky would have collapsed (it had no support and no power at all) but what would have replaced it is anybody's guess, though a soviet government (i.e. a coalition of socialists) was the only real alternative. Kerensky's blunders over Kornilov and finally on 24 October when he tried to suppress the Bolsheviks ensured their victory. In many ways he initiated the insurrection by forcing the Bolsheviks to defend themselves. But while the October Revolution bore all the classic hallmarks of a *coup d'etat* [swift overthrow], it was more than that: it was a response to the popular movement. The troops stood by and allowed the Bolsheviks to take over, in the name of the soviets, in the name of the people. But this turned out to be a massive deception.

The Provisional Government Failed

Thus it can be argued that the Provisional Government was almost doomed to failure from the start. The propertied classes had removed the Tsar to prevent a revolution but their vision of a liberal democracy which would maintain their position of privilege in no way corresponded to the wishes of the people. Perhaps it was intellectual arrogance that made the bourgeoisie feel the people could not have an agenda. In any event, the people did have an agenda (peace, land, bread, etc.) and this was the revolution from below. The government failed to respond to the people's wishes and even came to resist them. But it had no power to do so. Power rested with the people but they in turn needed a responsive government. Eventually after the failure of the Mensheviks and SRs in coalition many turned to the Bolsheviks. After August Kerensky's government had no power and Lenin stepped into his place in October. But whereas the people saw the Bolsheviks as a vehicle for achieving their aims, for Lenin popular support was a vehicle for achieving his messianic vision of world revolution and world socialism. Accordingly there was bound to be a dramatic clash between these two perceptions. "Where the people thought they were taking power for themselves, they were actually handing it over to a new, authoritarian leadership with almost unlimited aims." This became clear as the Bolsheviks struggled to retain power.

Because the whole mechanism of state control had collapsed, the principal objective of the Provisional Government should have been to restore the authority of the state; but it could not. It had no coercive power and the link with the localities had been broken. In fact state authority was not to be re-established until some time after the Bolsheviks had seized power and then they were only able to do so by reverting to the methods of the old regime. This of course explains the paradox at the heart of the Revolution—how an oppressive, bureaucratic police state under the Tsar was replaced by an oppressive, bureaucratic police state under the Communists. There was a truly popular revolution in 1917, but the Provisional Government failed to respond to it. The Bolsheviks did, but only to pervert it. The Russian people are still living with the consequences.

Modernization and Terror: The Campaigns of Joseph Stalin

Theodore von Laue

After the Bolsheviks took power, the Russian, now Soviet, government was faced with a nation plagued by poverty and unemployment. The new Soviet Union was considered backward by Western standards. The society promised by Soviet leaders was a daunting challenge as Russia remained in a state of chaos. Lenin offered a solution. He established a model of centralized totalitarian rule fueled by the Marxist vision of a perfect society. To solidify the government, Lenin launched a terror campaign against perceived enemies of the regime and mobilized the population in an attempt to modernize Russia.

Lenin's plan was driven by a fear of Western aggression from the outside and domestic chaos on the inside. The Soviets stayed the course of Lenin's terror in an attempt to catch the industrialized and economically secure West. Lenin's successor, Joseph Stalin, continued to use terror and propaganda beyond what Lenin had envisioned. Stalin, though, hoped to westernize peasants and modernize Russia while securing his own dictatorship. Theodore von Laue, professor emeritis at Clark University, argues that Stalin was an extraodinary person. While many condemn Stalin's methods, von Laue points out that Stalin turned a chaotic and backward nation into a modern industrial empire. The author sees Stalin's terror and "reculturation" process as a necessary evil in the critical times he faced.

A profound shift in political ambitions on a global scale began in the late nineteenth century. Fueled by a desire for

Theodore von Laue, "A Perspective on History: The Soviet System Reconsidered," *Historian*, Winter 1999. Copyright © 1999 by Phi Alpha Theta, History Honor Society, Inc. Reproduced by permission.

economic and industrial expansion, the British empire set the example, inspiring worldwide imitation by other European countries and the United States. During the First World War, the European powers' pursuit of victory led to unprecedented mobilization and collective sacrifice. Casualties totaled over 12 million civilians and 37.5 million soldiers, setting the tone for the postwar years when power politics became global. What did individual human lives count when the fate of a country was a stake? The European war effort thus served as a model for ambitious postwar regimes like Fascist Italy or Hitler's Germany, whose citizens were becoming politicized as never before: In 1927 the Japanese prime minister Tanaka dreamed of expanding Japanese power even into Europe. In 1917, U.S. President Woodrow Wilson had proclaimed American democracy as the model for the world; by 1918 he predicted another world war.

Russia Looks Toward the Future

Viewed in this broad context, how did the Soviet regime, established only since the revolution of 1917, fare? The Russian Empire emerged from World War I disheartened by its defeat and saddled with massive poverty and unemployment. When Lenin signed the humiliating peace treaty of Brest-Litovsk in March 1918, ceding extensive territory to Germany, he announced his intention to "make Russia cease to be wretched and feeble and become mighty and abundant in the fullest sense of the term." But its vast Eurasian territories, populated mainly by uneducated peasants, did not contain the cultural resources necessary for building a modern state capable of holding its own with western European countries and the United States. The Russian writer Anton Chekhov in 1897 had condemned the peasant population as "rough, dishonest, filthy, drunken"; but, given the adversities of climate, territorial distances, the heritage of serfdom and pervasive poverty, how could it have been otherwise? As for the Western-oriented Russian intellectuals, a small minority, they suffered from a strong sense of inferiority to the West and sought to overcome their country's backwardness. . . .

Lenin Launches the Terror

Inspired by Marxism, Lenin defined humanity's goal as Communism.

But how could Russia overcome its challenges to becoming that world leader? In 1902, while living in exile in London, Lenin had formulated a theoretical prescription for a totalitarian recasting of Soviet Eurasia: "[W]hat is to a great extent automatic in a politically free country must in Russia be done deliberately and systematically by our organizations." The liberal prescription, suspended during the war even among democratic countries, made no sense among what he perceived as brute Eurasian masses. In the collapsed post–World War I Russian empire, Western humanitarian values were an invitation to defeat. Peace and order, let alone territorial security for his country, could be established only by a determined dictatorship; popular support would follow.

Thus, in early 1918, when Lenin advocated terror against perceived enemies of the state, it seemed a minor cruelty amidst the continuing battles of the war. After the peace of Brest-Litovsk and a nearly successful assassination attempt against him, Lenin escalated his terrorist policies with the help of the Communist Party, the Cheka (secret police), and concentration camps for perceived enemies of the state. As Lenin's prescription of 1902 began to take shape, anarchy and civil war endowed it with the ruthlessness bred by the world war just concluded.

Lenin's brutal repression, evidence of which has been well publicized in the West, has led to widespread vilification of his policies. But Western experience, evolved in relatively small and much more integrated countries, is inapplicable to the Soviet Union. No European country had suffered as much as Russia in the First World War; Soviet leaders were fighting to save their country from utter collapse in the face of popular incomprehension. Moreover, brutality had long been part of Russian life, and never more than during the Russian Civil War of 1921. . . .

Regard for individual life was a necessary sacrifice in Lenin's ambition to enhance life in the future. In Russia, necessary changes could be accomplished only by a highly centralized dictatorship mobilizing the Russian masses with the help of the semireligious Marxist vision of human perfection. In the West, individual freedom had always been anchored in powerful if ethnocentric nation states; under the circumstances, ideals of individual freedom would have been an invitation to disaster in the Soviet Union.

Can we then condemn a Russian patriot, determined to surpass the influence and success of Western nations, for wanting in 1920 to spread the Soviet model and reveal "to all countries something of their near-inevitable future"? After the collapse of the Russian empire, in short, the Leninist model offered the only rational alternative to chaos if Russia were to regain some standing in global politics.

Stalin Looks to Catch the West

Like Lenin, his successor Josef Stalin (1897–1953) dreaded a repetition of the chaos of 1917. Stalin was terrified by the dangers to his country posed by expansionist nations like Italy and Japan. Germany soon would follow, he feared, and American influence loomed ever larger. Stalin therefore determined to modernize the Soviet Union in the shortest time possible, whatever the price. He frankly stated his primary intention in 1931 in utterly un-Marxist terms. After citing all the defeats Russia had suffered, he warned his peoples: "Now we are fifty or a hundred years behind the advanced countries. We must make good this lag in ten years. Either we accomplish this or we will be crushed."

Obviously, assessing the world scene in these years of unprecedented change was a risky business, and egregious misjudgments by all political leaders were a curse of the decades between the wars. Modern Russian intellectuals' blindness about world affairs is appalling; none of the exceptionally gifted intellectuals who condemn Stalin's policies—Alexander Solzhenitsyn foremost—have shown any sensibility about their country's external insecurity at that time. In his grasp of global realities, Stalin clearly outshone all his contemporaries. Carrying Lenin's prescription to its extreme, he aimed at total control not for his own ego but to guide his ignorant country firmly through a necessary cultural transformation unprecedented in history.

In attempting to transform anarchic peasants into cooperative urban-industrial citizens, Stalin forced them against the grain of tradition into a pattern of life utterly incomprehensible to most of them. That drastic cultural revolution in the lives of millions of peasants, westernizing them by anti-Western methods, was designed to wipe out deeply cherished agrarian habits of mind and action. Rural landscapes of individual peasant farms and local villages were forcibly transformed into huge collectivized state farms, while workers were often drafted and sent to urban areas where they were forced to become industrial workers in state factories. Inevitably collectivization provoked resistance, both unconscious and deliberate, and in his solitary vision and lonely life Stalin was haunted by real or imagined threats. Remembering his adversaries in the early days of Soviet rule, Stalin had reason to distrust his comrades, especially in this time of perilous change. Even Stalin's closest associates were uneasy, increasing Stalin's insecurity as well as spreading instability in society at large. The conflict produced an existential void in Russian minds. The customary ways of thinking that had given meaning to life were discredited, and the new ideology did not fit human reality. . . . And Stalin's daughter, Svetlana Alliluyeva, complained in 1963, "No revolution ever has destroyed so much of value for the people as our Russian revolution." But given the threat to the country's survival, how much of the anachronistic and individualistic tradition was worth preserving in this backward country threatened with political extinction?

Reculturation Was a Bold Experiment

Obviously, collective reculturation, involving rapid industrialization through a series of Five Year Plans and, more drastically, transforming anarchic and passive peasants into conformist workers like Western citizens, was a highly fragile experiment. Catastrophic mistakes and chaotic mismanagement were inevitable given the urgency of the change, the total lack of experience, and the vindictive temper of the times.

Yet Stalin's style of leadership, although crude by Western

standards, was persuasive among his disoriented peoples. The sophisticated design of Soviet totalitarianism has perhaps not been sufficiently appreciated. However brutal, it was a remarkable human achievement despite its flaws. The Marxist ideology helped suppress the ethnic and national diversity within the Soviet Union in a common membership in the proletariat [laboring class] that promised a glorious communist future to follow.

The party thus imposed a sense of Soviet superiority designed to match Western arrogance. In order to sustain that artificial pride, all subversive comparison with the outside world was suppressed. Soviet Communists promoted idealistic dedication, especially among young people, to help speed up the Stalinist transformation of Russian society. In addition, following fascist practice, the party idealized Stalin in order to promote emotional unity; ever present, he was "the beloved father, dear guide and teacher, greatest leader of all times." But though he knew how to act his public role, Stalin himself retained a sense of fallibility and imperfection, remaining remarkably humble. During cheers at a banquet in honor of his 70th birthday in 1949, his daughter Svetlana heard him say about the guests: "they open their mouths and yell like fools."

Stalin has been greatly criticized for the extent to which he used terror as an instrument to transform traditional attitudes and to force submission to the discipline imposed by the Communist Party—far greater than under Lenin. There is no need here to go into detail on this subject as it has been highly dramatized. Suffice it to point out that Stalin had reason for fear. The experiment of reculturation in the 1930s was at its peak. In addition, external dangers were mounting: Japanese aggression in China, German rearmament under Hitler. While a terrorizing shakedown enforcing loyalty and discipline had been part of Bolshevik statecraft from the start, now the need became especially urgent.

Stalin had plenty of assistants in his campaign of terror, among them [heads of the secret police] Genrikh Jagoda, Nikolai Yezhov, and Laurentia Beria, not counting the guards in the gulags. Their wolfish brutality was rooted in Russian life, as Solzhenitsyn noted in his *Gulag Archipelago:* "Where does this wolftribe appear from among our people?" he asked. "Does it really stem from our roots? Our own blood?" And he answered devastatingly: "It is our own." Under the circumstances, a slower pace of reculturation, as suggested by some critics, would only have encouraged anarchy and retarded the process of mobilization just when external threats were rising. In any case, by 1938 the terror was scaled down, and Stalin himself admitted that "mistakes" had been made.

The Soviets Are Caught Off Guard

Stimulated by the new widespread literacy the Soviets promoted, which offered new job opportunities, and motivated in part by a sincere idealism for the Soviet cause, industrial productivity in the Soviet Union had increased by 1940. In addition, popular entertainment and cultural pursuits continued in Moscow and elsewhere; even under Stalin, Soviet citizens had access to music, ballet, and theater. Physicists and engineers were trained for the future glory of the Soviet Union, and all citizens enjoyed a degree of economic security promised by socialism.

Having hoped for cooperation with Hitler, Stalin was taken off guard when the Nazi leader invaded the Soviet Union in June 1941. Stalin had profoundly misjudged Hitler's plans. War justified Stalin's frantic effort to reculturate the Soviet population, as Hitler threatened the very identity of Russians. In October 1941, Hitler said, "We are absolutely without obligations as far as [the Russians] are concerned. . . . Look upon the natives as redskins." Hitler intended to Germanize the Soviet Union, and terror under German rule would have been even worse than under Stalin.

Despite devastating losses and months of battle, the Soviets were victorious at Stalingrad in February 1943, greatly boosting the morale of both Soviet troops and civilians. Essential resources were available to the Soviets for fighting the most devastating and cruel battles of World War II. By engaging the bulk of Hitler's armed forces, Stalin's soldiers not only preserved their own country but also assisted the victory of their Western allies as they invaded France in

1944. Thus the Soviet Union emerged as a victor in World War II and as master of Eastern Europe, more powerful than the tsarist empire had ever been.

Should Stalin now have slowed down his drive to catch up to Western superiority? His country was still poor and backwards, having suffered greatly during the war. Stalin therefore continued his basic course, now challenging the United States during the Cold War by matching its nuclear weapons. Thanks to scientists like [Soviet physicist and hero of socialist labor] Andrei Sakharov, he succeeded. When Stalin died in 1953 the Soviet Union was an incipient nuclear superpower with a strong ideological appeal in Asia and even Africa.

Though in Stalin's last years the terror lessened under [Stalin's police chief Lavrenty] Beria's guidance, the chaotic strains through which he had guided his country for so long led to increasing paranoia. As [Stalin's successor Nikita] Khrushchev overheard him say in 1951, "I am finished. I don't trust anybody, not even myself." In any case, the news of his death moved most Soviet people to tears; in Moscow people were mortally crushed in the crowds gathering for his funeral service. Although the price was brutal, Stalin had opened to them a source of confidence and patriotic pride; their country was respected in the world. Moreover, for the first time Russian Eurasia was safe from the hostile attacks that had endangered its civic stability in the past.

Stalin's Success Was Bittersweet

How then are we to judge Stalin? Viewed in the full historical context Stalin appears as one of the most impressive figures of the twentieth century. Born in obscurity, he rose to historic significance, a fallible human being of extraordinary qualities. He supervised the near-chaotic transformation of peasant Eurasia into an urban, industrialized superpower under unprecedented adversities. Though his achievements were at the cost of exorbitant sacrifice of human beings and natural resources, they were on a scale commensurate with the cruelty of two world wars. With the heroic help of his uncomprehending people Stalin provided his country, still highly vulnerable, with a territorial security absent in all its history. Always incited by the Western model, he accomplished this historic turning point in Russian history under circumstances utterly alien to the Western experience. Given the utter novelty of Stalin's effort to reshape the peoples of the tsarist empire in a world of unpredictable change, profound mistakes on his part were inevitable. But we, the proud source of Stalin's model, can hardly condemn the improvised imitation under non-Western conditions in perilously critical times.

In the postwar Soviet Union, profound changes in global politics were wrought by the defeat of the Axis powers in World War II. The United States, in surprising cooperation with Stalin's Soviet Union, set the tone for a new era in 1945 by sponsoring the United Nations as a tool for peaceful worldwide cooperation. That vision was backed up by the Universal Declaration of Human Rights that reaffirmed basic humanitarian values for the conduct of human affairs.

Despite the tensions of the emerging Cold War, the spirit of the United Nations penetrated into the Soviet leadership. Stalin's atrocities became a moral burden as the country benefited from its new external security; the dread of Russia's collapse faded from memory, replaced by moral outrage against Stalin's efforts to prevent it. A speech in November 1956 by Nikita Khrushchev, Stalin's successor, revealed Stalin's cruelties to a shocked communist audience. The compulsions maintaining political unity remained in force, however, although gradually they were scaled down. The pretense of Soviet superiority was upheld for a time by Soviet triumphs in space exploration, and under Leonid Brezhnev, who followed Khrushchev, the Soviet standard of living rose to its highest level within memory.

Gorbachev Discredits the Soviet Message

Yet as contact with the West increased, the Soviet system's hold over its population diminished as inevitable comparisons undermined the communist message. When Mikhail Gorbachev took over as head of state in 1985, the Soviet experiment gradually was discredited. In 1989 Soviet control over Eastern Europe was ended, and by 1991 the Soviet Union had fallen apart.

Now Russia and other former members of the Soviet Union are conducting their protracted post-Soviet experiments, attempting to build civic communities and democratic governments in the vast Eurasian lands and among their divided peoples just liberated from the Soviet dictatorship. The Federal Republic of Russia, the heir to the Soviet Union, possesses helpful assets: unprecedented external security, an urban-industrial society created by the Soviet experiment, and considerable natural wealth. But it still suffers from its size, lack of civil cohesion, and economic fragility. The traditional divisiveness persists, aggravated by profound cultural disorientation and deepening poverty. Gone is the relative economic security granted under Soviet socialism, and violence still is part of life. [The first president of post-Soviet Russia] Boris Yeltsin, in uncertain health, faces the hopeless task of mobilizing his people for a common purpose. High-living financial oligarchs in charge of outdated industries control most of the economy, and young people seek Western standards of living, especially visible in the artificial splendor of Moscow. Such standards are sustained by foreign loans, but the money lent to help the Russian economy flows back into private accounts in Western banks. While the prospects for the future look grim, nostalgia prevails for Russia's past eminence in world affairs; Russians yearn for the self-assurance that goes with global prestige.

Chapter 3

Communism in Asia

Mao Rose to Power Through Peasant Discontent

Olivia Coolidge

The failures of the Kuomintang nationalist party in 1918 led China into economic and social ruin. The success of the Bolshevik movement in Russia inspired a small study group from the University of Peking to look to Moscow for answers. One of these students was the son of a peasant from the rural province of Hunan named Mao Tse-tung. Mao preached communism as the panacea to the disparities in Chinese society.

By 1921 Mao had returned to his home province of Hunan and was focused on forming peasant associations. His peasant organizations grew quickly. Mao understood the plight of the peasant. His intimate knowledge of rural China and his revolutionary zeal made him a natural leader of the peasantry. However, the peasantry was not the proletariat, and according to the orthodox Marxist-Leninist viewpoint, the revolution must begin with working class from the urban industrial centers of a nation. This made Mao an outsider among the Chinese Communists and Moscow.

Mao's peasant army held strong through years of battle against China's Nationalist Army led by Chiang Kai-shek. After several failed attempts by the Chinese Communists to mobilize the proletariat in the cities, they turned to Mao. Decades of fighting had solidified the peasant army as a powerful fighting force, and Mao was becoming confident as a military leader. When civil war had engulfed China in 1931, Mao's forces overtook Chiang Kai-shek's army, and the Kuomintang was forced to flee to Taiwan. Mao formed his own government and emerged as the hero of China.

Olivia Coolidge, *Makers of the Red Revolution*. New York: Houghton Mifflin, 1963. Copyright © 1963 by Olivia E. Coolidge. Reproduced by permission of Russell & Volkening as agents for the author.

Author Olivia Coolidge points out in the following selection that Mao's imagination, unorthodox strategy, and leadership abilities allowed him to understand that a successful socialist revolution could be built upon peasant discontent.

Olivia Coolidge is the author of an ecclectic array of historical works. Her books include *Roman People* and *Winston Churchill and the Story of the Two World Wars.*

In 1911, after the death of the old Empress, the rule of the Manchus collapsed like a house of cards. It was brought down by a partly westernized doctor called Sun Yat-sen whose vision for China was a vague, but liberal one derived from the West. His supporters had for years been the overseas Chinese and the new business classes rising to wealth in the Chinese ports. These were receptive to the slogans of the American world. The new Chinese republic was initiated with great hopes. Much was promised about democracy, public welfare, and freedom from the exploitation of foreign powers.

Much was promised, but nothing was done. Sun Yat-sen had a great reservoir of good will, but he lacked the machinery of power, which had under the Manchus been the army and a classically trained civil service. Without an army, Sun was soon driven out of Peking [the seat of China's government] and after many adventures established himself in Canton. There, for lack of a trained bureaucracy with western standards, his administration was by no means a shining example to the rest of China. The country, meanwhile, was split up between various warlords—these consisting of everyone who could get together an army and establish himself in control of some vast province. Naturally all had their intrigues and their wars, so that to the evils from which China previously suffered there were now added anarchy and civil war, together with the extortions of military adventurers whose existence depended on keeping ahead of their neighbors. Faced with this situation, the foreign powers in the treaty ports were more concerned with gaining extra concessions to protect their nationals than in handing over the rights which they had extorted from the Chinese.

China Looks to the Bolsheviks

For all these reasons, the Chinese revolution, which had started in 1911, had produced by 1918 complete disillusion. The little group at the University of Peking was not anti-western as such. They were indeed highly critical of the failures of the Chinese. But they were nationalist, too, and aware that western civilization had by no means always showed its pleasant side in China. At the moment, all China was outraged by the political situation at the end of the First World War.

In the First World War, Japan had been a highly useful ally to America and Britain in the Pacific. Many Pacific islands had been German colonies in 1914, and it had been helpful of the Japanese to occupy them. Somebody had to patrol the oceans, and the submarine menace in the Atlantic had made assistance elsewhere specially welcome. Now, in 1918, Japan desired her reward: the Pacific islands, or some of them at least, and the German concessions along the coast of China. Very naturally the Chinese were deeply offended, since they had been neutral and done no harm to the Allies. Yet after the victory, Japan was to be rewarded at their expense. No wonder that patriotic Chinese looked very seriously at what was taking place in Russia, where the Bolsheviks [radical socialist party] had simply defied the West. Moreover, the Russians were talking of the brotherhood of man, the end of colonial exploitation, and even promising to relinquish their extraterritorial claims in China, including control of the Trans-Siberian railway. . . .

The Communist Party Is Founded

According to [socialist philosopher and writer Karl] Marx, the evils of colonial exploitation are directly due to capitalism. In the atmosphere of 1918 and in the situation of China, this view expressed with all the headlong vehemence of Marx carried conviction. In addition, the vigor and success of the Bolsheviks was in striking contrast to the anarchy and powerlessness of China. The Peking group progressed from interest to direct contact with Russia. Under instruction in the revolutionary methods of [Communist leader Nikolai] Lenin, they began quite remarkably to lose their sense of detachment. By 1921, they were ready for federation with a few other similar groups in large towns. Mao [Zedong], for instance, had drifted back to [his home in the rural province of] Hunan and was now working in the capital of Changsha, where he had made himself a prominent student leader. He was among some twelve or fifteen people who met, by connivance of the watchman, in a girls' school in the French concession of Shanghai which was closed for the holidays. Here, and afterwards on a pretended boating excursion, the Communist Party of China was officially founded. . . .

The Kuomintang Befriend Russia

While all this was going on in Peking, Shanghai, and elsewhere, the affairs of the Kuomintang, or Nationalist Party, founded by Sun Yat-sen were going very ill. Isolated as he was in Canton and dependent for his authority even there on the good will of Cantonese warlords, Sun still pretended to be the government of China. The foreigners, however, in the treaty ports did not agree. So far were they from interfering in the affairs of China to support his claim that they even made difficulties about turning over to him the customs revenues of Canton, which were by an old agreement collected by their agents. Their treaty, they pointed out, had been made with Peking in the time of the Manchus. The existence of a rival government in Canton was no real reason for changing the place to which they made their payments. Such being the attitude of the foreign powers, it was not surprising that Sun Yat-sen, despite his sympathies with the West, did not succeed in obtaining the extensive foreign loans he needed, both to develop his area and to reconquer China. In desperation, he took a step from which he had previously shrunk and opened negotiations with Russia.

The alliance of an Asiatic neighbor might be of great importance to Russia, friendless and emerging devastated from the civil war. Nor had Lenin any democratic scruples about interfering in a local contest for power. The Chinese Communist Party, which had clashed with the Kuomintang on numerous occasions, was by no means anxious to make friends with it. Policy, however, was dictated from Moscow. Chinese Communists were to join the Kuomintang as individuals, keeping their own party organization, which would support the combined cause. Russian advisers, technical experts, army equipment, and so forth poured into Canton. The Kuomintang army made a start at modernizing through the foundation of Whampoa Military College, a Chinese West Point presided over by a useful, youngish professional soldier named Chiang Kai-shek who had attached himself to the Kuomintang rather than setting up as a private warlord. Being an organization more or less under Communist auspices, Whampoa had its political adviser, too, in the person of Mao Zedong, by now a member of the Central Committee of the Communist Party and also rising by sheer ability in the ranks of the Kuomintang.

The union of the Communist Party with the Kuomintang seemed highly profitable to both, though in different ways. For Sun Yat-sen it meant the possibility of a disciplined army of his own and an expedition to conquer Peking in the north. For the Communists, it meant the chance of infiltrating and gaining the Nationalist movement. More and more as he accepted Russian help and Russian money, Sun Yat-sen became the prisoner of his allies. The Kuomintang was well on the way to becoming Communist in all but name when the process was interrupted by the deaths of Lenin and Sun Yat-sen in 1924. . . .

Chiang Kai-shek Launches a Coup

Chiang Kai-shek [who became Sun's successor], as it happened, was quicker to act than Moscow. His northern expedition and the conquest of Peking took place in 1927. Once the operation was launched, he turned on the Communists before his victory should encourage them to take over. All the leaders he could get into his power were shot, the rest driven into hiding. From this time, Chiang turned to the merchants for support. In Peking he set himself up as the government of China, though he only controlled eight provinces and "ruled" the remaining twenty by negotiation with the warlords in possession. Such as it was, however, Chiang's new government did give him a chance to speak for the Chinese nation and to work on the reconstruction of the country.

Chiang Kai-shek's coup had made it obvious that the leadership of the Communist Party had blundered. By Communist reasoning, the fault could not lie in Moscow, even though the alliance with the Kuomintang had been dictated from the very first by Russia. It was necessary for the Chinese leaders to admit they had been at fault and to be replaced. As

The Cradle of China's Revolution

Mao Tse-tung lived in a cave in the little town of Yanan, China, from 1937 to 1947. Yanan, therefore, has a sacred significance to Chinese Communists. In recent years, the town hoped tourism would bring wealth to the remote and impoverished town. As a writer for The Economist *points out, the tourism boom never materialized, leaving Yanan as both a symbol of China's national pride and its backward countryside.*

The town of Yanan, tucked between the yellow hills of Shaanxi Province, is a symbol of the Communist Party's greatest pride and of its greatest embarrassment. This is where the Red Army took refuge from bombing raids at the end of the Long March and where Chairman Mao made his home in a cave from 1937 to 1947. Yanan is the glorious cradle of China's revolution.

Mao's faithful white pony is stuffed in the local museum, the Great Leader's saddle still on its back. Groups of tourists from state industries gaze in awe at the cave dwellings and the rooms where the party's Central Committee met. Last year 480,000 people made the pilgrimage, bringing some money into the town. But these are slim pickings. While the big cities and coastal provinces prosper, Yanan is a reminder of the backwardness of much of China's hinterland.

The town is polluted with filth from factory chimneys. Many factories were set up before 1949 and still use ancient machinery. The biggest is state-owned and makes cigarettes. A Taiwanese company—surely Mao would turn in his grave—has set up the only joint venture in Yanan, producing cigarette lighters.

For foreign investors, Yanan seems too remote to consider

1927 coincided with the period when [Soviet dictator Joseph] Stalin had definitely forced [Russian revolutionary and writer Leon] Trotsky and the left wing out of power, it was also possible for him to change his policy in China and, without acknowledging his debt, to enforce Trotsky's. From this time on it was decided in Moscow that a violent explosion of the proletarian [industrial labor class] masses in the big coastal ports of China was imminent, and that it was the duty of the

---

when China offers many more accessible places. From the provincial capital of Xian it is a day's drive over mountain roads. There is a railway, but only one train runs each day. Yanan has an airport, but flights were stopped last year [in 1992] because the route was said to be unprofitable.

About half of Yanan's people still live in simple cave dwellings built into the hillsides. Power cuts and water shortages are commonplace. The top people in Beijing appear to feel a sense of shame about life in the revolutionary heartland, once extolled as the custodian of the Yanan Spirit, self-reliance and hard work. Last year the party leader, the president and the prime minister all made donations to a campaign called Send a Little Love to Yanan. Apart from love, Yanan gets a "poverty subsidy" of more than 12m yuan ($2.1m) a year. Wages are reckoned to be about half those of Xian. Poverty prevents about 10,000 children from going to school.

City officials yearn for Yanan to make it big. One says, "We grow apple trees, but nobody makes apple juice here. I've spotted the ideal location for a juice-processing plant." He pleads, "I know it is not your job, but if only you could find someone to invest." The deputy mayor, Feng Yi, is sure that Yanan will prosper once it is allowed to adopt the "preferential policies" enjoyed by the coastal regions.

Perhaps. But some people in Yanan believe that its most famous asset—its revolutionary links—is holding it back. The Yanan Spirit these days seems to be a preoccupation with the past.

"Mao Was Here," *The Economist*, June 19, 1993.

Communist Party to supply the spark.

No notice was taken of a remarkable brochure issued at this point by Mao Zedong entitled *Report on an Investigation of the Agrarian Movement in Hunan*, which ignored the city workers completely, bluntly proclaiming that "the force of the peasantry is like that of the raging winds and driving rain. It is rapidly increasing in violence. No force can stand in its way. The peasantry will tear apart all nets which bind it." In the last year or so, Mao had devoted more and more of his time to Hunan, where his lifelong knowledge of the countryside had fitted him to understand the peasants' problems. In a land where three and a half acres had long been riches, where cottage industries had been driven out by western manufacturers and the peasant had no work for half of the year, where beggary and brigandage [organized plundering] were the only resorts of the landless, where the devastation of civil wars drove wealthier people into the towns to live there on their rents as absentee landlords, where all administration of justice came from above and was all corrupt, the rage of the peasant, which had broken out through various mass movements in the nineteenth century, was rising again. It had found this time as its spokesman a leader of a new kind, no longer a peasant, though one in origin, no longer even a Marxist in the strictest sense of the term, but an opportunist. Just as the local warlords built their power on outcasts and brigands who had nowhere else to turn, so Mao was ready to enlist the peasants, not with the object of gaining for them what they desired. He merely saw his chance in their misfortunes. A new dictatorship of the proletariat might be built in China on a new principle, since it would come into existence without the aid, with hardly even the knowledge of a proletariat.

The Proletariat Fail to Seize Power

It is a Communist foible to work on preconceived notions, and the unimaginative mind of Stalin dominated countries which he never understood. China did possess a proletariat, microscopic in comparison to the country at large and concentrated in the great ports along the coast where industrialization had come with western influence. This proletariat was miserably poor, housed in shocking conditions, and must in the nature of things be discontented. It was ignorant and lacked leadership, which the Communist agent was anxious to provide. Looking on these facts, and perceiving in addition the difficulties of Chiang Kai-shek with local warlords, Stalin took for granted a widespread discontent which would only, as he reasoned, come to a head in the big cities. Marx had said so, and the experience of Lenin had borne him out. But in actual truth, the city proletariat was loyal on the whole to the Kuomintang, which had attempted to reform its lot by introducing government-sponsored unions. The proletariat neither at this nor at any time was really ready to play the part assigned to it by Marx. The consequence was that when the Chinese Communist Party in obedience to orders from Moscow attempted to seize power in the cities, it merely ran head-on into trouble. It was not strong enough to maintain itself against the forces that the local warlords could collect against it. After having, therefore, subjected a city to mob rule for a few days or a week, Communist-led forces were extinguished, driven out, or hunted down, while their popularity was terribly damaged by their wild behavior. . . .

Mao Builds a Peasant Army

Mao's work in Hunan in 1920 and '27 had been concerned with the forming of peasant associations. These spread like wildfire through the province and were followed, conditions being what they were in China, by the appearance of irregular armies of unemployed peasants, bandits, and deserters from the Kuomintang. The end of 1927 saw a series of risings, all unsuccessful, relying on terror and put down with savage force. The countryside, split up by poor communications, was too disorganized to face the local military power based on urban centers. The Chinese Politburo [Communist executives committee], unwilling to believe in rural uprisings and hardly consulted by Mao in all that he had done, was disillusioned. Mao was expelled from their number. With such members of his peasant bands as had nowhere else to go, he took refuge on the mountain of Chingkanshan which, being situated on the borders of Hunan and a neighboring province, would require the cooperation of two warlords to drive him out. Here he settled down, taking over the local Buddhist temples to house the thousand or so whom he had with him, while he built up the area of Chingkanshan as a base.

Mao's methods of appealing to the peasant were simple. On the face of things, he had much to offer. He distributed the lands of the absentee landlords, never in American terms very large, but an appreciable part of the countryside nonetheless. He freed the villager from the burden of debt to the local moneylender. He repudiated the taxes and exactions of the warlords. He encouraged the beginnings of local government through the formation of peasant associations and somewhat later by the election of Soviets. The price for all these benefits in peasant terms was small. It was the support of an army which immediately swallowed up the local bandits and similar parasites who had long preyed on the countryside, besides providing employment for the surplus rural population. Moreover, the army was not merely a burden. It was useful. During its periods of leisure, it turned to, drained swamps, cleared land, and generally undertook labors for the common benefit, well understanding that the food produced by the countryside supported the army. Meanwhile, the necessity for equipment of all sorts encouraged the beginning of simple manufactures, which were undertaken in Communist fashion as a community project.

For all these reasons, the little Communist army on the side of the mountain grew. The local warlords with their city bases and their power complexes were far more expensive and did nothing for the countryside. Mao's guerrillas, often living in caves or makeshift huts, fared no better than the country folk themselves. If the soldiers could not expect to make their fortunes from plunder, they had the advantages of high morale. It was in his relations with the peasants and guerrillas that Mao began a practice which he later developed on a great scale. Like all manipulators of men, Mao was a propagandist. The minds of the ignorant and the illiterate in China were a vast blank. With proper attention, a clever leader could inscribe on them what he pleased. Thus both in the army and among the poorest of the poor, Mao created the nucleus of the famous Communist cadres [small disciplined units]. These men, indoctrinated parrot-fashion with simple concepts, were used to mobilize groups. They acted, informally at first, as overseers. They were entrusted for the first time in their lives with responsibility. They responded with fanatic devotion to their new cause.

The situation on Chingkanshan was not considered of much importance by the Chinese Communist Party. Peasant guerrillas were not a proletariat. Marxian revolution could only come by a rising in the cities. However, an army of any sort was not to be despised. Perhaps eventually it would be strong enough to take Changsha [the capital of Hunan province]. Naturally the Central Committee expected to direct it as they had directed Mao since 1921, as absolutely as the Comintern [Soviet-based organization of international Communist parties] directed them. However, it soon appeared that control of an army was not the same sort of thing as control of a party. Emissaries of the Central Committee arrived in Chingkanshan. Somehow or other they got to the front of skirmishes and were killed, or they died of infections. On the face of it, Mao was as dutiful as ever; but the Committee found they had to consider what he said.

A Power Struggle

His early beginnings in Chingkanshan did not induce the Central Committee to restore Mao to the Politburo. His small successes were causing them to value him less than ever. In the age of Stalin, it was essential to hold the right "line." The right line in China was that the revolution would be built on the proletariat in the cities. As a peasant leader, Mao was really outside the pale. It did not suit the party to expel him, since an army of sorts can always be an asset. Similarly it did not suit Mao to sacrifice the backing of Russia or the party. He was, it must be remembered, a Communist of long standing who had been indoctrinated in the Leninist principles of party organization. However, from quite early stages a power struggle developed which for a long time was fought out under the surface. Up to a point it was possible for Mao to tell the Central Committee what he could do. Beyond that point he would have to obey orders. It was by these means that he was brought eventually to commit himself to an attack on Changsha.

Within a year after his reaching it, Mao had already found the mountain of Chingkanshan too small. He had fought fifty-seven skirmishes and thirteen sizable battles. He had won confidence in himself as a guerrilla leader. He commanded about eleven thousand men and was concerned about their food supply. In January, 1929, his little army, still in its cotton uniforms, his men lice-covered and with hair falling to their shoulders, came drifting through the nearby country, infiltrating the upland villages of Kiangsi. Here after a year or so and despite continuous fighting, there were several Communist "armies" in existence, armed mainly with bayonets or agricultural tools, but disciplined and led by experienced men.

The opportunity for a raid on Changsha was created by a conflict between Chiang Kai-shek and one of the powerful warlords, which caused the chairman of the province to send off the bulk of his troops to the aid of Chiang. The Communists took the city and called on the proletariat to rise. However, it soon appeared that the Central Committee had been misinformed. The proletariat was by no means organized for a rising, and the forces against it were stronger by far than had been calculated on. There were foreign gunboats on the river, protecting foreign interests in the town. The Nationalist armies were hastily retracing their steps and could be expected to make short work of the Communists, confused by the strange town and not in any case equipped to withstand a siege or win a pitched battle. The Communists withdrew after two days, leaving behind them the proletariat to face reprisals.

This fiasco at Changsha was shortly followed by a still more unsuccessful attempt in which Mao's armies were repulsed from the walls of the city. Notwithstanding, these failures made not the slightest difference to the attitude of the Central Committee or of Moscow. They did, however, carry the rivalry between the Committee and Mao into a further stage. The Committee's difficulties at the time were very great. The rising in Changsha and other abortive attempts had decided Chiang Kai-shek to get rid of the Communists. He had started a reign of terror against them in Shanghai, their headquarters at present. The members of the Central Committee were personally occupied in dodging the police. What was worse, their organization was moribund [dying] in all the big cities. They were becoming financially dependent on remittances from Mao. It was easy for Mao to suggest that they move to the area occupied by his guerrillas, where they would be safe from Chiang, but in his own power. . . .

Chiang's Campaigns

While Mao was building up his strength in Kiangsi, Chiang was attempting to grapple with the problems of China at large. Had he really possessed the over-all power he claimed and had the business classes who backed him taken a broader view, he might just possibly if he had been left alone have saved the country from chaos. As things were, though he achieved a good deal, his task was hopeless. He knew it himself; and because he was a military man of limited imagination, the primary problem which presented itself to him was the problem of power. He must become master. In this spirit he struggled valiantly to control the warlords and expended his strength against the Communists. By late 1933, he had already directed four campaigns to exterminate Mao, who had by now set up his own government, raised the number of his troops to a hundred and eighty thousand, and controlled a rural area which was rapidly increasing. Since, however, his men were still lightly armed and he had no industrial bases, the resources of Chiang with his modernized army and control of the trading ports were very much greater. It was merely a question of bringing these resources to bear.

It is never easy to put down a guerrilla force, but with the systematic deployment of immensely superior armies it can be done. The importance of his fifth campaign in Chiang's mind may be measured by the tremendous effort he made, even though his making it was, as he knew, unpopular through the country. Educated Chinese, who had originally formed the backbone of the Kuomintang, were widely saying that instead of fighting the Chinese Communists, Chiang should be defending the country against the Japanese.

The Japanese, whose power in the Pacific had been immensely increased by the First World War, had never ceased since 1918 to act aggressively towards China. In 1931, they had invaded Manchuria in the north. This huge province was now permanently lost to the Chinese nation, which naturally blamed Chiang for doing nothing about it. Chiang for his part had trained as a soldier in Japan. He knew that his own army was hopelessly inferior to the Japanese. All he could do was redouble his efforts to be master in his own house, since it naturally followed that when the Japanese had digested Manchuria, they would be hungry for more. It was in these circumstances that with an enormous expenditure of manpower and money he made a final effort to put down the Communists in Kiangsi. He nearly succeeded.

Mao Leads the Long March

He did not capture Mao and did not annihilate the Communist army, but he succeeded in making it impossible for them to stay where they were. Mao escaped with a hundred thousand men. By four hours' marching, four hours' rest day and night, he managed to get a start on his pursuers. The question was, where should he go? He needed a base if possible close to Russia, since Chiang's communications with the coast would then be bad and since the Communists in emergencies could dodge across the frontier. The possible places were six thousand miles away by any route he could take to them, since he would need to skirt the edges of the country instead of plunging straight across. Chiang had bombers at his command. Besides, a hundred thousand guerrillas were insufficient to fight their way across China, where every warlord would throw his armies in their path.

Mao's own army was exhausted, cumbered with sick and wounded, laden with spoils it did not like to relinquish, and short of pack animals. It went plunging eastward towards the trackless country of the Himalayas, always pursued and often faced by local armies which had been called up by Chiang. Mao's own wife was with the marchers, and her sufferings were typical of theirs. Three of her children had to be abandoned to peasants on the road. They all disappeared. While she was pregnant, she was dreadfully wounded by shrapnel and did not recover for more than a year. Even then she was lucky to be counted one of thirty women who lived to arrive out of several hundred who had started. . . .

When the Long March ended in Shensi in the remotest part of China, there were twenty thousand of them left. But the Communist Party of China was welded together as never before. It had turned its back on the cities. It had accepted Mao for its chief, not at the bidding of Moscow, but perforce. It was committed to the conquest of China by Mao's guerrillas.

War with Japan

Mao settled in Shensi in 1935. Chiang let him alone. The Japanese menace was looming. . . .

War with the Japanese was to destroy the old China. It was the terrible climax to a long series of indignities which China had suffered at the hands of every nation aspiring to power. Nationalist feeling, which had always been strong, was rising to frenzy. Chiang, unfortunately, had nothing to gain from provoking Japan. He could only lose. This was not by any means true of Mao. The Japanese mainly garrisoned towns and strongpoints. Mao's guerrillas had in any case no use for these. It was easy for Mao to put himself forward as the champion of China. By so doing, he began to attract a stream of young idealists from the universities all over the land. The Communist movement, though firmly based on peasant discontent, was taking on the airs of a crusade. Once more Chiang, clinging blindly to his concept of unification, moved against it. . . .

The Japanese full-scale invasion of China proper began in 1937. Its effect on Chiang was ruinous. He lost immediately the rich and populous areas of the coast and was driven back on Chungking, a small inland center too remote for the Japanese to penetrate it. Here he was cut off from the majority of his own supporters and also from the outer world, whose communications with him were restricted to the winding, long, and vulnerable Burma Road. Perhaps Chiang had been right when he insisted that the chances of his regime for survival depended on power. At all events, without it his followers lost heart. The ideals and hopes of the Kuomintang for a new China faded away. The Chungking government degenerated into another warlord regime, distinguished only by being more corrupt than many. Perhaps the inactivity of Chiang against the Japanese contributed to this. He clearly dared not provoke them, since he could not face them in the field. Mao, meanwhile, entrenched in an area which the Japanese could not possibly want, was extending his tentacles through the countryside, publicly proclaiming a crusade against the Japanese and preying on them, as a guerrilla must do, for the weapons he needed. . . .

The end of the European war did arrive, and Stalin's forces began to mass on his northeastern frontier. This was a maneuver which naturally took time. As it happened, the collapse of Japan came much more rapidly than either Americans or Russians expected. No Russian onslaught and no campaign in China proved to be needed. The problem was rather to send the Japanese home and to establish administration in the newly reconquered areas. The Americans poured in through the coastal ports, while the Russians for their part swept down and occupied Manchuria.

America Offers Chiang Assistance

Chiang Kai-shek, his army splendidly re-equipped at American expense, was ready and waiting to take over. Very shortly he established himself in Peking. To the north of him lay the province of Manchuria, still occupied by the Russians. This province had been in Japanese hands since 1931. It had been industrialized by them and further used as a base for the conquest of China. It contained besides industrial wealth a tremendous arsenal of Japanese weapons. The Communist Chinese, far nearer to the Manchurian border than Chungking, were reported not to be waiting for an official take-over, but to be pouring in. Chiang's American advisers were inclined to let Manchuria go or at most to put pressure on the Russians to keep the Chinese Communists out. It was beginning to look as though China was going to be torn by a civil war which nobody wanted.

The Russians on the whole were fairly correct. They had never openly supported the Chinese Communist aims. In deed, there was some question in everybody's mind as to how far Mao was a Communist at all. His unorthodox approach to the Chinese problem put him in a category of his own. The Russians therefore acknowledged the right of Chiang to enter Manchuria. They merely put difficulties in his way.

Chiang for his part was determined to play for all or nothing. His national feelings were deep and fierce. To him, China was all of China, not the greater part. He had been struggling through his entire career to unite China under his rule. With effective support from America, it might be done. What if by grasping at too much he might lose all? It was worth the risk.

Chiang had reckoned unfortunately without the people of China. He had sat too long in Chungking doing nothing, had let too many people entrench themselves in his government who did not believe in its future. Intent on feathering their nests, these men descended on the reconquered provinces like hungry locusts. The value of Chinese currency fell shockingly low and was going lower. It was too much. The Nationalist Party had led the country since 1911, and during that period it had consumed an immense amount of good will. It had achieved little. Chiang had no positive program, no new deal to offer. The Communists had. According to rumor, they were hardly Communists at all, merely land reformers with a new economic program. They were not corrupt. Nor were they backed up by foreign arms. A genuine surge of enthusiasm passed through the country.

Militarily Chiang was extending himself too far as he tried to reach for control in Manchuria. He had made himself vulnerable. People began to desert his cause. Even his troops deserted it, first on a small scale, and then on a large scale. The Communists were arming themselves from Japanese dumps in Manchuria. Pretty soon they were also using American equipment brought in by deserters. All of a sudden, Chiang collapsed like a dam giving way before the weight of flood waters. He made his escape as best he could, while all over China people were dancing in the streets, on the banks of the rivers, in the villages, in the fields. The civil war was over before it had time to get properly started. The Chinese revolution, which had been thirty-eight years in process, was over, too. The People's Republic could wipe that old sheet clean and start afresh.

Mao Insisted That the Proletariat Lead the Revolution

Nick Knight

In the following article from the *Journal of Contemporary Asia*, Nick Knight argues that Mao Tse-tung was not an unorthodox Communist leader who relied on the peasant population to achieve a socialist society. Mao was, in reality, a hard-line Marxist-Leninist who believed that a socialist society and a modern industrialized nation could only be achieved if the proletariat class led the revolution. The problem was that the working class made up only a small portion of China's population. Still, Mao took steps to ensure that the proletariat would lead the revolution. He altered the Soviet election process so that more working-class people would be represented, encouraged workers and farm laborers to join the "Poor Peasant League," and insisted that the working class head the Red Army.

Nick Knight works for the School of Asian and International Studies at Griffin University.

From early 1949, the leadership of the Chinese Communist Party began to turn its attention from revolutionary struggle based primarily in the countryside and premised on the support of China's peasants to the construction of a modern, industrialised nation-state directed politically and economically from the cities. The focus of the Chinese revolution thus appeared set to undergo a fundamental shift, both in terms of location and objectives. As Mao commented in March 1949, "From 1927 to the present the centre of gravity of our work has been in the villages—gathering strength in the villages, using the villages in order to surround the

Nick Knight, "Working Class Power and the State Formation in Mao Zedong's Thought, 1931–1934," *Journal of Contemporary Asia*, vol. 32, March 2002, p. 29. Copyright © 2002 by Journal of Contemporary Asia Publishers. Reproduced by permission.

cities and then taking the cities. The period for this method of work has now ended. The period of 'from the city to the village' and of the city leading the village has now begun." Nowhere was this shift more apparent than in Mao's determination that the Chinese Communist Party expand its working class membership and reduce the proportion of peasants within its ranks. A halt was called to indiscriminate recruitment of Party members and some "unusable peasant elements" were expelled. Indeed, working class participation and leadership were now stressed across many dimensions of new China's political and economic life. This was in conformity with Mao's vision for China, central to which was modernisation, a process in which industry and the working class were central. Mao also believed that the class composition of the Party had to be brought in line with the insistence of Marxism-Leninism that a communist party be the vanguard of the proletariat [laboring class], led by and primarily for the working class. From this perspective, the very large numbers of peasants in the Party, while a reflection of the need for peasant support during its period of revolutionary struggle in the countryside, were an impediment to the Party's goal of the creation of a socialist society with a modern industrialised economy. For this goal to be achieved, the industrial proletariat would not only be central to new China's economic efforts, but to the class composition of its leadership as well.

This shift—from the countryside to the cities, from the peasants to the working class—was genuine enough, although it took the Party a considerable time to redress the imbalance in its ranks between peasants and workers. Indeed, by 1957, despite a concerted drive to recruit workers, they still constituted less than 14% of Party membership. Nevertheless, the Party's capture of the cities in 1949 did provide Mao the opportunity to realise a long and deeply held conviction that the Party, in order to perform its historical role, had to be constituted primarily of members drawn from the working class. While force of circumstances had obliged Mao to rely on the peasants as the "main force" of the Chinese revolution from 1927, he had never relished this reliance. The peasants were not, he felt, capable of envisioning a future of modernity and industrialisation in the way that the working class could. He had consequently attempted wherever possible to strengthen working class representation in the Party, and the leading role of the working class had, since the mid-1920s, remained central to his perception of China's revolution as a modernising revolution. . . .

An Orthodox Marxist-Leninist

Had Mao experienced a conversion to Marxist orthodoxy in 1949, or was this just another example of the contradictory character of his thought? The answer is neither of these. Mao had not suddenly discovered (or rediscovered) the working class in 1949. Rather, Mao's call for increased number of workers in the Party, particularly to fill leadership positions, was a manifestation of a long and consistently held view that the working class was the leading class of the Chinese revolution. The peasantry, he believed, while of immense importance to the successful prosecution of the revolution, could not play that leading role. The peasantry's class limitations made it less effective in organisational and leadership roles within the Party, and limited its vision of the revolution's goals. Despite his admiration for and reliance on the peasants, he was under no illusions that the realisation of China's future—modernisation, industrialisation, socialism—depended on the working class. . . .

Mao attempted to ensure that the working class was strongly represented numerically in leading positions within the state, and that the nature of state institutions reflected the interests of the working class. Mao did not accept that the unfavourable social and political context in which he found himself, one in which the peasants remained the very large proportion of the population and in which modern industry was poorly developed, justified "turning his back on the working class." To the contrary, Mao felt it necessary, precisely because of the inauspicious setting for the creation of a modernising state which the Jiangxi Soviet [1931–1934, the rural base where Mao held out against Nationalist attacks] represented, to compensate for the numerical weakness of the industrial working class. He attempted to do so through strategies of recruitment, electoral policies and processes of institution building that expanded worker representation and influence in the new state beyond their diminutive numbers in society at large. . . .

Involving the Workers

The question arises, in light of the [Russian] Comintern's powerful influence on the Chinese Communist Party at the time of the creation and development of the Jiangxi Soviet, whether Mao's utterances and policies on working class leadership were merely a tactical deference to the Comintern line, and not a genuine expression of his own views. That this is not the case can be demonstrated by examining his views on working class leadership and the peasantry in the years preceding the establishment of the Jiangxi Soviet. From 1927–1930, during the very years in which Mao's revolutionary strategy was being forged, he continually stressed the importance of working class leadership of both the Party and the Chinese revolution. He also identified the large numbers of peasants, recruited from necessity into the Party and Army, as the source of the numerous political, organisational and ideological problems that afflicted those organisations. Thus, his admiration for the revolutionary potential of the peasants was balanced by a realistic assessment of their shortcomings as a class, and their urgent need for leadership by the working class and its vanguard party. His words then were certainly not those of a revolutionary who willingly embraced rural revolution and uncritically revered the revolutionary potential of the peasantry. They were, rather, the words of one who finds himself forcibly separated from the cities and the working class, and compelled to find a strategy which could exploit the dissatisfaction of the peasantry and channel their revolutionary impulse in the direction of a modernising revolution. Mao did not, therefore, lose sight of the need for working class leadership of the Chinese revolution, and his words and policies of the Jiangxi Soviet are consistent with those of both the 1927–30 and post-1949 periods. . . .

With the establishment of the Central Soviet Republic

[an organization representing regional Soviet councils], Mao moved to improve and extend the system of soviets that were to constitute the fundamental building blocks of the new state. The hierarchy of soviets rested on a foundation of xiang soviets, which administered a local area that incorporated several villages and included a population ranging from several hundred to several thousand people. The structure of the xiang soviet and its relationship to mass organisations at the grass-roots level varied somewhat between 1931–34. However, it was the Representative Congress that theoretically stood at the pinnacle of xiang organisation, with a Presidium of five to seven persons, chosen by and from among the Representative Congress, which oversaw the implementation of policy between meetings of the Congress. What is significant about the xiang Representative Congress, from the perspective of Mao's views on working class leadership, is the manner of its election. In a Directive of January 1932, Mao ordered that the deputies to the xiang Representative Congress be elected from different class constituencies, and that these constituencies be given different weightings. Every fifty poor and middle peasants and "independent labourers" (*duli laodongzhe*) had the right to elect one deputy, whereas every thirteen workers, coolies [unskilled workers] and farm labourers could elect one deputy and, from 1933, were given the right to hold electoral meetings separate from those of the peasants. This deliberate institution of electoral imbalance in favour of workers had a significant effect on the class composition of the xiang Representative Congresses. In some xiang Congresses, almost half of the deputies were defined as "workers," this in a context in which "workers" (even broadly defined in the manner Mao referred to them) were a small percentage of the population.

This class "gerrymander" [advantage given to one party] was repeated at every level in the hierarchy of soviets. In elections to township soviets, there was one deputy elected for every twenty "workers, coolies and farm labourers," whereas one deputy was elected for every eighty of the remaining classes. The same electoral ratio applied in city soviets subordinate to the provincial soviet. Here, every one hundred "workers, coolies, and farm labourers" elected one deputy, whereas four hundred urban poor and local peasants could elect one deputy. At the level above the xiang, the district (*qu*) soviet, whose deputies were drawn from xiang and township soviets, Mao prescribed that "workers, coolies and farm laborers" make up a total of 20% of the deputies. Mao stipulated that "rural and urban soviets as well as congresses at the two levels of district and xian must all pay attention to the components from the workers, coolies, farm laborers, and Red Army."

At the next level in the hierarchy of soviets, the xian (or county) soviet, the number of "workers, coolies and farm labourers" was increased to 25%, and deputies elected to this level from towns were to be 50% "workers, coolies and farm labourers." The same principle was also applied at the level of provincial soviet congress, which stood immediately below the Soviet Central Government. Elections to the provincial congress allowed one deputy for every five thousand rural residents and one for each two thousand urban residents. This ratio was altered, in 1933, to provide even greater representation to urban residents, who now elected one delegate for every fifteen hundred residents, compared to one delegate to every six thousand rural residents. This electoral imbalance, in favour of those living in urban areas (and therefore by implication in favour of the working class), was established at each level, from the xiang soviet to the National Soviet Congress. At the latter, there was one deputy for each ten thousand urban electors, and one for each fifty thousand rural electors.

The Temporary Soviet Election Law of August 1933 (which appeared over Mao's signature) made quite explicit its intention to entrench the leadership of the working class. There is, here, no deference to the suggestion that each voter's vote should be equal, or even approximately equal, to the votes of all other voters. . . .

In his Report of the Central Executive Committee and the Council of People's Commissars of the Chinese Soviet Republic to the Second National Soviet Congress (January 1934), Mao summed up the class intentions of the machinery of soviet elections, and their achievements over the previous two years, as follows:

> They [soviets] should arouse class struggle among the workers, develop the agrarian revolution of the peasants, and heighten the activism of the worker and peasant masses under the principle of a workers' and peasants' alliance led by the working class. . . . [C]oncerning the balance of class composition: To guarantee that the proletariat will be the mainstay of leadership within the soviet regime, we applied the method under which thirteen workers and their dependents elected one representative, and fifty peasants or poor people elected one representative, and the same composition is used to organize conferences of deputies at the city and township level. At all levels of deputies' congresses and executive committees from the district to the central level, an appropriate ratio of workers' and peasants' deputies was established. This has guaranteed the alliance between workers and peasants in the organization of the soviet regime, and ensured that the workers occupy the leading position.

The principal institutions of government, composed of a hierarchy of soviets from the level of the xiang to the National Soviet Congress, were not, therefore, intended to represent the population of the Jiangxi Soviet equally. Rather, the electoral process that brought the soviets into being was deliberately structured in a manner intended to favour one particular section of the population: the working class. This was in part to compensate for the diminutive size of the working class; it was in conformity, too, with the electoral practice of the Soviet Union. It was also, however, in conformity with Mao's own insistence that the working class play an active and leading role in the establishment of the new state. Moreover, within the soviets themselves, attention had to be given to ensuring that the members of the working class were elected onto leadership committees. As Mao urged, "[a]t the time of electing executive committee members, special attention should be given to worker activists, and large numbers of such elements should be elected to the executive committee to strengthen the leading force of the proletariat in the soviet." This would serve to consolidate "the soviet political power of the dictatorship of the workers and peasants, and to strengthen the leadership of the proletariat."

The Poor Peasant League

Under Mao's administration, electoral mechanisms were therefore set in place to reinforce working class leadership of the newly established institutions of the fledgling Soviet state. However, his commitment to working class leadership was not limited to the formal institutions of the state, constituted of the hierarchical system of soviets. It extended to mass organisations that helped channel information to and from the state, and which facilitated linkage between state and society. Of particular importance was the Poor Peasant League. Despite its title, the Poor Peasant League was not limited to the class whose name it bore. As Mao pointed out in July 1933, "The poor peasant league is not an organization made up purely of a single class, but a mass organization of poor peasants within the jurisdiction of the township soviet." Importantly, leadership of this organisation, and by extension, the poor peasants themselves, was not in the hands of the poor peasants, but the working class; and where this had not occurred, Mao stressed, steps had to be taken to ensure that it did. As he pointed out, "workers in the countryside must join the poor peasant league and form a workers' small group to play an active leading role in the league and unite the broad masses of poor peasants under the leadership of the proletariat, turning the league into the most reliable pillar of the political power of the soviets."

One of the most important functions of the Poor Peasant League during the Jiangxi Soviet was the Land Investigation Movement, although it was only one of several of the Soviet's organisations involved in it. The Land Investigation Movement . . . was not merely a strategy in the agrarian revolution that had been unfolding in the Soviet area since 1930. While its objective was certainly to resolve agrarian problems using class analysis and class struggle, its purpose was also to reorganise and reform government structures and mass organisations to facilitate the mobilisation of the masses. It was thus an extremely important and broadly based campaign, which had both socioeconomic as well as organisational objectives. Nevertheless, the Poor Peasant League was crucial for the success of the Land Investigation Movement, and Mao moved to ensure it pursued an appropriate line by strengthening the representation of the working class and labour unions within it. One of the clearest indications of his perception of the limitations of the Poor Peasant League under the leadership of the poor peasants themselves was articulated in July 1933. Here, Mao makes it abundantly clear that working class leadership of this supposedly peasant organisation was absolutely essential:

> Only under the leadership of the Communist Party and the soviets can the poor peasant league correctly accomplish all its tasks, and avoid being influenced by the rich peasants or dominated by all sorts of backward peasant consciousness, such as the ideas of absolute egalitarianism and localism. . . . The unions of agricultural workers and craftsmen should try to pass motions at their own congresses about having their membership join the poor peasant league in a body, so as to bring about a constant leading role for the proletariat in the poor peasant league.

Mao was adamant that the Poor Peasant League, crucial to the success of the Land Investigation Movement, would not succeed if left to the leadership of the poor peasants themselves. It was particularly important, he felt, to encourage "farm laborers," who were the "brothers of the urban proletariat in the countryside" to join the Poor Peasant League and form independent small groups of workers within it. These workers groups "should be an active leader of the organization," and their presence would have the effect, he believed, of uniting poor peasant activists and developing the League generally. He pointed to the example of the township of Shanhe. Here, the Poor Peasant League had not been able to get the Land Investigation Movement started. It was only when the rural labor union and the handicraft workers' union became involved and provided leadership that the Movement got under way. The experience of Shanhe should, Mao believed, be applied in all rural areas. Consequently, the labor unions' leadership should "treat the task of land investigation as one of the important missions of the labor unions." Indeed, the purpose of the involvement of workers in the Poor Peasant League during the Land Investigation Movement was to "establish the leadership of the working class in the countryside." Thus, while the Poor Peasant League remained, as Mao asserted, the "central force" of the Land Investigation Movement, he exhorted the workers in the countryside to join the League "so as to lead the development of the land investigation struggle." For, "the labor union is expected to be the leader of the class struggle in the countryside, while the poor peasant league is expected to be the pillar of the struggle."

This formulation—the peasants as the "main" or "central" force, with leadership provided by the working class—is typical of Mao's understanding of the relationship between the peasantry and working class in the Chinese revolution, and also the roles of each class. Even in a policy area dedicated to change in rural areas, as the Land Investigation Movement appeared to be (particularly the elimination of feudal class relations), Mao was not prepared to leave its leadership to the peasants. Only "a constant leading role for the proletariat in the poor peasant league" could ensure that the League avoid being "dominated by all sorts of backward peasant consciousness.". . .

Workers Lead the Red Army

While Mao had much reduced control over military policy during the years of the Jiangxi Soviet, he was still concerned to ensure that leadership of the Red Army and the militias remained, where possible, in the hands of workers. . . . Mao took comfort from the fact that many members of the Labour Unions were also members of the Soviet's military organisations. In a directive of September 1932 on expanding the Red Army, Mao had insisted that investigation of class status was important in recruiting for the Red Army. Those who become Red Army soldiers, he declared, "must be the healthiest and most enthusiastic elements among the worker and peasant masses. Only in this way can the Red Army be qualitatively strengthened." However, while Mao welcomed "healthy" and "enthusiastic" peasants into the ranks of the Red Army, it would not be they, ideally at least, who would lead it. This was the prerogative of the working class. To achieve this goal, Mao directed that each military district recruit large numbers of worker cadres "so as to strengthen the leadership of the working class in the Red Guard armies." In his Report to the Second National Soviet Congress of January 1934, Mao reported that his policy had been generally successful: "Worker cadres [small, cohesive units] have increased in number [in the Red Army] and the political commissar system [organized around loyal, propagandist administrators, or commissars] has been universally instituted, so that control of the Red Army is in the hands of reliable commanders." Nevertheless, more remained to be done, and Mao exhorted further consolidation of the Red Army in the hands of workers. As he pointed out, "more people with worker backgrounds should be promoted to positions as military and political commanders at all levels." This was important, as it was necessary for people with "clear class consciousness and strong leadership ability" within the Army if mistakes were not to be made. . . .

Limiting the Impact of Peasant Weaknesses

Mao believed that, if the organisation and policies of the Soviet Government were to operate effectively, the weaknesses of the peasants as a class had to be recognised and action taken to limit their impact. Mao attempted to achieve this goal through several means. First, he formulated and implemented electoral laws that determined the membership of the soviets at all levels in a way that quite overtly favoured the working class and those who lived in cities, and which discriminated against peasants and rural dwellers. The hierarchy of soviets, from the level of the xiang soviet to the National Soviet Congress, was thus founded on the assumption that workers should be represented in the core institutions of government in numbers far greater than existed in the population at large. Mao was quite explicit in his purpose here. The peasants needed working class leadership, and a class bias in the electoral system was required to achieve it. Mao's writings on this subject reveal no false romantic sentiment about the peasants and their importance to the revolution, and there is no apologetic tone for the class discrimination that his electoral system instituted. If anything, Mao's utterances go in the opposite direction, bemoaning the impediments that stood in the way of electing sufficient workers into the soviets and leading positions within them.

Second, Mao attempted to ensure that members of the working class led the mass-based political institutions of the new Jiangxi Soviet. The Poor Peasant League is an excellent example, and reveals only too clearly that even the poor peasants, the most trusted and reliable stratum of the peasantry, required working class leadership. Mao exhorted workers to join this organisation, establish their own groups within it, and become active in its leadership. Only if they were successful in doing so would important campaigns, such as the Land Investigation Movement, be successful. . . .

Finally, Mao urged greater working class representation in and leadership of the Red Army and the militias. In 1929, he had complained that many of the organisational problems in the Red Army were a result of the large numbers of peasants recruited into it. The source of the "incorrect tendencies" in the Army lies, "of course, in the fact that its basic units are composed largely of peasants and other elements of petty bourgeois origin." During the period of the Jiangxi Soviet, Mao continued to perceive the organisational problems besetting the Red Army as deriving from the same source; and attempted to overcome these problems by increasing the recruitment of workers into the Army, and by promoting them to positions of leadership.

The Sino-Soviet Rivalry

Richard Lowenthal

When Mao Tse-tung and the Communists took over
mainland China, they were a force to contend with globally. They were neither a Soviet outpost or a small anticolonial movement. China established itself as a Communist superpower. The nation shed its backward rural
origins and built an impressive military force and economy.

As ideological schisms developed between China and
the Soviet Union, the West anticipated the possibility of a
battle between these two powers. Author Richard Lowenthal looks at the root of the Sino-Soviet rivalry. He points
out that Mao's innovative road to communism did not
portend a break between China and Russia. Rather, he argues that the ideological schism was founded in competing national interests in which both nations vied to reach
a higher form of communism.

When in 1949 the Chinese Communists established their
rule over the whole of mainland China, they changed not
only the world-wide relation of forces between the Communist "camp" and its opponents; they also transformed the nature of that camp itself. For the new state they had created
was not merely one more satellite of Stalin's Russia, but an
independent power born out of an independent revolution;
and its founders were conscious of owing their victory
chiefly to their own efforts and wholly to their own decisions—decisions taken, sometimes against [Soviet dictator
Josef] Stalin's advice, by the first Communist leader who
had, in Stalin's reign, won control of his party without
Stalin's investiture: Mao Zedong.

Henceforth there existed two Communist Great Powers.

Richard Lowenthal, *World Communism, the Disintegration of a Secular Faith*. New
York: Oxford University Press, 1964. Copyright © 1964 by Oxford University Press,
Inc. Reproduced by permission.

For though only the Soviet Union was a world power, Communist China soon established herself as a great regional power in Asia. Her intervention in the Korean War demonstrated quickly how formidable a military force the new dictatorship had built up in a country that had for decades been helpless in the grip of foreign aggression and civil strife. Her appearance at the Geneva conference of 1954 showed that, whether diplomatically recognized or not, Peking's delegates could confront the representatives of other Great Powers as equals when Asian affairs had to be settled, and did in fact exert a major influence on the terms of the Indochina armistice. By state visits to neutral Asian countries and by [Chinese minister] Chou Enlai's performance at the Bandung conference in 1955, the Chinese Communists achieved a considerable impact on the public opinion, and even on the foreign policy, of the merging "Third World" of ex-colonial nations. Finally, when [Stalin's successor Nikita] Khrushchev's overthrow of the Stalin idol was followed by a grave crisis of the Soviet's European empire, by popular revolt in Hungary and by the popularly backed change in the leadership of the Polish Communist regime, an astonished world watched how the Chinese Communist leaders during 1956–57 threw their intact authority into the scales to preserve the cohesion of the Communist bloc and world movement under Soviet leadership— the first effective intervention of China in the history of modern Europe. Poor and backward China, so obviously dependent on Russian military and economic aid, had seemingly demonstrated to its powerful protectors in the Kremlin that they in turn had become dependent on Chinese ideological support.

It was natural that so impressive a display of Chinese independence should give rise to Western speculations about the possibility of eventual conflict between the two main Communist powers; and these speculations increased interest in the accumulating evidence that the Chinese Communists under Mao's leadership had a way of solving their problems that differed persistently from the Russian Bolshevik model. Moreover, the Chinese Communists themselves had increasingly come to emphasize these differences in their strategy for conquering power, in their style of inner-party work, and in their methods for "building socialism," as achievements due to Mao Zedong's creative adaptation of "Marxism-Leninism" to the conditions of an underdeveloped, semi-colonial Asian country; and they had also proclaimed the Chinese road as the appropriate model for the Communists of other parts of the underdeveloped world. Hence when clear evidence of Sino-Soviet disagreements—both over questions of foreign and military policy and over the new Chinese "people's communes"—began to reach the West during 1958 and 1959, the question naturally arose as to what extent these disagreements reflected not only differences of national interest or personal and national rivalries for leadership within the Communist bloc and world movement, but also differences of ideological emphasis and inner-party style rooted in the different histories and conditions of development of the Soviet and Chinese Communist parties.

Ideological Schisms Led to Conflict

By now, this question ought to have been settled by events. For as the half-hidden Sino-Soviet disagreements of 1958 and 1959 have grown into open, full-scale conflict, both sides have formulated their positions on each disputed issue in ideological terms, until finally two complete rival systems of interpretation of the Marxist-Leninist doctrine have come to be developed by Moscow and Peking. This does not, of course, prove that the historic differences between the outlook and approach of the two ruling Communist parties, and even the tendency to erect them into rival models for the revolutionaries of other countries, would by themselves have been sufficient to cause the present conflict; I believe that it was an increasingly acute divergence of national interest that brought about the first critical change from differences of opinion to conflict of policies. But the further crucial transformation, by which these practical conflicts of interest gave rise to an ideological schism between two rival versions of the creed, seems hardly conceivable without that historic difference of outlook and approach: clearly, it was that preexistent difference that made it possible for either side to erect a coherent ideological structure out of the materials furnished by various practical disagreements.

Yet in Western specialist discussion, the recognition of this historical and structural element in the present Sino-Soviet conflict is still to some extent obstructed by the long-standing controversy about "the originality of Mao Zedong" or about the existence of a specifically "Maoist" strategy for the conquest of power. While one group of scholars has from an early stage emphasized the new features by which Mao adapted his strategy to Chinese conditions and the differences between this Chinese version of Leninism and the Soviet version as interpreted by Stalin, another school has attempted to prove that in all his practical innovations Mao has kept strictly within the framework of Leninist, and indeed Stalinist, orthodoxy.

It is clearly not possible to discuss the historical background to the Sino-Soviet schism without taking sides in this controversy. This does not, however, require that we should enter into a detailed examination of the various disputed historical facts; for a study of the relevant literature shows that the heart of the matter is not in historical disagreements about the relation between Soviet and Chinese Communist policies at particular times, but in methodological differences about the relation between political decisions and their justification in terms of doctrine.

Mao Was an Innovator

Those who deny Mao's "ideological originality" apparently believe that the Leninist doctrine is by itself sufficient to determine the proper strategy for any given situation; hence statements justifying a major policy decision in doctrinal terms may be taken as adequately indicating the actual motives of that decision. This method of interpretation is dogmatic in the sense that the understanding of the actions of Communist leaders is reduced to the immanent exegesis [critical explanation] of the dogma they profess.

By contrast, those who regard Mao as an innovator assume that no political doctrine can possibly anticipate all the major choices by which its followers may be faced: at crucial moments, "ideological" politicians are forced to give preference to one element of the doctrine over another with which, owing to unforeseen circumstances, it has come into conflict. Whichever decision has been taken will henceforth be justified by emphasizing the corresponding aspect of the doctrine; hence it is not the unchanging doctrine that has determined the decision but the decision that determines the further evolution of the doctrine. This method of interpretation is functional and critical in the sense that the doctrine is seen as a justifying ideology as well as a motivating force, and it is truly historical in focusing attention on the preferences that determine the crucial choices—even if those preferences may not yet have found a mature formulation.

In siding with the latter view, I do not have to assume that Mao was ever consciously heretical, or even that he clearly saw himself as an innovator as soon as he actually started to explore new roads. He was confronted with situations unforeseen by the orthodox theory, and he took new decisions in meeting them; whether his decisions were "orthodox" is therefore a secondary, and in some cases a strictly meaningless, question. What cannot seriously be disputed is that, in taking new decisions to meet new problems, Mao imparted to Chinese Communist strategy and organization, and *therefore* also to Chinese Communist ideology, new characteristics differing from those of Soviet communism. Our concern here is to try and identify these distinctive characteristics, to trace their origin in the conditions in which Chinese communism rose to power, and to point to their consequences for the later course of relations between the two leading Communist parties.

Sino-Soviet Ideological Differences

When a wider non-Communist public first became aware of the existence of major differences of outlook and approach between the Soviet and Chinese Communists, the impression was contradictory and confusing. Thus when the Chinese Communists advised Khrushchev during the winter of 1956–57 to tolerate the new leadership of the Polish Communists headed by Gomulka and to grant its demand for increased autonomy in shaping the Polish state and the Polish economy in return for a pledge of bloc discipline in foreign policy, this was generally viewed as proof that Mao represented a more "liberal" type of communism than the Soviet leaders. At the time, this interpretation seemed to be confirmed by Mao's famous instruction to his party machine to "let a hundred flowers bloom, let a hundred schools contend" in intellectual discussion, and by his sensational admission of the existence of "contradictions between the leadership and the masses" within his regime, which were to be kept in a "non-antagonistic," that is, non-explosive, framework by opening safety valves for the expression of legitimate grievances. Yet as early as the summer of 1957, this period of domestic relaxation was followed in China by a new drive to purge the critical intellectuals, which in turn considerably exceeded by its ruthlessness the corresponding post-Hungarian reaction period in the Soviet Union. During the following year, the Chinese Communists took the most intolerant and aggressive position in the Soviet bloc's new conflict with Yugoslavia; and finally, in trying to achieve a sudden total revolution in the living and working conditions of hundreds of millions of Chinese peasants by means of the "people's communes," they acted with a degree of doctrinaire utopianism that provoked the criticism of the Soviet leaders and produced results that soon forced a partial correction.

Clearly, then, our alternatives of tolerance or intolerance, liberalism or dogmatism, relaxation or rigidity do not get to the root of the underlying ideological differences. To uncover this root, we have to go back to the historic beginnings of Chinese communism as an autonomous movement—beginnings which we may date from Mao Zedong's stepping forward as leader of an independent unit of Communist partisans toward the close of 1927.

Revolution Through Peasant Uprising

At that time, Stalin's Chinese policy of the 'twenties had ended in a catastrophic defeat. On Stalin's instructions, the Chinese Communists, while maintaining their separate party organization, had individually entered the revolutionary nationalist party, the Kuomintang, and had systematically supported the organization of its Canton power base and its Northern expedition for the unification of China; by this "united front from within," they had aimed to develop mass organizations of the workers and peasants under their own control, to occupy key positions in government and army, and to cement the alliance between the Soviet Union and the emerging Chinese nationalist government. Yet with the victorious advance of the nationalist armies and with the unfolding of the revolutionary peasant movement, conflicts between the Kuomintang leadership and the Communist-directed workers' and peasants' unions had multiplied. While the Communists were still following Stalin's orders in searching for compromise, Chiang Kai-shek, as commander in chief of the nationalist army, had suddenly broken with them and begun to destroy their organizations and exterminate their cadres [units of loyal followers]. After a period of confusion, the Communists reacted with desperate attempts at insurrection in several South Chinese cities; but the discouraged workers no longer followed their slogans, and the isolated little bands of armed Communists were defeated everywhere without difficulty.

It was in this situation that Mao, then no more than an important Communist Party official in Hunan province, led the remnants of his armed followers—rebel units from the nationalist army, proscribed Communist workers, and uprooted peasants—to temporary safety in the mountain stronghold of Chingkanshan. At first this was hardly more than an act of self-preservation; instinctively the peasant's son fell back on the ancient Chinese tradition of peasant risings. Even before the final break with the Kuomintang, Mao had warned the party against underestimating the elementary force of the peasant movement; now, in defeat, he chose the road of rural partisan warfare for which few other Communists saw a future. But Mao knew as well as his comrades that China's traditional peasant risings had never been victorious unless leaders from outside, that is, from the educated classes, had enabled them to overcome their limited local horizon and to merge into a nation-wide movement; now, he developed the concept that this would have to be the role of the Communists in Chinese conditions. Lenin had built up his Bolshevik Party as a centralized organization of professional revolutionaries, in order to "introduce" the conscious revolutionary struggle for political power into the young Russian labor movement; just so, the Chinese Communist cadres were henceforth to give political leadership and military unity and mobility to the peasant partisans. The eventual fruit of this concept was not only the creation and expansion of large "Soviet areas" deep in the rural hinterland of China, but the successful "mobilization" of many thousands of uprooted peasants, their transformation into an army of partisans who were to prove their ability to fight far from their native region in the ordeal of the now legendary "long march" from the Southern "Soviet areas" to Yenan in the far Northwest. . . .

A New Brand of Communism

Naturally, the fact that the Chinese Communists followed a different road to power was also noticed by many Western observers at an early stage; and just as many Communist doctrinaires, both in Russia and in China, doubted for years the "orthodoxy" of Mao's strategy, many of those Western observers at first believed that Mao and his men were not "real" Communists, but were merely leading a militant movement for agrarian reform. The underlying error, common to both views, consisted in defining a modern Communist Party in Marxian terms as a representative organ of the industrial working class, and not in Leninist terms as a centralized party organized for total power. In fact, the Russian Bolsheviks' pretense of being a working-class party had never been true either, even when industrial workers constituted the majority of their membership—because their form of organization made them independent of the actual support of the bulk of the working class and enabled them to change their "social basis" as occasion required: only parties with a democratic structure can truly be class parties, for only they are permanently tied to the particular social soil from which they have grown and from which they draw their nourishment. Rather, the Bolsheviks are a modern totalitarian cadre party, led by "professional revolutionaries," which originally relied on the support of a section of Russia's industrial working class, but as a ruling party has long since merged with the bureaucracy of the Soviet state and mastered the totalitarian art of balancing between the various classes of Soviet society and manipulating them all. Just so, Mao's Chinese Communist Party never was a class party of the peasants; it is a totalitarian cadre party which during the civil war relied primarily on peasant support, but as a ruling party has long since proved its ability to manipulate and, if necessary, oppress the peasants no less effectively than it manipulates and oppresses China's other social classes. . . .

Mao Supported Soviet Authority in Eastern Europe

Throughout this development, the Chinese Communists acted as the pioneers of a new, successful Asian policy for the whole Soviet bloc; yet their "vanguard role" did not then take organizational form. As far as we know, the technical links of most Asian Communist parties continued to be with Moscow rather than Peking, and Peking does not seem to have asked for more direct organizational control at that time—except over parties whose members were of predominantly Chinese nationality, as in Malaya. But the formal dissolution of the Cominform [league of international Communists, held in Russia] in April 1956 was bound to revive debate over the proper form of international contacts among Communists; and it occurred at a time when Khrushchev's disclosures about Stalin's crimes [purging of rivals and execution of untold numbers of dissidents and innocent civilians] had shaken the authority of the Soviet Union throughout the world Communist movement, and when many a major leader of European communism took the road to Peking in order to find comfort and ideological assurance in the unbroken authority of Mao—the victorious leader of a great revolution and not a successor's successor like the men in the Kremlin. As the year proceeded and the Polish and Hungarian events made the crisis of Communist ideology and Soviet authority increasingly manifest, those Communist pilgrimages to the Peking oracle became more and more frequent.

By the winter of 1956–57 it appeared that the overcoming of the crisis and the future cohesion of the bloc might depend to a considerable extent on the intervention of Mao's intact authority; and the Chinese Communists had far too large a stake in the working of the economic system of Soviet-controlled Eastern Europe to think of withholding such intervention. In the theoretical debate, it took the form of their second statement on Stalin's errors, in which they acquitted the Soviet Union of any charge of structural degeneration, thoroughly condemned the Hungarian popular revolt as "counter-revolutionary," and rejected the cautious and hesitant doubts raised by the Yugoslavs about Soviet military action in Hungary [to suppress anti-Soviet uprisings]; in the field of practical diplomacy, it was supplemented by Chou En-lai's European visit and his assumption of the role of mediator between Khrushchev and Gomulka's new team in Poland. . . .

The Soviets Criticize China

The Chinese Communists had begun to prepare for . . . ideological rivalry. In April 1958, they founded their first experimental "people's commune," and they ominously baptized it "Sputnik"—as if, by alluding to Mao's words, they now wished to stake a claim to equality in leadership after all.

We may only speculate about the reasons for this change. We know that the "people's communes" were formed in an attempt to solve the urgent problems of Chinese industrialization despite an extreme shortage of capital; and we also know that one of the causes for that attempt was that the Soviet Union, though willing to sell China considerable amounts of new industrial plant, had offered no new loans for that purpose since 1956. It was thus partly the Soviet Union's fault that China had to rely on her own resources for her "Great Leap Forward" and to devise her own original methods for that purpose. Hence this leap really originated as an effort to increase China's economic capacity and

power more rapidly than the Soviets considered possible—
or even desirable. When, in August, the Chinese leaders decided that the first unpublicized pilot communes had been a
success and proceeded to proclaim a policy of transferring
the entire rural population into these new units, their ideological enthusiasm made it seem natural to present this revolutionary emergency measure as a direct short cut to the
higher stage of communism. It seemed natural because of
the Chinese Communists' traditional inclination to leap
over objective conditions and to believe that nothing was
impossible to a determined will guided by a clearly conceived aim; but it also seemed natural because resentment
against the slowing down of China's development by insufficient capital aid from Russia increased the appeal of an idea
that implied that China, thanks to the genius of Mao Zedong, was about to catch up with the Soviet Union and even
surpass it on the road to the higher stage of communism.

Thus by the last four months of 1958, the ideological rivalry between Peking and Moscow had become fairly open.
While Peking's campaign for the new communes was at its
climax, Moscow at first kept silent about the affair, then
published some remarkably detached reports stressing the
heroic primitivity of the rural furnaces and the "war Communist" atmosphere of work in the communes, and finally
began a theoretical discussion about the Soviet road to communism. Its participants never mentioned China but emphasized in article after article that progress toward the
higher stage of communism was only possible on the basis of
the highest technical productivity. . . .

Ideological Rivalry

The chief counter-action by the Soviets, apart from the unpublicized intervention in various Communist-governed
countries at which we may guess, was taken in the context of
preparations for the Twenty-first Congress of the CPSU
[Communist Party of the Soviet Union]; and there are indications that this Congress—an "extra-ordinary" one, that is,
one not yet due under the party statutes—was called chiefly
for this purpose. The only point on its agenda, the new

seven-year plan, could just as well have been decided on and popularized by different means; the plan only became a subject for a party congress because it was treated not as a purely economic project, but as the first step in laying the foundations for the higher stage of communism, and the Congress itself was announced as "the Congress of the builders of communism." The preparations thus furnished to the Soviet leaders ample opportunity for explaining again and again their orthodox Marxist version of the interdependence between the raising of productivity and the standard of living and the transition to a classless society, and also for stressing both the need for maintaining differential incentive wages and the role of money as a yardstick of cost and return all along the road to communism. Every one of these arguments was a blow aimed against the claims of the Chinese Communists and against their idealistic tendency to leap over the objective conditions—even though the Chinese were never mentioned by name. . . .

But just as surely as the distinctive characteristics of Chinese Communist ideology and strategy are rooted in the difficulties of modernizing an underdeveloped and overpopulated country, so the utopian hopes raised among the Chinese Communists by the campaign for the "people's communes" must have found an echo in the hearts and minds of many other Communists throughout Asia. In future debates, these Asian Communists would find the Chinese of Mao and his followers easier to understand than the Russian of their Soviet comrades—a language that to their ears has become Westernized with the progress of Russia's industrial technique.

Ho Chi Minh Unified Vietnamese Communists

Douglas Pike

Ho Chi Minh was a well-educated, well-traveled Vietnamese revolutionary. An eager socialist, Ho was given orders in 1925 by the Russian-based Comintern (international organization of Communists) to start a Communist revolution in Indochina. He embraced the challenge and set out to create a Communist organization from Vietnamese patriots living in exile in Canton, China.

Communism, then, was imported to Vietnam from the various radical émigrés living in Southern China in the 1920s. Ho had formed the Thanh Nien, whose membership was a mixture of Socialists and Nationalists. The Thanh Nien suffered from ideological differences and eventually disintegrated into different factions. The disputes centered around whether the national revolution or the world revolution should take priority. In 1929, Ho was given orders by the Comintern to unify these factions into one Communist Party. This goal was achieved at the historic unification conference at a soccer stadium in Hong Kong on January 6, 1930, where the Vietnamese Communist Party was born.

In the following article, Douglas Pike points out that it was Ho Chi Minh's experience and organizational ingenuity that brought the Nationalists and the Communists together in an effort to mobilize a revolutionary movement in Vietnam. These efforts would be slow to take, as Vietnam was still a French-controlled colony through the 1930s. And in 1940, the Japanese seized the nation in their bid for conquest of Indochina. In 1945, however, when Japan was defeated at the close of World War II, Ho Chi Minh and other Communists declared the rural, northern

Douglas Pike, "The Birth of Vietnamese Communism," *History of Vietnamese Communism, 1925–1976*. Stanford, CA: Hoover Institution Press, 1978. Copyright © 1978 by the Board of Trustees of the Leland Stanford Junior University. Reproduced by permission of the publisher.

half of Vietnam to be an independent Socialist country.

Douglas Pike was the director of Indo-china studies at the University of California, Berkeley, from 1982–1996.

Vietnamese communism was born, if so amorphous a development as a modern mass movement has a fixed time and place of birth, in Canton in 1925.

Although it was a historic moment, there in south China, it was only recognized in retrospect that a fundamental change had occurred in Vietnamese history, the mantle of destiny passed from Vietnamese reformer to Vietnamese revolutionary. The first generation of anticolonialists, who had so largely determined the degree and kind of opposition offered the French [who had colonized Vietnam and controlled it until the 1950s], was fading from the scene, its doctrine in disgrace, its organizational techniques now scorned. [Vietnamese militant] Phan Boi Chau was in jail, Phan Chau Trinh [who fought to end Vietnam's feudal system] was dead—typical fates of the initial leaders. Vietnamese radicals of all stripes, many of whom were living in Canton at the moment, suffered varying degrees of disillusionment over the failure of the cause to advance much under the banners of [socialist organizations such as] the Tan Viet, the Tam Tam Xa, and lesser groups then in operation.

It was a propitious moment for the arrival on the scene of a new figure representing a new force in world history. He was a well-traveled, Moscow-trained communist revolutionary, experienced beyond his years. And he arrived in Canton with the authority of a full Comintern agent able to claim as a base of power both the USSR and the Communist Party apparatus in south China. He was the man the world came to know as Ho Chi Minh. Assigned as a liaison agent in the Comintern mission to the [nationalist party] Kuomintang (KMT) of China, to work directly under the even then legendary [Soviet state and party leader] Mikhail Borodin, Ho's orders were to begin a systematic and intensive effort to develop a communist movement in Indochina, using as his nucleus the various Vietnamese émigré radicals in Canton.

Ho Chi Minh Establishes Vietnamese Communism

Ho was a wise choice in such a venture. Boldly he struck out in new organizational directions and created the first of what proved to be a long succession of complex, involuted, overlapping structures, yet with an unchanging essence. This first structure had three elements.

The first was the Oppressed Asian People's Association (Bi Ap Buc Dan Toc Lien Hiep Hoi), what today would be called a communist-led mass organization. Its cofounder was the famed early Indian communist figure, M.N. Roy. The association was designed to be Asian-wide and to include Koreans, Chinese, Indochinese, Indians, and Indonesians. It apparently reflected a grandiose Comintern ambition to create a pan-Asian (or Nan Yang/South Seas) Communist movement. The association, as well as the broader Comintern effort, came to little. It was broken up by police in the respective countries; it never did get the support required to make it a success; and it lasted only a few years. This was Ho's first experiment in united fronts and served, if nothing else, to help school him.

The second element was the (Vietnamese) Young Revolutionary Youth League (Thanh Nien Cach Mang Dong Chi Hoi, originally without the term dong chi), or Thanh Nien for short. It was not a communist party nor a simple front organization but something of both, a nationalist-socialist movement (as Ho described it) incorporating certain party organizational techniques. It was never large, numbering perhaps 50 at the time of its formation, 300 by 1928, and 1,000 by 1930. Two-thirds of its members were in Vietnam, the rest in China.

The third element was an informal but disciplined inner group, the Communist Youth League (Thanh Nien Cong San Doan), which was the beginning of the Party. . . .

At the time of its formation, the Thanh Nien Cong San Doan consisted of Ho and six to eight youths. Even later it was only a lateral organization, that is, a cluster of communist cells made up of select members from the Thanh Nien working through that organization and reporting directly to Ho

Chi Minh. It was the proto-Communist Party of Vietnam.

This two-tier arrangement—that is, half Party and half non-Party—was dictated by Ho's estimate, one shared by the Comintern, that Vietnam was too backward for a regular communist party. Reportedly Ho argued in Moscow in the summer of 1927 against formation of a communist party in Vietnam on the grounds that no one in Vietnam understood the word *communism*. Deception apparently was not part of his purpose, for Ho at that time was embracing the idea of communism publicly. For example, in the May 1926 issue of *Thanh nien* (the organization's official publication) he wrote that "only a communist party can assure the [eventual] well-being of Annam [i.e., Vietnam]."

Of course, the wheel-within-a-wheel arrangement did permit a more sharply disciplined and orthodox approach both to doctrine and to organization because, as Ho expressed it, in the "Cong San Doan were comrades properly ideologically armed."

The two-tier arrangement also became geographic. Head and body were born in Canton. It was necessary to transplant the body to Indochina and graft onto it all available local revolutionary sentiment. The head remained abroad and would stay there for another decade and a half.

Far more than the various nationalist movements, then, communism came to Vietnam as an import, the result of alien initiative. As an institution it was conceived outside Vietnam, launched from foreign soil, managed from abroad during its formative years and, to a degree, fostered and sustained by interests largely irrelevant to Vietnam. . . .

Thanh Nien Approaches Collapse

By 1930 the Vietnamese proto-Communist movement had on its rolls 250–300 cadres [small, well-disciplined units], plus 1,300–1,500 members or close collaborators. This organizational force was concentrated (70 percent of the strength) in Tonkin (the North), chiefly in the two cities of Hanoi and Haiphong and the three provinces of Nam Dinh, Thai Binh, and Bac Ninh. It was weaker (20 percent) in Annam (the Center), existing there mainly in the city of Hue and the province of Binh Dinh. Activity (10 percent) in Cochin China (the South) centered around the three major cities of Saigon, My Tho, and Can Tho.

But the Thanh Nien was disintegrating. This was due chiefly to ever-widening fissures—triggered by personality clashes and doctrinal differences—in the cadre corps and in the rank and file. Absence of the strong guiding figure of Ho Chi Minh was also a contributing factor. A third reason was geographic regionalism, the influence among members of the ever-present North-Center-South sense of identification.

At the time of its formation, the Thanh Nien was a group in fairly close doctrinal harmony. Its chief theoretical guide was [Russian leader Nikolai] Lenin. His theory of imperialism adequately explained the Indochinese situation to most Thanh Nien followers. Ho added his own ideological contribution, *Revolutionary Road* (1925). His major points:

• The revolution must have a proletarian [laboring class], mass base; the worker is the unit, the city the vortex (the peasant was yet to be brought to center stage).

• Marxist-Leninist organizational principles must be employed, that is, organization stressed over personalized leadership, the vanguard principle, the party as elite, the central committee—cell hierarchical structure.

• All policies must conform to the wishes of the Third International [Comintern].

This last principle never was acceptable to all members and eventually became a chief cause of the Thanh Nien's collapse. Within the question of obedience to proletarian internationalism three specific doctrinal disputes developed.

Which comes first, the world revolution or the national revolution, and which should be favored in the allocation of resources? The Comintern held for the former. Involved here was the issue of emancipation of Vietnam versus development of a worldwide class struggle.

Should the revolution be one-stage or two-stage? The Comintern held for two-stage: first comes the bourgeois [middle-class property owner] democratic revolution that wins independence from colonial rule, then the socialist revolution against the bourgeois democratic regime.

What is the proper relationship of the movement to less radical organizations, particularly to non-Communist revolutionary groups?

Beneath the doctrinal debate was a deeper consideration: the general sense—shared mostly by those who came to be known as the Tonkin Group—of the current of historical development. In the past half decade, it was said, some members had developed along progressive lines and had become increasingly proletarian-minded; others had not moved in this direction and were as bourgeois as ever. Further, because of parochialism, some members did not (and could not) adjust to the mandatory imposition of Comintern discipline. The future belonged to the centrally directed, proletarian-based revolutionary; the failure in the Thanh Nien was that some members simply could not see the road down which Vietnam was traveling.

Thanh Nien Splits

An effort to heal this doctrinal breach, doomed before it began, was made at the Thanh Nien congress in Hong Kong in May 1929. Rather than unifying the membership, it set loose forces that resulted in a three-way split of the Vietnamese proto-Communist movement.

The Indochinese Communist Party (Dong Duong Cong San Dang) was officially proclaimed in June 1929. This was the Tonkin Group, based in Hanoi, urban-centered and industrial-worker-oriented. It set out to be a classic by-the-book communist movement. Major figures included Ngo Gia Tu, Nguyen Van Tuan, Tran Van Cung, Trinh Dinh Cuu, Nguyen Phong Sac, Quoc Anh, Do Ngoc Du, and Tran Tu Thinh (Bang Phong). It published *Bua liem* (Hammer and Sickle) for rank and file, *Bon-se-vich* (Bolshevik) for cadres, and *Co do* (Red Flag) as organ of the Red Trade Union composed of urban proletarians.

The ACP, the Annam Communist Party (Annam Cong San Dang), was formed, a creation of the original Thanh Nien Central Committee (whose leaders for a period operated under both flags). Smaller and less proletarian in composition than the ICP, it was led mostly by teachers and intellectuals. Also, it was more indigenous and less émigré in character than the ICP. It published *Do* (Red Journal) and a newspaper, *Bon-se-vich* (Bolshevik).

The ICL, the Indochinese Communist League, or Al-

Ho Chi Minh Appealed to Nationalist Sentiment

Ho Chi Minh's first political organization was called the "Association of Vietnamese Revolutionary Youth." Author Lea E. Williams points out that the name appealed to a mass audience primarily because it avoided the term "communism."

Collaboration between the Chinese Communists and the Kuomintang [Chinese nationalist] during the mid-1920's enabled Ho to base himself at Canton [in China]. The site was attractive because of its proximity to the Tonkinese frontier [border between China and Vietnam] and because it had become a haven for a handful of Vietnamese who had been linked to nationalist stirrings and forced into flight by the colonial regime. Working among his compatriots in the southern China city, Ho assembled a following that in 1925 banded together as the Association of Vietnamese Revolutionary Youth, a body that was directly ancestral to the Vietnam Communist Party born five years later. It is worth noting that Ho's first political organization bore a name designed to appeal to the widest possible audience, for the technique of suggesting nationalist coalition through the use of labels that avoided direct mention of communism was to be repeated.

The climate of discontent in Vietnam in 1930 prompted the Communists, as it had the VNQDD [Vietnamese nationalist party] earlier in the year, to turn to violence, with peasant rage harnessed to the Marxist-Leninist cause. Rebellious outbreaks in the countryside and urban work stoppages profoundly alarmed the authorities but never menaced their ability to react. Military assaults on rural pockets of upheaval caused heavy loss of life; police sweeps netted thousands.

Lea E. Williams, *Southeast Asia: A History.* New York: Oxford University Press, 1976.

liance (Dong Duong Cong San Lien Doan), also arose. It included some Thanh Nien residue but was mainly a continuation of the militant Tan Viet. Its major figure was Tran Phu, and its members were mostly students and teachers; thus it was more bourgeois than either the ICP or the ACP. For several years the ICL and its predecessor organizations represented a separate stream of rather impure communist thought, or, as Ho Chi Minh expressed it, having only Marxist tendencies. Through the 1920s, however, this element maintained close relations with Ho; in fact, most of its cadres were trained by him. Doctrinally, the ICL was more utopian and in some ways more bloody-handed than either the ICP or the ACP.

The Comintern Stressed Unity

Both the ICP and the ACP sought the Comintern seal of approval and each tried to get Ho Chi Minh to plead its case. The Comintern, after issuing a patronizing criticism of the existing factionalism, ordered Ho to Hong Kong to effect a unification and upgrading of the Indochinese communist movement. . . .

The Comintern directive (October 27, 1929) that ordered the formation of the ICP officially determined that Indochina was ready for a normal communist party.

> Divisions among various Communist groups . . . cannot be tolerated. . . . The most urgent important task of all Communists in Indochina is to form a revolutionary party with a proletarian class base, that is, a popular Communist Party of Indochina. It should be the only Communist organization in Indochina. . . .

The Comintern's position was that the Thanh Nien's indecisiveness and lack of self-discipline was engendering disunity, the movement's greatest danger. It asserted that objective conditions for a capitalist revolution did exist in Vietnam and that the consciousness of the workers there had been raised to a level such that creation of a communist party was not only possible but urgently required. Actually, it is not clear whether the Comintern ordered formation because it truly believed Indochina was ready for a regular party or simply saw it as the best means of ending organizational disarray and competition. The Comintern did make it clear who was the wooer and who the wooed, setting down twenty-one conditions to be met before the proposed party would be admitted into the world communist fraternity.

The Unification Conference

The historic unification conference began in a soccer stadium in Hong Kong (some reports place it in a rural Kowloon barn) on January 6, 1930, and lasted several weeks. Ho Chi Minh presided, and attending were about a dozen individuals representing the ICP and the ACP. The ICL was not present officially, although apparently some of its members were. The Vietnam Communist Party (Vietnam Cong San Dang) was formed with a chapter membership of 211, according to official history; this included 85 members from the ICP or Tonkin Group, 61 from the ACP, 11 from the ICL, and 54 other Vietnamese communists living abroad, mainly in Canton and Hong Kong.

The results of the conference and the actions that followed it were these:

- It unified the disparate organizational elements into a single, formal communist party, proclaimed the Vietnam Communist Party on February 3, 1930. It established a nine-man Central Committee with Tran Phu as secretary general.
- It integrated the Vietnamese communist movement into the regional and worldwide communist system and arranged a formal liaison mechanism. At the lowest (or national) level, the Party was equal to the Siam and Malay Communist parties. These three were coordinated laterally by the Comintern's Southern Bureau in Singapore, which administratively was under the Comintern Far Eastern Bureau in Shanghai. The Shanghai Bureau reported directly to the Communist International (Comintern) in Moscow.
- It arranged the Party's incorporation into the network of international front and collaborationist organiza-

tions, chiefly those involving trade unions. The primary organization in Asia for this activity was the Pan-Pacific Trade Union, a communist front headquartered in Shanghai, submember of the Red International of Labor Unions of Moscow. This front linkage also involved connections with the Unitaire Confederation Generale du Travail (Unitary CGT) in Paris. The Unitary CGT was an arm of the French Communist Party, hence there was established early a strong and in some ways peculiar connection between the communist parties of Indochina and France.

- Internally, it created a network of overlapping front and mutual-interest organizations, an institutional approach that was to become a Ho Chi Minh hallmark. These included the National United Front against Imperialism (Mat Tran Dan Toc Thong Nhat Chong De Quoc), the smaller Antiimperialist League (Hoi Dong Minh Phan De), the Red Peasant Association (Nong Hoi Do), the Women's Liberation Association (Hoi Phu Nu Giai Phong), the Party youth organization formed in Saigon on March 31, 1931, and initially called the Communist Youth Group (Thanh Nien Cong San Doan), plus a welter of of basic-level elements: assistance associations; organizations of workers, small traders, and owners of small industrial concerns; sports and training associations; reading societies; harvest, rice-transplanting, and roof-rethatching teams; burial societies; hunting and fishing clubs; feasting societies (during Tet [Vietnamese holiday]), and others.

- It received and ratified Ho Chi Minh's famous "Political platform and outline of strategy" (Chinh cuong sach luoc van tat), a philosophic rather than program-oriented outline of future Party policy. . . .

- It arranged systematic financial support for the movement, soon including an annual Comintern appropriation of about $25,000 (U.S. equivalent) per year.

- It ordered the formation of a newspaper, *Tien len* (Forward), which became the initial Party organ and was distributed widely during the crucial years of 1931 and 1932.

- In sum, the conference, in the official view, unleashed a new force in Indochina.

Name Change

The Comintern was not entirely satisfied. Being oriented toward pan-Asianism rather than toward national-level communism, it was particularly displeased with the parochial choice of name: the Vietnam Communist Party. . . .

In response—and apparently over the demur of Ho Chi Minh, for whom this represented a political setback—the Party Central Committee met in October 1930 and changed the official name to Indochinese Communist Party (Dang Cong San Dong Duong). Thereupon, it was granted national section status by the Comintern at its Eleventh Plenum in April 1931.

The rechristening came at the Party's First Plenum (October 1930), at which Party representatives also formally elected Tran Phu and the nine-man Central Committee and added detail to earlier instructions by accepting Tran Phu's "Political program" (Luan cuong chinh tri). The program: (a) acknowledged that the Vietnamese and world revolutions were a seamless web; (b) accepted the two-stage revolutionary scenario for Vietnam; (c) fixed as the Party's two chief tasks ending imperialism and ending feudalism in Vietnam, to be accomplished so as to skip one of the Marxist stages of development—the capitalist stage; (d) broadened the revolutionary base to root the struggle in a worker-peasant alliance. As to intra-Party matters, the Party determined:

> The essential conditions for assuring the victory of the revolution is to have a Communist Party to use Marxism-Leninism as the ideological foundation, to have the correct political line for leading the revolution, to organize in accordance with democratic centralism, to have strict discipline, to maintain close contact with the masses, and to mature in the process of revolutionary struggle.

The plenum also addressed itself to the membership problem. There had been considerable fall-away in the summer after unification. A recruitment drive was ordered, with specific instructions to concentrate on proletarians and particularly on factory workers.

A few conclusions and judgments can be offered about the Vietnamese proto-Communist movement of the 1920s.

- It had, for a variety of reasons, a breadth of vision and because of this was able to create a first-generation, sophisticated revolutionary organization, one that appealed to the most promising Vietnamese youths but was so structured as effectively to hold its members in line.

- It had the services of Ho Chi Minh—not only his organizational genius, but also the guidance, assistance, and experience he could summon in the international fraternity of revolutionaries. This was an invaluable connection, which by comparison made indigenous revolutionary movements seem parochial and naïve.

- Relative to earlier groups, it was unified, solid in structure, and resilient and was able to reduce, at least at its core, the most serious internal weakness of revolutionary movements: meandering, argumentative disunity.

- Its day-to-day activities were based on mass action and intensive agit-prop work among the proletariat, which—whatever the effect or lack of it on the ordinary Vietnamese worker—was of enormous benefit to the cadre and Party members involved, for it provided both purpose and experience.

- It had a corps of dedicated revolutionaires, carefully recruited, well trained, skillfully led, and lacking only practical experience that time alone could produce.

- It had international support, from the Comintern and from China. The importance of this can easily be exaggerated, for communism in Indochina in the 1920s was no well-ordered operation run from Moscow or Canton. In fact, it seemed at times as if the Comintern in particular had no real interest in what was happening in Indochina. Yet the movement did receive aid, both material and psychological, from both sources and without it could have died before taking root.

- Events of the 1920s largely shaped the direction the Party would take in the decade that followed. It began to shift from a bourgeois alliance to a more orthodox Marxist relationship with the proletariat, not yet having grasped the full meaning of rooting a revolution in the peasantry, although glimmerings of this notion already were clear by 1930. Proselyting of intellectuals began in earnest, along with the necessary dissembling of Party lines in order to appeal to diverse elements. Experimentation with the techniques of the united front were well under way. Finally, stress began to be placed on the idea that the Vietnamese revolution, to succeed, could not depend on the Chinese or on any other outside source of support (even though such support would in fact be necessary).

Ho Chi Minh Was a Master Opportunist

Robert F. Turner

The Russian Revolution and its leader Vladimir Ilyich
Lenin had a major influence on Vietnamese revolutionary
Ho Chi Minh. Ho saw Lenin as a guiding light for the
people of Vietnam, who suffered under French colonial
rule in the early decades of the twentieth century. Ho traveled abroad for nearly thirty years, absorbing Leninist
thought, before returning to begin a revolution in Vietnam.
    The author of the following excerpt, Robert F. Turner,
maintains that Ho Chi Minh's greatest attribute was his
ability to navigate between the French colonialist forces and
the Vietnamese nationalists who wanted a free Vietnam but
not a Communist one. Ho managed to turn his rivals
against each other, leaving time and room for communism
to take hold in the people of Vietnam. Robert F. Turner was
the regional editor of *Yearbook on International Communist
Affairs* in 1973–1974 and was a lecturer in law, government,
and foreign affairs at the University of Virginia.

The establishment of a Communist movement in Vietnam
resulted primarily from the efforts of two individuals,
Vladimir Ilyich Ulyanov, better known to the world as
Lenin, and Nguyen Tat Thanh, better known as Ho Chi
Minh. Lenin's contributions included his founding of the
Third or Communist International (Comintern) in 1919,
and his appreciation of the role Asian colonies would play in
the world revolution. Ho Chi Minh was responsible for the
application of Leninism to Vietnam.
    To Ho Chi Minh, Lenin was "our father, teacher, com-

Robert F. Turner, *Vietnamese Communism, Its Origins and Development.* Stanford,
CA: Hoover Institution Press, 1975. Copyright © 1975 by the Board of Trustees of
the Leland Stanford Junior University. Reproduced by permission of the publisher.

rade and adviser," Leninism was "not only a miraculous 'book of the wise,' a compass for us Vietnamese revolutionaries and people," it was also "the radiant sun illuminating our path to final victory, to socialism and communism."

For Vietnamese Communism, "Ho Chi Minh was the founder, leader and educator of our Party, the builder of the Democratic Republic of Viet Nam and the National United Front, the beloved father of the Vietnamese people's armed forces. He was the very soul, the shining banner that led our entire Party, our entire people, our entire army to unite as one man and struggle gallantly, thus writing the most glorious pages in the history of our Fatherland." The history of the Communist movement in Vietnam therefore begins with Ho Chi Minh.

A Leader Is Born

Ho Chi Minh apparently was born Nguyen Tat Thanh on 19 May 1890 in Kim Lien hamlet, Hoang Tru village, Nam Dan district, Nghe An Province, of what is now North Vietnam, although official accounts differ. During the following years he was variously known by at least nine pseudonyms, and probably by a dozen more. To avoid confusion, he will be identified hereafter by his two best-known names, Nguyen Ai Quoc and Ho Chi Minh.

Ho was the third child of a "patriotic scholar" and a "gentle and hard-working woman who devoted her life to tilling the fields and educating her children." His father, Nguyen Sinh Huy, was reportedly a personal friend of Phan Boi Chau, a prominent Vietnamese Nationalist. With his father's encouragement, Ho at fifteen served as a messenger for "patriotic scholars" who were actively opposing French rule of Indochina. He left school when he was twenty and soon traveled south to Saigon.

In late 1911, at twenty-one, Ho took a job in the kitchen of the French ship SS *Admiral Latouche-Tréville*. He left his native Vietnam and was not to reenter the country for thirty years. Until 1917 he traveled widely, visiting France, England, Africa, the Americas—including the United States—and other areas of the Western World. He supported himself on such jobs as those of waiter, gardener, photograph printer and retoucher, snow-sweeper, and stoker.

Introduction to Leninism

Ho returned to France in 1917 and became active in left-wing political circles. He joined the French Socialist Party, and shortly thereafter founded the Association of Vietnamese Patriots, a politically-left group of Vietnamese living in France. According to his official biographers, the Russian October Revolution had a great influence on him.

Ho Chi Minh first achieved prominence in June 1919 when he rented a tuxedo and appeared at the Versailles Conference with an eight-point petition entitled "The Rights of Nations." It was at Versailles that he first used the name Nguyen Ai Quoc, misspelled "Nguyen Ai Quac" on the petition. He was unsuccessful in his attempt to meet with President Wilson and other conference participants, but his exploit brought him publicity and a certain amount of fame among Vietnamese and left-wing groups in France.

On 6 March 1919 Lenin founded the Communist International in Moscow. At the Second Congress of the Comintern in July–August 1920, Lenin's *Theses on the National and Colonial Questions* was adopted, stating in part:

> [W]e must carry out it policy of realising the closest union between all national and colonial liberation movements and Soviet Russia. . . . [T]he international policy of the Communist International cannot limit itself to a mere formal verbal declaration of the recognition of the equality of nations, which does not involve practical obligations, such as has been made by the bourgeois democrats who styled themselves socialists. . . . It is likewise necessary . . . to support the revolutionary movement among the subject nations (for example, Ireland, American negroes, etc.) and in the colonies . . . [A]bove all we must strive as far as possible to give the peasant movement a revolutionary character, to organise the peasants and all the exploited into the soviets, and thus bring about the closest possible union between the Communist proletariat of Western Europe and the revolutionary peasant movement of the east and of the colonial and subject countries. . . .

Perhaps more than any other single factor, this document converted Ho Chi Minh to Leninism.

The last months of 1920 found the French Socialist Party in the midst of a major debate between those favoring affiliation with the Comintern and those wishing to remain in the Second International. Ho, still known as Nguyen Ai Quoc, was confused by all of the discussion. He "loved and admired Lenin because he was a great patriot who liberated his compatriots" but had read none of Lenin's writings. Forty years later Ho was to reflect:

> What I wanted most to know—and this precisely was not debated in the meeting—was: which International sides with the peoples of colonial countries?
>
> I raised this question—the most important in my opinion—in a meeting. Some comrades answered: It is the Third, not the Second International. And a comrade gave me Lenin's "Thesis on the national and colonial questions" published by *l'Humanité* to read.
>
> There were political terms difficult to understand in this thesis. But by dint of reading it again and again, finally I could grasp the main part of it. What emotion, enthusiasm, clear-sightedness and confidence it instilled into me! I was overjoyed to tears. Though sitting alone in my room, I shouted aloud as if addressing large crowds: "Dear martyrs compatriots! This is what we need, this is the path to our liberation!"

This was the beginning of Ho Chi Minh's conversion from a nationalistic patriot to an international Communist.

At the 18th Congress of the French Socialist Party in Tours, held from 25 to 30 December 1920, Nguyen Ai Quoc sided with the French Marxists and voted in favor of joining the Third International. He was in the majority, becoming a founding member of the French Communist Party and the first Vietnamese Communist.

Ho joined with a number of individuals from French colonies in 1921 and, under the guidance of the French Communist Party, formed the *Union intercoloniale*. Elected to the Central Committee, he became a Standing Member of the

Union, in which he represented the Indochinese people. A year later he was editor, publisher and manager of the *Union's* newspaper, *Le Paria* (the outcast) (Paris). He also contributed articles to other French Communist publications including the main Party organ, *Humanité*, and wrote *Le Procès de la colonisation française* (French colonization on trial), a pamphlet which was to increase his prestige in the years which followed.

Ho Leaves for Moscow

According to French *Sûreté* [secret police] reports, Ho Chi Minh left France for Moscow in June 1923. That October he was delegate of the French Communist Party to the Congress of the Peasants' International (Krestintern), and was elected as colonial representative on its permanent Executive Committee. He remained in the Soviet Union for a year and a half in this capacity, writing articles for *Pravda* and the Comintern's *International Correspondence* (Moscow), and studying Marxism-Leninism and Bolshevik tactics at the Eastern Workers' University.

While in Moscow Ho attended several Communist congresses dealing with trade unions, youth, women, and other subjects. The most important of these was the Fifth Congress of the Comintern, 17 June–8 July 1924. As an official delegate of the French Communist Party to that Congress, Nguyen Ai Quoc read a report which concluded: "If at present the peasants remain inactive, the reason is that they still lack organization and leaders. The Communist International must help them to revolution and liberation." Before the Congress had adjourned, Nguyen Ai Quoc had been appointed a Standing Member of the Eastern Department of the Comintern, directly in charge of the Southern Section.

Mission in China

In December 1924 Ho was sent to Canton, China, ostensibly as an interpreter on the staff of Mikhail Borodin, the Comintern's emissary with [Chinese general] Chiang Kai-shek's revolutionary government. It was his first major assignment as a Comintern agent, and events have established that his actual mission was to organize movements in Southeast Asia that were loyal to the Communist International.

The residents of Canton included a number of young Vietnamese revolutionaries, many of whom had been drawn there by the presence of Vietnam's most renowned revolutionary, Phan Boi Chau. Phan, who has been characterized by the late Bernard Fall as "Vietnam's Sun Yat-sen [in reference to China's first revolutionary leader]," is today considered a national hero in both North and South Vietnam. Directly, or indirectly through his teachings, during the first quarter of this century he was responsible for nearly every act of anti-French resistance in Vietnam.

Ho's activities in Canton are described in an official biography: "appraising Phan Boi Chau's patriotic organization . . . [and another organization of Vietnamese revolutionaries in Canton], President Ho Chi Minh highly valued their patriotic spirit but clearly saw the weak points of their leaders, who 'know little about politics, and even less about the organization of the masses.'" He made a selection of young patriots from those organizations . . . gave them political training to turn them into revolutionary cadres, and sent them back to the country to propagate Marxism-Leninism among our working class and people."

This particular biography makes no reference to what occurred next, but it is explained in an earlier Party publication: "In 1925 he [Phan Boi Chau] fell into a trap set in Shanghai [in China] by the French colonialists and was condemned to live in forced residence in Hue [in Vietnam] . . . where he died on October 29, 1941." What this account neglects to mention is that it was Comintern agent Ho Chi Minh who arranged for Phan to be in Shanghai on 30 June 1925, and for the French to be there to greet him. Phan was the number one target of the French colonial authorities because of his revolutionary activities, and they were happy to pay Ho Chi Minh 100,000 piasters for Phan's betrayal. Ho sent Phan an invitation to meet and discuss ways for the two to work together in furthering the anti-French resistance movement, and to participate in the founding of the Vietnamese branch of the World Federation of Small and Weak Nations. When the invitation was accepted, Ho informed the French who intercepted Phan at the Shanghai railway station and returned him to Haiphong for trial.

To his Communist associates, according to P.J. Honey, Ho justified the betrayal of Phan on three grounds:

(1) Phan Boi Chau was a Nationalist, not a Communist, and would prove to be a rival to the Communists in their plan to take control of the Vietnamese anti-French resistance movement. In betraying him he had disposed of a future rival.

(2) The reward money which he had received from the French could be put to excellent use in forwarding the Vietnamese Communist movement.

(3) The execution of Phan Boi Chau would create the required atmosphere of shock and resentment inside Vietnam.

Phan Boi Chau was tried and on 23 November 1925 sentenced to death. Because of widespread public protest, the sentence was commuted to life imprisonment and finally to life under house arrest. His life was spared, but his career as a revolutionary was ended. He was no longer a rival to Ho Chi Minh, and his followers in Canton were without a leader.

Ho had anticipated the atmosphere of unrest created by the arrest and trial of Phan. One potential Vietnamese revolutionary was Nguyen Luong Bang, now Vice President of North Vietnam, who later wrote: "I left my motherland after the arrest of Phan Boi Chau. I seethed with discontent and wondered who could take charge of state affairs if such talented men as Phan were arrested one after the other." Another result of the trial of Phan Boi Chau was the creation in 1927 of the Vietnam Nationalist Party, *Viet Nam Quoc Dan Dang* (VNQDD).

Strengthening the Thanh Nien

In mid-1925 Ho Chi Minh founded the Vietnam Association of Young Revolutionaries (*Viet Nam Thanh Nien Cach Mang Dong Chi Hoi*), its membership consisting largely of people recruited from Phan Boi Chau's organization and similar groups in Canton. A handful of hard-core members of the new organization were gathered into a Communist group,

Tan Viet. In the name of the association Ho published a weekly paper, *Thanh Nien* (Youth), a title widely used to identify the organization; 88 issues appeared between June 1925 and April 1927. He also helped found the Union of Oppressed Asian Peoples, with a Vietnamese section, which published a collection of Ho's political training lectures as a book entitled *The Revolutionary Road (Duong Cach Mang)*.

In addition to strengthening his own organization, Ho Chi Minh worked actively in the late 1920's to undermine Nationalist opposition. The VNQDD was founded in 1927, and within two years it grew to become numerically the strongest party in Vietnam. It was one of several anti-French organizations in Vietnam to regularly send promising young men to China for training at the Whampoa Academy [Chinese equivalent of West Point]. These men were to be the future leaders of their respective parties.

Upon arrival in Hong Kong or Canton, however, each new recruit for the academy was required to submit two photographs in order to complete his files. The young Nationalists were approached at the academy by Ho or his agents and invited to abandon their parties and join the Thanh Nien. Those who accepted were allowed to return to Vietnam and became the nucleus around which Ho would later built a Leninist party. The Nationalists rejecting the invitation never returned to their organizations inside Vietnam. Ho arranged for their photographs and travel plans to fall into French hands, and they were arrested upon crossing the border. The money Ho obtained from the French for these betrayals was used to further his Communist activities in Canton. Thus he financed his operations and eliminated his future competition at the same time. He used a similar approach in maintaining discipline among his subordinates: those who questioned their leader's orders or directives were reported to the French *Sûreté*, which was always willing to assist Ho in punishing recalcitrant young revolutionaries.

Ho's Blueprint for Revolution

The split in the Chinese [Chinese Nationalist government] Kuomintang between the followers of Chiang Kai-shek and the Communists forced Ho Chi Minh to leave Canton in April 1927. He stopped briefly in Hankow, where he reportedly attended the fifth Congress of the Chinese Communist Party, and then returned to Moscow. There he argued that the creation of a Communist Party was impossible in Indochina at the time, because "no one [there] as yet understood the significance of the word communism." He concluded, however, that it was "possible to constitute an Indochinese nationalist-socialist and revolutionary party whose leaders would be responsible for bringing all its members step by step to orthodox Marxism." Ho believed that the Vietnamese revolution should take place in two distinct stages: a "Democratic Revolution" would come first, to be followed by a "Socialist Revolution."

He soon left Moscow for Brussels to attend the Conference Against the Imperialist War, and then stopped briefly in Switzerland and Italy. In the autumn of 1928 he was sent by the Comintern to Siam (now Thailand), where his objectives included reorganizing the Comintern's Southeast Asian network. In 1930 he traveled to Hong Kong to represent the Comintern at the founding of the Vietnam Communist Party, and shortly thereafter returned to Thailand. There he headed the Southeast Asian Department of the Comintern's Orient Bureau in 1930 and 1931, in control of the Communist organizations in Indonesia, Malaya and Thailand. In April 1930 he attended the Third Conference of the South Seas Communist Party in Singapore as the representative of the Comintern's Orient Bureau. Returning to Thailand a short time later, Ho published a newspaper, *Than Ai* (friendship), among his other propaganda activities.

Ho was arrested by British authorities in Hong Kong in June 1931 because of his Communist activities in Southeast Asia. According to the files of the Hanoi *Sûreté*, the French Communist Party organ, *Humanité*, and the Soviet press, Nguyen Ai Quoc died in prison in Hong Kong. In reality he was apparently set free in the spring of 1933, returned to the Soviet Union soon after and entered Lenin University, the foremost institution for key Comintern cadres from around the world. While in Moscow he is reported to have worked at the Comintern's Research Institute on National and Colonial Problems. In July 1935 Ho attended the Seventh Comintern Congress that set forth the "united front" policy which was to become so instrumental in future Communist successes in Vietnam.

Lenin's Influence

Ho was initially attracted to Communism by Lenin's *Theses on the National and Colonial Questions*, as mentioned above, which led him to vote with the majority of the French Socialist Party in affiliating with the Comintern, and later to spend many years of his life as a key Comintern agent. Few elements of his political strategy were void of Lenin's influence.

One of Ho Chi Minh's greatest talents was his ability to maneuver between various enemies, reaching a temporary compromise with one in order to attack another. This was the basic strategy behind the various united fronts so useful to the Communists in gaining control of the Vietnamese resistance movement. Later, as the leader of North Vietnam, Ho still followed Lenin's instructions. An excellent example of the application of a fundamental principle of Leninism was the North Vietnamese program of land reform. . . .

Another key element in Ho's strategy was the concept of the "opportune moment." Lenin explained: "To tie our hands beforehand, openly to tell the enemy, who is at present better armed than we are, whether we shall fight him, and when, is stupidity and not revolutionism. To accept battle at a time when it is obviously advantageous to the enemy and not to us is a crime: and the political leader of the revolutionary class who is unable to 'manoeuvre, agree, and compromise' in order to avoid an obviously disadvantageous battle, is absolutely worthless." These two principles are of course interrelated, and both were apparent in decisions such as the preliminary accord which Ho signed with the French on 6 March 1946.

Even in those instances when Ho's policy appeared to differ from the instructions of Lenin, the fundamental principles of Leninism were usually present. Ho was fond of citing Lenin's *Appeal to the Revolutionaries in the East*, which charged:

"You have before you a task which was unknown to the Communists in the world: relying on the theory and common practice of communism, and applying them to specific conditions which do not exist in Europe, you must know how to use them in the conditions in which the peasants are the basic masses and the task is not to struggle against capitalism, but against medieval vestiges."

By late 1929, Vladimir Lenin and Nguyen Ai Quoc had set the stage for the founding in Vietnam of a Communist Party.

Chapter 4

Latin American Revolution

Castro's Classless Revolution in Cuba

James O'Connor

As a young man, Fidel Castro abandoned conventional political struggle in favor of armed revolution. He led the guerrilla movement that ousted Cuban dictator Fulgencio Batista in 1959. Then Castro, the brash hero of the rebel army, assumed control of the new revolutionary government made up of many opposing factions. Castro initially kept control by playing the factions against each other and refusing to make his brand of socialism based on the dominance of one class of people.

Author and Latin American historian James O'Connor argues that Castro's success as a revolutionary leader was due to his ability to minimize his opposition and make bold decisions when initiating economic or social reform. His reforms were often vague and contradictory, but necessary. Eventually Castro's economic policies alienated the wealthiest Cubans, and class conflict—so long absent in the first stages of the revolution—came to characterize its later phases. Castro carefully molded the conflict into an impassioned nationalism that viewed capitalism, both internally (landowners) and externally (the United States), as Cuba's greatest threat. With patriotism running high, Castro secured nationwide support for his socialist programs, and Cuba joined the ranks of the world's Communist nations.

All nations, in some eras of their history, and some nations, in all eras of their history, unashamedly and uncritically idolize their revolutionary heroes. Cuba belongs in the second

James O'Connor, *The Origins of Socialism in Cuba*. Ithaca, NY: Cornell University Press, 1970. Copyright © 1970 by Cornell University. Reproduced by permission.

category: Conservatives as well as liberals and radicals worship the memory of José Martí. The heroic (and some not-so-heroic) leaders of the struggle against Spain automatically became the political chieftains of independent Cuba. The army enlisted men's hero, [Fulgencio] Batista, was a strong and hence popular executive before he began to rule by intimidation and terror [as Cuba's dictator from 1952–1959]. Side by side on the walls of *bohíos* in rural Cuba are pictures of Jesus Christ and Fidel Castro.

Castro has all the qualities and accomplishments required to endear him to the Cuban people as an authentic hero in the Cuban revolutionary tradition: victory in military struggle, the will and ability to be a strong leader, an uncanny capacity to establish empathy with individual workers, farmers, and students as well as with masses of people at a public rally, great oratorical prowess, unusual physical strength, integrity, *machismo*. That he is impatient with detail, sometimes fails to compromise when compromise would serve his aims, often makes unilateral decisions that take his colleagues by surprise, hates paper work, restlessly moves from place to place—these and other qualities authenticate him even more as a man among men.

But Castro's most "revolutionary" quality is his capacity, indeed his need, to lead, to take and keep initiatives and make far-reaching decisions with the utmost confidence of success. This is readily confirmed by a backward glance at the major steps of his rise to power.

Castro's Rise to Power

The first was in 1953 when Castro took up arms against Batista. A young lawyer, the son of a well-to-do cane grower, and a member of the Ortodoxo party's national assembly, Castro was a congressional candidate in the elections that Batista annulled after his seizure of power in March, 1952. Castro petitioned the Supreme Court to declare the Batista government unconstitutional. The petition was denied. The electoral road to power closed by Batista, the army, and the Court, Castro without hesitation turned to armed struggle.

He struck the first blow on July 26, 1953. At the head of

a small column of young men, most of them student activists, Castro attacked the Moncada barracks at Santiago de Cuba and three minor targets. The rebels expected to hold the barracks until the Cuban people rose up against the illegal regime and restored constitutional democracy. But the rebellion was a military and political failure. The barracks put up a successful resistance, and Castro had grossly overestimated the Cuban people's antipathy for unconstitutional government.

The attack on the barracks and the political trials that followed made Fidel Castro's name a household word in Cuba. "Sentence me," Castro cried at the end of the now-famous five-hour speech in his defense. "It doesn't matter. History will absolve me." Released in May, 1955, in a general political amnesty, Castro returned triumphantly to Havana. His personal popularity was growing, his party, the Ortodoxos, was torn apart by factional struggles and personal rivalries, and within two months Castro decided once again to abandon conventional political struggle.

The second way station of Castro's political journey was his decision to go into exile in Mexico and plan another armed rebellion. He raised money from Cuban exiles in the United States and other countries, recruited and trained men for guerrilla warfare, made the friendship of Ernesto ["Che"] Guevara, an Argentine doctor and revolutionary. In December, 1956, Castro and his men reached Cuba in an old yacht. Of eighty-two rebels, only twelve survived to reach their destination—the remote, mountain forests of the Sierra Maestra. Fidel and Raúl Castro and Guevara were among the survivors.

For two years Castro's guerrillas attacked police posts and army patrols, built up a base among the local peasants, and transformed themselves into an experienced, effective guerrilla army. Partly inspired by the accomplishments of the guerrillas, partly as a result of parallel, independent efforts, an urban resistance movement grew swiftly. Student groups, business, church, and professional organizations, and factions within labor unions arrayed themselves against Batista. Many leaders of the established political parties opposed

Batista, and some went into exile. There was a major split between moderates and activists. The former pressed for negotiations, new and honest elections, and peaceable change. The latter took up arms against the most immediate symbols of oppression: police stations, army posts, and other government buildings. Batista attempted to suppress all opposition, at times ignoring the moderates, at times not distinguishing them from the activists. He opposed counterrevolutionary terror to revolutionary terror. Isolated, demoralized, politically bankrupt, military on the defensive, Batista and his followers finally fled the island on January 1, 1959.

Forty-eight hours after Batista's flight, Castro's 26th of July Movement, now a loose coalition of oppositionist forces of all political shades and colorations, seized control of Havana. Castro stepped forward as the head of the Rebel Army and the undisputed leader of the movement. He had maintained his independence from the older, established anti-Batista politicians who had been jockeying for the leadership of the rebellion. He was the universally popular guerrilla leader, the man who had started the uprising.

The third step of Castro's rise to power was his determination in early 1959 not to let the political initiative slip from his grasp; most of the urban rebels and city politicians were unknown quantities, and he felt that he could trust only his closest companions. This decision had three profound implications. First, it meant that he would personally make the major political decisions for the foreseeable future. Second, it meant that the new government, in particular the Cabinet, would be little more than window dressing and that major policy decisions would be made behind the scenes. Third, it meant that Castro would eventually be compelled to confront the United States government, together with those groups within Cuba that were dependent upon United States–owned businesses or mainland trade or were otherwise in a subordinate position.

Thus, the Revolutionary Government's first and second presidents, Manuel Urrutia and Osvaldo Dorticós, were Castro's personal choices.

Thus, Castro personally ordered the political reforms of

1959: the postponement of elections; the dismissal of Congress; the purge of Batistianos [supporters of Batista] from the judiciary, local government office, and the police; the discharge of over 3,000 government employees; and the total reorganization of the armed forces.

Thus, Castro's men wrote the revolution's basic economic and social law, the Agrarian Reform Law of May, 1959, behind the backs of the Cabinet.

Thus, Castro initiated most of the revolution's major economic and social policies during 1959–1962, in particular sugar policy, industrialization, and education planning.

Thus, Castro personally conducted the economic and diplomatic war with the United States which flared up in 1959–1960 and personally led the Rebel Army and militia against the invaders at the Bay of Pigs in April, 1961 [when CIA-trained Cuban exiles staged a seaborne invasion of Cuba that failed miserably]. . . .

The Absence of a Revolutionary Class

The Cuban Revolution went through two basic stages, one characterized by class harmony, the second by class antagonism and conflict. Needless to say, Castro guided the revolution through both stages.

In the last analysis, the 26th of July Movement originally consisted of diverse, potentially antagonistic elements, reflecting the contradictory character of the Batista regime. Castro opposed himself to a politics in which every major economic class was to one degree or another organized and entrenched in the state bureaucracy. The rebellion at first did not set class against class, but out-groups against in-groups, unorganized against organized, men who either did not want or could not acquire access to the public treasury against those who did, constitutionalists against anticonstitutionalists, youth against age, and, last but not least, idealists against pragmatists and opportunists. Segments of each class stood to lose, while others could only gain, from the annihilation of the Batista regime. There was therefore no single revolutionary class that conducted, or at least gave momentum to, the political rebellion. There were no Cuban counterparts to the peasants in the Mexican and Chinese Revolutions, the urban working class in the Russian Revolution, or for that matter, the urban merchants in the American Revolution.

The Cuban Revolution was neither bourgeois revolution, lower-class rebellion, nor peasant uprising. "It has never been a revolution of the upper classes," Castro said in 1962. "Not a single representative of the upper class took part in the revolution, not a single rich man." This is true—and unexceptional. "All the participants . . . were young men with a modest, working-class background; workers and peasants, the sons of working people, employees." This is not true; the kindest interpretation is that Castro was deliberately employing the language of the common man, whose social categories were normally confined to the "rich" and the "poor."

The analogy of the blind men and the elephant is not inappropriate. In Havana the rebellion resembled a middle-class democratic revolution with the aim of restoring constitutional government. In Santiago de Cuba the revolution seemed to be a working-class rising against a brutal state power and state administration. In the Sierra Maestra the rebellion appeared to be a peasant war against a combination of greedy landlords and corrupt state officials.

In the Havana area middle-class students, intellectuals, and professionals were the main protagonists. Employees in tourism, "privileged" workers in the labor "aristocracy," politically inexperienced recruits for the urban work force fresh from the countryside, domestic servants, and white-collar workers constituted the vast majority of the Havana working class. None of these groups had any overriding incentive to engage in hard, risky political struggle. Worker participation in the rebellion was also limited by the fact that the top-heavy, conservative union bureaucracy was based in Havana. . . .

The economic program of the 26th of July Movement reflected the contradictory forces at play during the political rebellion. The program revealed that the movement lacked a unifying political theory or ideology and a coherent program of economic and social development. This was one "unprecedented hallmark of the revolution . . . the logical product of pre-revolutionary society."

Central to movement policy was, in fact, an idea already seized and acted upon by Batista: the participation of all sectors and groups in economic planning. Undoubtedly this slogan was partly a tactic designed to consolidate one united front against another united front (the out-group against the in-group), but it was actually much more significant. The movement knew that it could profitably appeal to varied groups because the existing political economy thwarted in

Castro Mythology

Fidel Castro's triumphant return to Cuban shores with a small group of dedicated followers and his protracted stay in the harsh environment of the Sierra Mountains made him a mythical figure. Author Georgie Anne Geyer points out in her column for World & I *that the growing mythology behind the Cuban Revolution was calculated and promoted by Fidel Castro.*

From Havana and his surprising release only a year and a half later [Castro] moved directly to Mexico with a small band of followers to train for "the return." This time, he knew exactly what he was doing. After two years of drilling and planning in Mexico City (and a few arrests), the group left the Caribbean coast of Mexico one dark and dramatic night in a small, leaky, uncertain craft named the *Granma*. After days of near-death at sea, they landed on Cuban shores, where again Castro, now el l'der, immediately began again replacing still more history with his own calculated myth: Although there were probably eighteen men who landed, Castro to this day insists they were the "twelve." Any intention in his mind to identify himself and his aura with the Twelve Apostles is a distinct possibility.

For two years, he and his small band stayed in the rough mountains of the Sierra Maestra, hiding from the army, engaging in occasional ambushes, but above all writing with their lives the new mythology of the Cuban revolution. The name Fidel Castro began to seep into the airwaves and newspaper columns of the world, particularly when, a mere two weeks after the landing, Castro very calculatedly had *New York Times* one way or another the realization of their interests. Had the dictatorship its own solid economic base, and had the movement its own, antagonistic base, the movement's appeal would have been unambiguously directed to the latter.

The authors of the program stressed two themes, one negative, the other positive. The negative theme was an attack on the state economic policy of the Batista government. The positive theme was the stress on mobilizing domestic capital and other resources for rapid economic development.

correspondent Herbert Matthews brought up to the Sierra to write glowing things about him. Meanwhile, many of the other, more serious revolutionaries, those who stayed in the dangerous cities to build real political structures and who might have become competitors to power, were dying, day after day, at the hands of [Cuban dictator Fulgencio] Batista's thugs.

Finally, the first week of January 1959, after Batista had fled the island, Castro marched across Cuba, slowly and deliberately. It was a march of victory, but it was also a march of warning: Castro was taking over, and Cubans were just beginning to understand that things would never be the same again. At that moment, the crowds were delirious with joy at their new leader. When, on the day of his entering Havana, a white [dove] landed on his shoulder as he was speaking to the masses, the crowds went utterly wild, shouting, FIDELFIDELFIDELFIDELFIDELFIDEL!

More trained and impassionate minds read other interpretations into these stunning events. "He had already easily induced the Cuban people, so long overwhelmed with failure, to suspend individual judgment and repose one's faith in the leadership of someone who conveys his conviction that he knows the way," American political psychiatrist Jerrold Post has observed. "He was saying, 'Follow me and I will take care of you.'"

But there was another message that he spoke over and over again in those euphoric days. It should have alerted people, had they really been listening: "Now, we are going to purify this country."

Georgie Ann Geyer, "The Unexpected Lives of Fidel Castro," *World & I*, May 2001.

Both themes were shot through with contradictions.

In the first place, one part of the program condemned Batista's policy of restricting sugar production. In another section, the program called for strengthening the marginal cane farmers by raising minimum quotas, that is to say, by fortifying the system of production restrictions as a whole. Secondly, Batista came under attack for his policy of building highly mechanized plants at the expense of jobs for workers. Elsewhere, the program asserted that agriculture should be mechanized in order to raise productivity and incomes in the countryside.

Nor was the positive aspect of the program free of contradiction. On the one hand, the emphasis on channeling domestic savings into productive investments and granting more protection to manufacturing industries appealed to local business. On the other hand, a proposed profit-sharing plan that promised workers in nonagricultural enterprises 30 per cent of net income won support in some labor union circles. Clearly, these proposals also were highly incompatible. . . .

Radicalization and Class Conflict

The second stage of the revolution, which was characterized by class antagonism and conflict, began around the middle of 1959. During the first five or six months of 1959, farmers, workers, and businessmen were all optimistic about the future economy and society. The large farmers and estate owners could not anticipate that the agrarian reform would wipe them out. The small farmers and peasants believed Castro's promise to "redeem" the countryside. The workers were asking, and getting, higher wages. United States capital "generally did not expect the change in Cuba's government to hamper their operations." Many foreign and Cuban companies prepaid taxes to help Castro consolidate his new government or planned to accelerate investment programs temporarily postponed during the rebellion. Business leaders who "as recently as one month ago were gravely concerned about the revolution" radically shifted their outlook.

Interclass unity and the resulting political euphoria speedily gave way to doubts about Castro's intentions, to honest confusion over the disparity between Castro's promises of "democracy" and "constitutionalism" and Castro's role of "maximum leader," and to fears about the consequences of his economic policies, in particular, income distribution policies which favored the poorer workers and farmers over the middle classes. The real reasons for the developing class conflict lie in the process of radicalization of the revolution. . . . In brief, the original agrarian and urban reforms triggered a complex interplay between middle-class opinions and actions, United States attitudes and policies, and Cuban government policy toward private business, the middle classes, and the United States. No one could anticipate the speedy radicalization of the revolution nor the socialization of the island's economy, because no one "caused" them; rather, they were the product of the *relationships* between individuals, groups, and classes. . . .

Thus, Castro pushed through reform after reform, yielding nothing to his opponents. Almost immediately he revealed his basic seriousness by seizing the Cuban Electric Company, which had been the target of many accusations of inefficient operations and monopoly profits. During the first nine months of 1959, there were no less than 1500 decrees, laws, and resolutions. Most of the early reforms were *capitalist* reforms in the area of rents, tariffs, taxes, money, and so on, although some reforms, in particular the collective aspects of the agrarian reform, contained a *socialist* bias. Despite the latter, all signs pointed to Castro's belief that a reformed Cuban capitalism (or a mixed economy) could perform in a satisfactory manner.

Nearly every measure, in particular those which affected the property system, deepened the commitment of some Cubans to the Revolutionary Government and antagonized others, leaving few indifferent. At the very least, the major changes—some examples are the cross-the-board rent reductions, the price-control laws, the seizure of the utilities, and the agrarian reform—touched on the day-to-day life of every Cuban, compelling him to question his economic and political beliefs. The most sweeping of these changes occasioned Cabinet crises, official resignations, arrests, and exile.

The basis for the demand to choose sides—for or against the revolution—was therefore laid by the Revolutionary Government's first economic measures.

To make such a demand required considerable confidence on Castro's part that the majority of Cubans would side with the Revolutionary Government. His decision to polarize opinion around the fundamental issues of Cuba's sovereignty and the government's economic and political programs was not the only path open to him. Instead of isolating oppositional elements and branding them with the label "counterrevolutionary," he could have allowed them to form into functioning interest groups. These groups probably would have ranged from the "left-opposition" of the small Cuban Trotskyite [follower of the socialist philosophy of Russian activist Leon Trotsky] movement all the way to the moderate right, consisting of the large sugar, cattle, banking, and commercial interests purged of their pro-Batista elements. Castro could have thwarted any majority coalition by playing one group against another, ceaselessly probing the weaknesses of each, and employing the tactics of divide and conquer. . . .

The Government Gains Mass Approval

There were four basic reasons why the Revolutionary Government was confident that its programs would win mass approval and alienate only a fraction of the Cuban people. In the first place, there was widespread recognition that "something had to be done" about the Cuban economy and that mild reforms were insufficient to get the economy off dead center. The Great Depression, war and postwar speculative booms and busts in sugar, and economic stagnation in the 1950's revealed to nearly everyone that development and prosperity required that the sugar economy undergo basic structural changes.

Increasingly, the rural workers and peasants were made aware by hunger and enforced idleness of the abundance of unused lands and badly cultivated fields; the teacher and doctor, by illiteracy and disease, of the backwardness of the education and health systems; the small businessman, by his sluggish profits, of state corruption and irrational labor, trade, and other laws; and the industrial worker, by his underemployment and lack of training, of inefficient operations and underutilized capacity in manufacturing and other industries. "For fifty years," a well-to-do importer said in July, 1960, voicing the attitude of many Cubans, "Cuban society has been decrepit and decadent. Of course Castro has turned a popular movement into a dictatorship. I don't know, perhaps it is necessary now. But believe me when I say that a revolution was both desirable and inevitable."

The second reason that the government's programs met with relatively weak opposition was that earlier government development schemes, in particular those of the Batista dictatorship, raised the expectations of the poorer classes, undermined respect for "free enterprise," and conditioned the average Cuban to accept a prominent role of the government in the economy. Related to this, the average Cuban understood the old electoral process to be totally corrupt, and hence there was little popular sentiment favoring a return to constitutional government. Moreover, the 1940 Constitution was viewed less as a document that established a basis for parliamentary government than as authority for a strong executive committed to deep-going social and economic change.

Third, government policy toward property owners whose wealth and income were adversely affected by the new economic programs was designed to minimize opposition. Urban landlords, retailers, and the middle farmers received compensation under the laws taking over apartment houses and office buildings, small stores, and medium-sized farms. To be sure, plantation owners, sugar companies, the large ranchers, and the big businessmen did not receive compensation, but these groups constituted only a tiny proportion of the island's propertied classes. Moreover, for reasons we have seen in the preceding chapter, these groups were not "permeated by a spirit of loyalty." In G.D.H. Cole's words, a man "will be able to act effectively in social matters only if he transfers his allegiance to some . . . group or class within which he can find like-minded collaborators. A class cannot be defined, when it is regarded as an active agent of social change, simply in terms of its common economic experience. It becomes fully a class, in this positive sense, only to the extent to which it is permeated by a spirit of loyalty."

Finally, and perhaps of greatest significance, due to the intimate ties between Cuba and the United States, government programs were nationalist, as well as reformist or socialist, in character. Cuban nationalism was the strongest thread that ran through both the class harmony and class struggle phases of the revolution. Nationalism was one issue that bound together the diverse elements engaged in the struggle against Batista. The 26th of July Movement's heavy emphasis on the mobilization of domestic savings for investment and economic development reflected the rebels' unwillingness "to compromise our economic and political future with the importing of capital." The fear of foreign influence and control was also reflected in the movement's stress on export diversification and the production of substitutes for imported commodities. Liberals and radicals, moderates and activists, reformers and revolutionaries—nearly every tendency within the 26th of July Movement was nationalist-minded.

During the class-struggle phase of the revolution, nationalism, now transformed into anti-imperialism, bound together the workers and farmers not only against the United States but also against the local middle classes. The hostility of the United States to many of the Revolutionary Government's programs and policies, together with the strong nationalist character of these programs, transformed nationalism from a theoretical issue into a practical one. The liberals and reformers within the movement looked to the national middle class to simultaneously reconstruct Cuban capitalism on a reformed basis and withstand pressures from the United States. But they failed to understand the implications of the absence of a large, unified, progressive national bourgeoisie: the political initiative must inevitably shift to the left. In brief, the reformers in the movement who involved themselves in a nationalist, anti-Yankee policies were unaware that they were playing with a loaded gun. The reformers and national middle class unwittingly helped the revolution along the path of socialism.

The Communist Drive for South America

U.S. News & World Report

In this 1964 article from *U.S. News & World Report*, the members of the news staff document the "Red Menace" that was spreading throughout South America. South America was seen as a prime target for a Communist takeover; many of its nations were poverty stricken, unindustrialized, and resentful of the United States. The Communists saw opportunity in Latin American misfortune. The article focuses on Castro's Cuba as the base of communism in Latin American as well as Castro's plans to export revolution throughout the region. From there on, the article moves through South America nation by nation to describe the political situation in each. For example, it describes the peaceful Communist revolution in Chile, the shantytowns and high unemployment in Venezuela, and the drive to move the Americans out of Panama in Central America. The article portrays the political instability in South America during the 1960s.

- In Venezuela, a bomb knocks out a U.S.-owned oil pipeline for the third time in three months.
- In Peru, surprisingly well-armed peasants stage a pitched battle against troops sent to halt illegal seizures of land.
- In Chile, key ports and railroads are paralyzed by a 24-hour strike, called to demand 70 per cent pay increase for civil servants.

These seemingly unrelated developments, it is now becoming clear, all have a common denominator: the Communist drive to get Latin America.

U.S. News & World Report, "How Communists Plan to Get Latin America," *U.S. News & World Report*, March 9, 1964, pp. 58–59. Copyright © 1964 by U.S. News & World Report, LP. Reproduced by permission.

That drive is using Fidel Castro's Cuba as a base for disruptive activities all through Latin America.

On February 24, investigators for the Organization of American States released documented proof of Castro's unsuccessful plot to overthrow the Government of Venezuela by armed violence. . . . Then, on February 27, Secretary of State Dean Rusk called for followed pressure on Cuba to prevent Castro's subversive activities elsewhere in the Hemisphere.

Latin-American experts are convinced that Venezuela is no isolated incident. In the words of a top specialist on Communist strategy in the Western Hemisphere:

"Castro has been unleashed by the entire Communist camp. He has been told he can go ahead with all of his plans for exporting revolutions.

"It's an over-all plan for Latin America. It doesn't depend on the take-over of any one specific country, even though Venezuela—because of its oil—and Brazil are key targets.

"But the Communists are now specializing in situations, not countries."

Communist Opportunity

To Communist strategists, Latin America is the "soft underbelly" of the Western Hemisphere—backward, frustrated, resentful of the U.S., ripe for sweeping change. To the Reds, no other area of the world offers such a target of opportunity, and such a chance to hurt the U.S.

Do the Communists have a master plan for using the same pattern in country after country?

Intelligence experts say no. Communist strategy, they find, has changed considerably in the five years since Castro seized power in Cuba.

At that time, the Reds seemed to think that Castro-type take-overs could be accomplished everywhere with just a minimum of cost. But a chain of abortive attempts to grab power in various countries taught them otherwise.

Today, strategy is far more subtle, based on recognition that Latin America is made up of 20 distinctly different countries, each offering its own opportunities to the Communists.

As you travel from one nation to another, you find Reds

working in many different ways to exploit the situations confronting them.

Red Chile

Nowhere in Latin America, for example, are the Communists acting in a more docile and nonviolent way than in Chile. Just a few years ago, Chile was the scene of bloody, Communist-led violence. At present, in contrast, the Chilean Reds publicly abhor terrorism of the Castro model.

Reason: They belong to a left-wing "Popular Front" of political parties that hopes to win power in the presidential election next September [1965]. This coalition fell only 35,000 votes short of victory in 1958, and the coming race among three entries promises to be just as close.

The Front candidate for President is Salvador Allende, a prosperous doctor in Santiago. An avowed Socialist, he has publicized his aim to make Chile a "free country" like Cuba, and to nationalize 1 billion dollars' worth of U.S. investments in Chile if he becomes President.

That is why fiery young Reds, just back from guerrilla training in Cuba, are donning suits and ties and electioneering, with smiles for the ladies and pats for the babies.

Venezuelan Oil

At the other end of the scale, there is Venezuela.

There, in cities and countryside, the Communist weapon of terror has been used to an extent found nowhere else in the Hemisphere.

For the Reds, Venezuela represents a special prize. It ranks as the world's largest oil-exporting country, and it is the major supplier of foreign oil to the U.S. Under President Romulo Betancourt, moreover, it has been moving ahead fast in agriculture, industry, schools, hospitals and housing. As an anti-Communist "show window," Venezuela is especially abhorrent to Cuba's Castro.

Since Betancourt ousted pro-Castro factions from the Government two years ago, terrorists have killed more than 50 policemen, U.S.-owned installations—oil pipelines, factories and stores—have been a special target. Damage from arson and sabotage runs to more than 10 million dollars.

The objective has been to make the Government look ineffective, thus encouraging a military take-over. Then the military, the Reds hoped, would make a mess of running things, and pave the way for a popular uprising in which they could grab control.

Terrorism has failed to gain in Venezuela so far.

For all the gains made under Betancourt, Venezuela's jobless still come to 12 per cent of the labor force. Crowded into the shantytowns surrounding Caracas, the capital, the unemployed are ideal targets for Red agitators. And there is a question whether President-elect Raúl Leoni has the ability to finish the job started by Betancourt.

Poverty Aids Reds

Elsewhere, too, Reds are finding choice targets in countries plagued by chronic poverty, illiteracy, overcrowding and land hunger.

In Brazil, for instance, living costs jumped more than 80 per cent last year [1963], and inflation is undermining the economy. Land seizures by peasants, encouraged by Communists, are rebuilding up tensions. Both peasants and landowners now have arms—and seem ready to use them. There have been clashes recently in several rural areas.

The Red cause also is being helped along by the apparent confusion of President João Goulart over just what to do about the Communists. A long-time friend of leftists and leader of the Brazilian Labor Party, he now is veering between attempts to win Communist support and attempts to marshal non-Communist forces behind him.

In that setting, Reds are frowning on violence—at least for the time being. Instead, they are using the twin tools of infiltration and agitation.

Communists hold several second-rung and third-rung jobs in Government. Communists have moved into key positions in several labor unions, too.

They took control of Brazil's biggest union, the Industrial Workers Union. This came when Goulart's own special assistant for labor matters worked hand in hand with a Red expert in engineering the take-over. Now the Government has recognized a Communist-dominated national federation of rural workers.

To exert more control on labor, the Reds organized a pressure group known as the General Labor Command. Constitutionally, this group is illegal, but Goulart has never tried to ban it.

Last September [1963] this group threatened a nation-wide strike of transport, maritime and port workers unless a few labor leaders arrested for illegal activities were released. Red trouble was averted when Gen. Peri Bevilacqua in São Paulo forced the labor group to pull back. But the General has since been removed from his post under leftist pressure—one of many Army leaders eased out.

U.S. officials say Brazil is in no immediate danger of a Red take-over. But they see Latin America's biggest nation as a prime target. One expert said:

"Brazil may yet become the Red China of Latin America."

Fomenting Unrest

Communists in Argentina are up against peculiar problems.

There the Communist Party is reported to be the largest in Latin America, with about 40,000 members. But, in wooing the working class, Reds find themselves in competition with followers of the ousted dictator, Juan D. Perón, who are far closer to Fascism than to a Castro-style revolution. Reds, as a result, hold control of only a few labor unions while trying to infiltrate the Peronista movement.

A far different opportunity presents itself in Peru, where Reds are capitalizing on unrest of Indian peasants who make up two thirds of the population.

At least two dozen Cuba-trained guerrillas reportedly lead armed peasants as they invade highland estates. Early in February [1964] about 20 persons were killed in a land-seizure battle near Cuzco, the old Inca capital close to the Bolivian border.

As appraised by experts on the scene, the Red aim is to spread unrest across the backlands before the Government can enact land reform—objective of President Fernando Belaúnde Terry.

Should that happen, some experts say Peru is a likely site for the same sort of guerrilla warfare that brought Castro to power. Though Peru is governed by a moderate and reform-minded Government, it has problems even greater than those that gave Castro his foothold.

Rural violence is an even older story in Colombia. There it became serious in 1948 as a result of bloody feuding between the Liberal and Conservative parties. Since then, terrorism has cost 300,000 lives.

Now Castro Communists are beginning to emerge in some bandit areas. For the most part, however, they have made little headway against entrenched leaders representing the older parties. What is more, they are feeling the brunt of the systematic Army campaign to bring law and order to the backlands. Mainly as a result of this drive, deaths from violence in rural areas of Colombia were down 36 per cent last year [1963].

Red Terror

Where Colombia's Reds are turning up more strongly these days is in Bogotá and other cities. Recently they set off a wave of bombings. One took place on the street next to the presidential palace, another in the garden of an American's home. While the bombs were noise weapons and did no harm, they went of with a co-ordination that suggested the work of Cuba-trained guerrillas.

In Bolivia, Reds are concentrating on labor unions. Already they are strong among tin miners who dominated labor ranks. Last December [1963], Communists precipitated an international crisis by capturing some U.S. officials and holding them as hostages. Bolivia's President Victor Paz Estenssoro forced the release of the hostages.

Now the question is whether he can go ahead with needed reorganization and refurbishing of the nationalized tin mines and get them out of the red. Communist-led miners are blocking the scheme in several big mines, because it would reduce the number of jobs.

A change of Red tactics may be in the offing in British Guiana, where "legality" brought Communists to power in the guise of Premier Cheddi Jagan's People's Progressive

Party. Stimulus to change is Jagan's fear that British will require, as a condition for the country's independence, an election based on proportional representation. Jagan won in 1961, under the unit system, with only 42 per cent of the popular vote, and his worry is that a new system might break his legal hold. In a showdown, it is thought, Reds may drop "legality" and turn to violence.

Central America

All through Central America, small republics find themselves having to deal with a Communist problem while trying to cope with entrenched problems of backwardness and poverty.

In Panama, Cuban-trained Reds spearheaded a bloody demonstration against Americans in January [1964] as the opening gun in their newest drive to dislodge the U.S. from the Panama Canal.

Popular uproar forced Panama's ruling families and Government to join the demand for a revision of the Canal treaty with the U.S. Now the feeling is that the Panamanian Government will find it hard to backtrack from that demand—and is not likely to get the big concessions from the U.S. that might be needed to quell Communist-inspired unrest in Panama. In that situation, officials say that Reds may try to stir another round of violence.

The Caribbean

Out in the Caribbean, another tempting target is developing in the Dominican Republic—still unsettled politically nearly three years after the long dictatorship of Rafael Trujillo came to an end.

A military revolt overthrew the elected Government of President Juan Bosch last September [1963]. In December [1964], the Government crushed a guerrilla movement in the mountains. But Castro-trained agents are known to be in the Dominican Republic, and propaganda broadcasts are beamed in daily from Cuba.

Even in countries now calm on the surface, Communists are finding situations to exploit.

In Costa Rica, traditionally stable and democratic, trouble for the future is building up as a population boom outstrips economic growth. In Nicaragua, pro-Castro sentiment is held likely to grow as a focus of opposition to the power of the [ruling] Somoza family. Similarly, military dictatorships in Guatemala and Honduras are seen as anything but invulnerable to Red troublemaking.

Losing Control?

Communists, it is found, are not having things all their own way in Latin America.

Evidence grows that Fidel Castro is losing some of his glamour because of his ties to Moscow, though Cuba continues as the major source of Red propaganda, guerrilla training and weapons.

Military men from many Latin-American countries are getting instruction from the U.S. Army on ways to cope with guerrilla warfare.

The American-sponsored Alliance for Progress, while not upgrading economies as fast as expected, is making some impact in Venezuela and elsewhere on such problems as housing and farming.

Over all, however, U.S. officials—and growing numbers of political leaders in Latin America—are coming to view the Communist menace as a growing one.

Conditions all across the vast regions to the south of the Rio Grande, they find, are inviting targets for the Communists.

By capturing Latin America, the Reds could deprive the U.S. of important markets and raw materials. Communism, triumphant in America's own back yard, would gain an overwhelming—perhaps decisive—boost in world stature.

To grasp this prize, Reds are following tactics that range from infiltration in some places to terrorism in others. Everywhere, however, the objective is the same: to get control of this vital part of the world.

Party Line Communism in Latin America

Robert J. Alexander

Since its origins in 1919, the Comintern (the international Communist headquarters based in Russia and China) influenced a wide variety of leftists factions in Latin America. The revolutionary rhetoric and possible financial assistance appealed to insurgents seeking to overthrow governments in Central and South America. But many radicals were less pleased by the Comintern's rigid ideology and methodology that was not always adaptable to Latin American causes.

Those organizations that did adhere to Comintern policy often alienated their own leftist support when the Comintern made questionable decisions, such as when the organization backed the Soviet-Nazi nonaggression pact at the outset of World War II. Once the Soviet Union entered the war against the Axis powers, however, the Communists gained prestige and widespread acceptance by setting themselves once again opposed to fascist tyranny.

In the postwar years, the Communists lost support again when they adhered to the Soviet anti-American agenda. Fellow leftists thought the revolutionary struggle should be focused on overhauling the ills of Latin America, not propagandizing against the United States. These other progressive groups in Latin America were catching the ear of the masses and further alienating the Communist cause. Author Robert J. Alexander points out that the Latin American Communists faithfully followed the ideology of the Comintern, but often to their own detriment. Alexander stresses that any notion that Latin American Communists were different, unique freedom fighters or land re-

Robert J. Alexander, *Communism in Latin America*. New Brunswick, NJ: Rutgers University Press, 1957. Copyright © 1957 by Rutgers, The State University. Renewed 1985 by Robert Alexander. Reproduced by permission of the publisher.

formers is false and misleading. Author Robert J. Alexander was a central player in U.S.–Latin American labor, political, and scholarly affairs after World War II.

In the beginning the Communist International attracted the attention and enthusiasm of very diverse groups in Latin America. The Brazilian Anarchists, the Uruguayan and Chilean Socialists, the Syndicalists of Cuba, the middle-class revolutionaries of Peru, the revolutionary generals of Mexico, were all attracted to the Comintern.

These groups regarded the new International as the home of all the more restless souls and idealistic radicals the world over. It was some time before the more rigid outlines of Bolshevik theory and organization became plain to the Latin American radicals and trade unionists. For different groups there were different events which tended to distinguish the "reformist" sheep from the Bolshevik goats.

One of these events was the issuing by the Comintern of the famous "Twenty-One Points" to which a party wishing to adhere to the International must agree. These points included the demand that the affiliating parties purge their more moderate leaders and the provision that each change its name to "Communist Party," regardless of what it had previously been. Particularly in the Latin American Socialist parties which were looking sympathetically toward the Comintern—those of Chile, Uruguay, and Argentina—this made many hesitate about joining the Third International [the latest Comintern congress]. In Chile and Uruguay the majority of the party decided to accept the Twenty-One Points, but in Argentina they refused to do so, and the tiny Partido Socialista Internacionalista finally became the Comintern affiliate, instead of the much larger Partido Socialista.

With the Anarchosyndicalists [workers' organizations and anarchists] an important turning point was the decision of one of the early Comintern congresses to permit affiliation of political parties only. Many Latin American Anarchists had followed the lead of the Spanish Anarchist National Confederation of Labor in hoping that the Comintern would consist of both political parties and trade union groups. However, the Comintern decided that it should consist only of parties and that a subsidiary group of Communist-controlled trade unions should be established, the Red International of Labor Unions (R.I.L.U.). This decision made many Anarchosyndicalists in Brazil, Argentina, and other countries turn their backs on the Comintern and affiliate instead with a new Anarchosyndicalist trade union center, the International Working Men's Association

Latin American Radicals Were Split

Because of their great distance from the center of world affairs and of Communist power, the Latin Americans were often slow to become aware of the fact that the Comintern had developed a very well-defined ideology and form of organization. For instance, it was not until he went to Europe and came into personal contact with the Communist Parties in Western Europe and Russia that the young Peruvian student leader, Victor Raúl Haya de la Torre, was convinced that the new American Popular Revolutionary Alliance (A.P.R.A.) which he had founded should not become part of the Comintern. His fellow countryman, José Mariátegui, almost equally ill-suited to the Comintern's type of organization and ideology, died in 1929 without having fully realized that the Communists had a definite "line" and approved method of organization. His attempts to establish what he conceived to be a proper form of Communist organization for Peru were rebuffed at the 1929 congress of Latin American Communist Parties, and it was not until some months later that a clear division occurred among Mariátegui's followers between those who were willing to adopt the rigidity required for membership in the Comintern and those who did not think it appropriate for their country and their continent.

The second phase in Comintern history was a period of intense struggle between different factions, not only in the Russian party, but in other important affiliates of the International, including the French, German, and United States Parties. This was also true in Latin America. The Argentine and Chilean Communists were plagued with factionalism during the 1920's and early 1930's. The same was true of the Uruguayans and of the Cubans.

In most cases these splits were the result of personal rivalries for power and prestige among the leaders of the local Parties. However, as in the case of the European, Asiatic, and United States Communist Parties, these local quarrels often merged with the titanic struggle in the Russian Communist ranks, and the Latin American protagonists took the side of one or the other of the Russian groups. Thus Manuel Hidalgo's faction in Chile, and Sandalio Junco's in Cuba, took the side of [extremely leftist Communist theorist and activist Leon] Trotsky, while the Laferte and Vilar groups in those countries sided with [Soviet dictator Josef] Stalin. . . .

The Stalin-Nazi Pact Isolated Latin American Communists

The Popular Front [1930s coalition of leftist parties against fascism] epoch marked the first period during which the Communist parties of Latin America really assumed political importance in the life of the hemisphere. Although their activities had previously had some nuisance value in Colombia, Costa Rica, and elsewhere, this was the first time that responsible politicians in more than one country were willing to enter into alliances and agreements with Communists, and that they began to acquire really serious followings among the workers and intellectuals of the Latin American countries. They sowed the seeds during this period which were to flourish and grow into sturdy plants during the latter part of the second World War.

The Latin American Communists were again plunged into sudden isolation as a result of the coming of World War II. With few exceptions, the Latin American Communist leaders followed the International in its support of the Stalin-Nazi pact [in the late 1930s] and in its general endorsement of the Soviet's benevolent neutrality toward Germany during the first phase of World War II.

The result was the isolation of the Communists from the other left-wing and working-class groups in Latin America. The Chilean Popular Front was broken up. The Communists in the labor movement of Mexico were isolated, and pro-Communist Vicente Lombardo Toledano was forced out of his position as Secretary General of the Confederation of Workers of Mexico, although he continued as President of the Confederation of Workers of Latin America (C.T.A.L.). The C.T.A.L. itself was deprived of the financial support which one or more Latin American governments had been giving it during the Popular Front period.

Groups which had been allied to the Communists turned against them. The Apristas of Peru, the Liberals of Colombia, the Socialists of Chile were violently in opposition to the Communists' pro-German line in World War II and attacked the Communists as tools of the Soviet State. In Argentina the pro-Communist Socialist Workers Party, which had broken away from the Socialist Party of Argentina in 1937 because of that party's unwillingness to work with the Communists, was decimated with the great majority of its members returning to the Socialist Party.

Fortunately for the Latin American Communists, the period of Soviet-German friendship was relatively short. The entry of the Soviet Union into the War in the middle of 1941 ushered in another period of Popular Frontism, on an even more exaggerated scale than that of the late 1930's. This was the period during which the Communists of Latin America made their greatest gains.

Sympathy for the Allied Cause

There were various reasons for the Communists' success during this period. First of all, there was general sympathy among the workers and middle-class elements of Latin America for the Allied cause in the second World War, and after June 21, 1941, the Communists became the most vociferous supporters of the Allies. There was widespread admiration among the politically conscious Latin Americans for the mighty struggle which the Russians put up against the Nazi invaders, and there was a general tendency, in Latin America as elsewhere, to regard this military prowess of the Soviet armies as an indication that the charges which had been made concerning dictatorship and tyranny in Russia were not true.

The Latin American Communists basked in the reflection of this sympathy for the Soviet Union. They made no secret of the fact that they represented in Latin America what the Soviet Communists stood for in the U.S.S.R. At the same time, since they seemed to be such good supporters of the Allied war effort, the Communists found that other pro-Allied groups were willing and anxious to cooperate with them.

The Communists took the lead in organizing committees for the support of the Allies, such as the Junta de la Victoria in Argentina. They actively campaigned for Latin American countries breaking relations with the Axis and even for declarations of war by the Latin American countries. They worked as equals with, and were accepted as friends and allies by Socialists, Liberals, Radicals, and others throughout the hemisphere.

During this period, of course, the Communists dispensed with talk of revolution and of dictatorship. They were democrats among democrats, and if they supported advanced programs of social welfare, they were only doing so because this was the best way to win popular support for the war effort—or at least, so they claimed.

As their European comrades were working in the Underground and in exile with liberal, anti-fascist Catholic groups, so the Communists were willing and anxious to work with such Catholic elements in the New World. The most notable example of their success in this direction was the agreement made in Costa Rica between the Archbishop of San José, Monseñor Sanabria, and the Communist Party.

The Communists played down their past. In several instances they changed their name for the purpose of forwarding the broad alliance which they sought to make with all other elements supporting the War. In Colombia the Communist Party became the Social Democratic Party; in Cuba the Unión Revolucionaria Comunista was rechristened the Partido Socialista Popular. The Communist Party of the Dominican Republic also became the Popular Socialist Party. In Costa Rica the Communist Party became the Vanguardia Popular.

The Communists resumed the policy which they had followed in the earlier Popular Front period of allying themselves with the Latin American dictators, if those dictators would declare themselves in favor of the Allied war effort. Thus the Communists of Ecuador for a considerable time were allied with dictator Carlos Arroyo del Río, those of Nicaragua, with Somoza.

Old alliances, such as those of the Cuban Communists with Batista, of the Peruvians with Prado, were resumed. Juan Marinello, prominent Cuban Communist leader, actually served for a time as Minister Without Portfolio in Batista's Cabinet, thus becoming the first Latin American Communist to serve in a Latin American government. In Brazil the Communists succeeded early in 1945 in making a very fruitful working agreement with dictator Getulio Vargas, who was now eager to have their support in his attempt to have himself renamed President in the elections which he could not avoid calling.

Perhaps most striking of all was the short-lived alliance between the Communists of the Dominican Republic and the hemisphere's most monolithic dictator, Generalissimo Rafael Leónidas Trujillo. Trujillo, like Vargas, was anxious to go through the motions of a new "election," so as to establish himself as a "democrat." The Communists were willing to lend themselves to this maneuver, and for a considerable period they were given freedom of action, so that they could run an ostensible candidate against Trujillo, a candidate who they and he knew had no chance of winning, or even of having a respectable number of votes counted in his favor. Once he had used them, Trujillo sent the local Communists packing into exile.

Communist "anti-imperialism" was forgotten during this period. When Communists spoke of "imperialism" it was only the Axis brand to which they were referring. They attacked those who still insisted on speaking about British or American imperialism as saboteurs of the war effort. They discouraged all strikes and other activities against American and British-owned firms.

Friends of the United States and Britain

As a result of this attitude, the Communists were able to build up the most friendly relations not only with managers of local American and British-owned enterprises, but with local Allied diplomatic personnel. Their cooperation was sought in Allied propaganda efforts. Communist leaders, such as Senator Salvador Ocampo of Chile, were welcomed with splendid receptions when they visited the United States. Vicente Lombardo Toledano, by then widely regarded as pro-Communist, if not a Party member, was treated in a very friendly fashion by State Department officials and other U.S. leaders on his several visits to the United States, though President Roosevelt refused to receive him.

This apparent friendship between the Communists and the [North American] Yanquis strengthened the position of the Communists in Latin America. The Latin American governments, always anxious to keep in the good graces of Uncle Sam, took these friendly relations to mean that they, too, should court their local Communists. Or, if they felt inclined to treat the Communists in a friendly way in any case, the local government officials could point to the United States' attitude as an indication that this was what Uncle Sam wanted of them.

The Communists made particular headway during this period in the trade union movement. Although they tended to discourage strikes and even to soft-pedal peaceful presentation of demands on employers, and thus stirred up a certain discontent with their leadership among the rank and file trade unionists, the Communists' attitude of class collaboration and passivity won wide approval among the governments and employing classes of the hemisphere. In a region where the government plays such a dominant role in labor relations, this cordial relationship between Communist trade union leaders and government labor officials won the former more advantage than was lost them by the discontent these policies engendered among the rank and file workers.

As a result, the Communists made tremendous gains among the trade unions of a dozen different countries in Latin America. Their influence in the labor movements of Chile, Cuba, Argentina, Uruguay, Mexico, Colombia, Peru, Venezuela, and several other nations was greater than ever before. Furthermore, after the Cali Conference of the

C.T.A.L. in December, 1944, the Communists formed a majority of the Executive Committee of the Confederation of Workers of Latin America.

The Latin American Communists were at the zenith of their power and influence during 1945 and 1946. Their Parties were legal or at least tolerated in virtually every country of the hemisphere. They had members of Congress in Cuba, Colombia, Peru, Ecuador, Brazil, Chile, Bolivia, Uruguay, Costa Rica, and members of lesser legislative bodies in several other countries. In the latter months of 1946 they had three members in the Chilean Cabinet, and seemed well on the way to achieving the first Communist government of the hemisphere in that country.

Communists Turn on the United States

Since that period they have suffered severe defeats in virtually every country in the hemisphere. There are various reasons for these setbacks. First of all, they have followed the Communist international line in turning violently against the United States, and hence against every government in the continent which is friendly toward the United States.

On the other hand, many Latin American governments have tended to follow the lead of the United States in turning against the Communists. Frequently they have gone much further than the United States in this reaction, but in any case, the turn has limited the freedom of action of the Stalinists.

Perhaps more important was the fact that other political movements caught the imagination of the masses of several countries in which the Communists had been powerful. These nations included Argentina, where the rise of Perón stopped the Communists in their tracks; Brazil, where the *mística* of Vargas rose as that of the Communist leader, Luiz Carlos Prestes, fell in the late 1940's; Cuba, Colombia, Venezuela, and Peru, where left-wing democratic political parties stole much of the Communists' thunder.

At the same time, the Communists lost their position of dominance in the labor movement. Splits, government persecution, the rise of non-Communist trade union groups, help to the non-Communists from the United States labor movement, all tended to weaken the position of the Communists among the organized workers of the hemisphere.

Only in one country did the Communists make notable gains during the post–World War II period—in Guatemala. There they made great advances, due to vigorous propaganda and organizational activity by Communists from abroad, the inexperience of local left-wing politicians, and the advent of a major social revolution which the Communists more or less successfully identified with themselves. By 1953 the Communists controlled the labor movement in Guatemala, were an influential element in the government, although there were no avowedly Communist ministers in the Cabinet, and were edging their way towards the seat of power in that Central American republic. Even here, however, their progress was checked, at least temporarily, by the revolution which upset the Arbenz government in the summer of 1954.

Communists Isolate Themselves

After World War II the Communists tended to become increasingly isolated. Few of the Socialists, Radicals, Liberals, and other moderate leftists with whom they had cooperated during the war were inclined to follow them in their extremes of anti–United States propaganda and conviction. In most instances these groups had continued a more or less covert struggle with the Communists for control of trade union movements and other mass organizations, and although they had cooperated with the Communists for the temporary ends connected with the war, the rivalry had never really disappeared. It broke out again when the war was over.

This renewal of old interparty strife was made all the easier because the Communists had shown on many occasions that they would be ruthless if they were once fully in control of the organized labor movement or any other organization. The most notable instance of this occurred in Chile during late 1946 and early 1947, when the Communists, having ministers in the government, began to act as if they controlled the whole administration—behavior which united almost the whole of the rest of the country against them.

There were other groups which had worked with the

Communists during the war and which now began to turn against them. Liberal Catholic elements, which had been more or less sympathetic with them so long as they were fighting the Nazis, were not willing to accompany them on an equally energetic crusade against the United States and the countries of Western Europe. As their trade union following narrowed, the Communists tended to become more isolated from the mass of the workers in most of the Latin American countries.

The Communists' anti–United States line turned them into vociferous "nationalists," bitterly assailing what they claimed were United States attempts to dominate the economies and politics of the Latin American countries. However, many groups which in the past might have listened more willingly to the Communist attacks on the United States were now impressed with the Communist Parties' complete subservience to Russia and their willingness to justify anything which the Soviet Union did. To many staunch Latin American nationalists and opponents of United States penetration, it appeared that the Communists were not really Latin American nationalists, but, rather, special pleaders for the U.S.S.R. and its rulers.

Nevertheless, the Communists spent a large proportion of their time in the post–World War II period on the various "peace" drives of the international Communist movement. Hundreds of thousands of signatures were collected throughout the hemisphere for the Stockholm "peace" petition. Delegates from a number of countries participated in the numerous Peace Congresses. Vicente Lombardo Toledano played a leading role in the Peiping Congress of 1949, which organized the Far Eastern center of the Communists' World Federation of Trade Unions.

By the end of 1954, then, the Communists' political influence in Latin America was less than at any time since the late 1930's. In public opinion, politics, and the trade union movement, they certainly had lost most of the ground which they had gained as a result of World War II. Although they were still a potential power in the region, they remained a major force only in Chile, Brazil, and Guatemala.

Latin American Communists Follow Party Line

Throughout their history the Latin American Communist Parties have followed the general pattern set by the international Communist movement. The Latin American Parties have faithfully reflected the changes in the "line," the internal dissensions, and the varying conceptions of strategy and tactics which have characterized the world-wide Communist movement. Any claim that the Latin American Communists are somehow "different," that they are "indigenous social reformers," that they are merely "agrarian reformers" or "anti-imperialists," is just so much nonsense. The Latin American Communist Parties are an integral part of the international Communist movement, and their role in Latin American affairs cannot conceivably be assessed with accuracy unless this basic fact is recognized.

Recognition of the true nature of the Latin American Communist Parties is all the more necessary, because the salvation of the region from the Communists lies precisely in the real indigenous social reformers, agrarian reformers, and radical nationalists or anti-imperialists. For it is characteristic of the Communists that they have grown to important proportions in exactly those countries where there have been no local, native radical movements which could catch the imagination and arouse the loyalty of the workers, students, and intellectuals of the nation.

Chapter 5

The Soviet Bloc

Turning | Points

IN WORLD HISTORY

The Postwar Revolution in Eastern Europe

Constantine Poulos

The Red Army moved into Eastern Europe after World War II, and Soviet officials guided nations such as Bulgaria, Rumania, Czechoslovakia, and Yugoslavia into socialist revolution. The revolution in Eastern Europe was facilitated by a reaction to fascism and economic disparity that plagued these nations for years. Author Constantine Poulos reflects on the state of Eastern Europe only three years after the Red Army drove out the Nazis and their fascist puppet leaders. Poulos gives the Soviets credit for helping the Eastern European nations move through the first phase of the revolution, but he condemns the Soviets for hindering the progress of the revolution with their policy of economic exploitation and political oppression, that, unbeknownst to the author, would last for decades.

An American journalist, Constantine Poulos was a Balkan correspondent for the Overseas News Agency and traveled in a jeep through Eastern Europe for more than a year before he wrote this article for *The Nation* in 1947.

In a few months it will be three years since the Red Army, driving the Wehrmacht [German army] before it, started its triumphant march into Eastern Europe and the heart of the Continent. Three years is not a very long time in the history of the region, but the tempo of change has been greatly accelerated, and out of the events and developments of this period a new Eastern Europe is evolving, and making a desperate effort to catch up with the world.

It is possible to generalize about Eastern Europe only if

Constantine Poulos, "Revolution in Eastern Europe," *The Nation*, June 1947.

honesty and fairness are sacrificed. Austria and Czechoslovakia are exceptions to any generalization about the political scene. The non-Slav states, Hungary and Rumania, with their peculiar economic backgrounds, are exceptions to the prevailing economic situation. Poland and Yugoslavia may appear to be under very similar regimes, but basic differences exist.

Albania, Bulgaria, Czechoslovakia, Hungary, Poland, Rumania, and Yugoslavia are all within the Soviet Union's sphere of influence. All have had revolutions. In both respects Austria will eventually have to be classed with them.

The revolution is not, of course, over, and it varies in form and fabric from country to country. Only Poland and Yugoslavia had a revolution in the classic sense, and this explains much of what has happened in those countries since the end of the war—just as post-war developments in the other countries are explained by the fact that their revolutions were brought about by the entrance of the Red Army.

Russia cannot be held wholly responsible for the revolution in Eastern Europe, which has nowhere gone exactly as Moscow would have liked. Whether it came from "above" or "below," the revolution was inevitable: the rotten political, economic, and social conditions could not survive the ferment of war and resistance. But one must give credit to the Soviet Union for guaranteeing the first phase of the revolution and saving it from being smothered in its cradle by Western-supported counter-revolutionary forces, as happened after the last war.

Obviously, neither the direction nor the method of the revolution has pleased the West. The still-born revolt of 1917–25 might have taken a "democratic" form which the West could have approved. But not this revolution. The difference between Western and Eastern democracy, on which we insist, is reflected in the difference between a Western and an Eastern revolution.

The present revolution was born of the collapse of German imperialism, native feudalism, and fascist oppression, amid physical devastation, economic ruin, and human misery. The fatuous, selfish, do-nothing nationalist regimes of the past have been replaced by governments whose leaders not only understand the social problems of their countries but have the ability and will to do something about them.

This revolution will not stop or recede. The youth of Eastern Europe is behind it. By their prodigious efforts in the past two years the workers have proved their devotion to it. The former landless peasants have a stake in it.

Difficult Transition

Admittedly not all the people are in favor of the new regimes. The old ruling classes, the old army castes, the professional politicians of the past don't count. But there are many others for whom the turn-about was too sudden. The gap between feudalism and socialism is a very wide one. Many people still do not understand the causes of their present difficulties. Nazi oppression in Austria, Bulgaria, Hungary, and Rumania was so carefully executed that large sections of the population never learned what it meant. Class distinctions were so savagely beaten into the submerged masses for so many centuries that some of them are still afraid to walk with their heads up.

In time these attitudes will change. Peasants here and there, in Yugoslavia, Poland, and Hungary, assail the regime but at the same time admit that its policies may improve agriculture. Old men object to new ways but with childlike enthusiasm crowd into the little school-houses and churches to benefit from the anti-illiteracy campaigns. Peasants in remote parts of Hungary who never dreamed of going to school watch with pleasure as the school comes to their children. Balkan women voting for the first time show they are acutely conscious of beginning a new life. People who never before in their lives could benefit from clinics and nurseries or enjoy sports clubs and canteens are increasingly willing to stand by the new governments.

Contrary to the widespread belief in the West, the people of Eastern Europe are not as concerned about political freedom as they are about economic security. That civil liberties are meaningless without economic security is a simple truism whose force is appreciated by the most backward worker or peasant. It would have been nice if, after the war, political and economic democracy could have been established simultaneously in Eastern Europe. But given the historical and sociological background of these countries, how could that have been done?

Parliamentary democracy is based on compromises between social classes and political parties. But the peoples of Eastern Europe at the end of the war were in no mood for compromise, and they had no long tradition of political cooperation to fall back on. The governments today are following patterns of political behavior which go back many decades.

Communist Leadership

The present tremendous economic and political upheaval in Eastern Europe is either ignored in the West or vilified as a Russo-Communist creation—which, strangely enough, the Russians and the Communists claim it to be. But it cannot be judged by Western standards or interpreted according to Dun and Bradstreet or Time, Inc.

Men who are working with the Russians and the Communists today because to do otherwise would be to lay out the carpet for the old order—the Socialists, radical peasants, independent leftists, and intellectuals who helped make the revolution—feel that the Communists have proved themselves able leaders, fully aware of the needs of the people. They give the Communists most of the credit for the phenomenal revival of industry and agriculture, despite three successive years of drought, in all these countries except Austria. On the other hand, it is they and not the men sitting outside, complaining, plotting, and running to the American and British embassies, who best know the mistakes and the weaknesses of the Communists. They have no illusions about the Communists or the Russians. They recognize and accept the Communists for what they are.

Except in Czechoslovakia and Yugoslavia the Communists have been in a tough spot. They have had to be the official apologists of the Soviet Union and all its policies. The exigencies of power politics have forced them into strange contortions—which they never seem to find painful: they have been obliged to embrace collaborators, to appease, to vacillate, to find scapegoats when things go badly. Like devout, dogmatic, cunning Jesuits, they believe in the righteousness of their cause and that all means to attain their goal are blessed and justified. In some countries they have been reluctant to assume power alone; yet by their very training and mentality they are "ill-fitted" to work in coalition governments. They become frightened and hysterical when unbelievers present programs or solutions which are better than theirs. This partly accounts for their dishonest efforts to make "fascism" and "reaction" synonymous, and for their unsuccessful attempts to monopolize the progressive socialist spirit of the workers. Try as they may, they cannot control the revolution. While many conditions are similar, Eastern Europe today is not Russia in 1917.

Not the least of the reasons why the revolution in Eastern Europe cannot follow a "Russian" pattern is the Soviet Union itself. It was to the interest of the Soviet Union that the power of the old ruling classes and the social order on which that power was based should be destroyed. But after the revolution passed through that first phase, the Soviet Union did little to help it—indeed, it has hampered it. Russia's relations with the countries of Eastern Europe since that time have been guided by the same cynical selfishness which is apparent in its relations with the big powers and which reveals its continuous sense of insecurity.

Soviet Exploitation

Not only has the revolution been hindered, but two years of wasteful requisitioning by the Red Army, undisciplined behavior by Russian soldiers, and ruthless economic exploitation have aroused a popular revulsion which has enabled the professional Russophobes and the old ruling classes to steady themselves. By protecting and preserving the first phase of the revolution, the Soviet Union automatically assured the execution of far-reaching reforms. But then its economic pressure and its removal of food, livestock, poultry, finished goods, and machinery prevented the new governments from extending their economic reforms and delayed the realization of their social aims.

The new regimes—including the Communist members, although the latter seldom speak about it—know that Russia's ruthless tactics have set them back many years. And thus another vicious circle is formed. The more the governments, which feel they have not been given a real chance to show what they can do, sense a wave of feeling against them the more reluctant are they to allow political freedom to the opposition. The Russians, aware of the same revulsion, hesitate to loosen their grip for fear that violently hostile governments will again be lined up on their borders.

The existing governments are really Russia's best friends. But Russian policies consistently serve to weaken them. It is the old story of the defenses, by their very nature, destroying what they were designed to preserve.

To protect and extend the revolution, the governments of Eastern Europe are looking more and more to one another, and in this lies the hope for the future.

The Invasion of Czechoslovakia

Roy Medvedev

By 1964, anti-Stalinist sentiment was racing through Czechoslovakia. Czechoslovakia was entering an era of reform and democratic change led by progressive right wing reformers, most notably Alexander Dubcek. The Soviets were at a loss on how to handle the situation, but they began making plans to intervene on behalf of their puppet leaders heading the Czech government. The political situation climaxed in a meeting between Czech Communist hardliner Vasil Bilak and Ukrainian leader Pyotor Shelest. The meeting had all the intrigue and mystery of a spy novel. Bilak requested immediate assistance from the Soviet Union so Czechoslovakia might avoid a bloody civil war or a counterrevolution. This request was given to Shelest in the form of a letter and delivered by a KGB (Soviet secret police) agent in a public toilet.

In the following article, author Roy Medvedev explains that Bilak's letter led to the Soviet military invasion of Czechoslovakia. The Czech people, however, offered peaceful resistance to the attack. With a passive enemy and no clear objectives, the Soviets were at a loss. With no easy solution, the Soviets deposed Alexander Dubcek and earned the enmity of the Czech people who favored his reformist ideals. Roy Medvedev is a contributing writer to *Russian Life* magazine. He is a noted historian and author of the book *Let History Judge*.

How farcical spy games, personal squabbles and a meeting in a Bratislava [a Czech city on the Danube River] men's room led to the invasion of Czechoslovakia . . .

The October 1964 Plenum [full parliamentary assembly]

Roy Medvedev, "A Very Hot Summer in Prague," *Russian Life*, vol. 41, August/September 1998, p. 28. Copyright © 1998 by Russian Information Services. Reproduced by permission.

which ousted [Soviet premier] Nikita Khrushchev signalled the end of political thaw in the USSR. But, in Czechoslovakia, the anti-Stalinist movement in ideology and culture was gaining momentum. Proposals were made for political and economic reform. Such a Soviet-Czech divergence should have warned leaders of impending conflict, but neither Moscow nor Prague [Czech capital] took notice. In the fall of 1967, a group of reform-oriented communists, headed by Alexander Dubcek [one of the most popular of the Communist leaders who wished to reform the oppressive Stalin-era Soviet policies], Deputy Prime Minister Oldrich Cernik and Josef Smrkovsky, who later headed the National Assembly, became very influential. The party and society were buzzing with calls for changes. [Czech Communist First Secretary Antonin] Novotny began losing control. . . .

In January 1968, Dubcek was elected First Secretary of the Central Committee of the Czechoslovak Communist Party. Two months later, Novotny would also lose the post of President. He was succeeded by the 73-year old general Ludvik Svoboda, who enjoyed wide popularity not only in Czechoslovakia but also in Soviet military circles—he had even met the then Major General Leonid Brezhnev [who would become Soviet president in 1977]. However, under the Czechoslovak Constitution, the mandate of the President was narrow, so real power was concentrated in the hands of Dubcek, whose public popularity was on the increase.

The Prague Spring

The campaign aimed at condemning Stalinism and political repressions of the past in Czechoslovakia gathered speed. The press published detailed materials denouncing the punitive organs of the Gottwald regime [Czech Communist leader 1946–53], and revealed facts on corruption within the party and state structures. Censorship was lifted first de facto and then formally; a free and wide exchange of opinions began taking place in the press; new magazines and newspapers were being founded. A radical economic reform was on the agenda.

April 1968 became, in many respects, a decisive month for

the "Prague Spring." Dubcek had stated that the country and the party were entering a new stage of socialist revolution, and that one needed to better organize and plan the process of renovation, in order to avoid extremism and revive the authority of the Czechoslovak Communist Party, which had become tainted in recent years.

A Plenary session of the Czechoslovak Communist Party approved their Action Programme, which gave a brief analysis of the crisis and outlined the way to a democratic restructuring of all aspects of social and economic life. Oldrich Cernik became the new head of government and Otto Sik and Husak became his deputies.

The mood of the nation was on the rise, thousands thronged in meetings held all over the country. The authority of the Central Committee of the Czechoslovak Communist Party skyrocketed; Alexander Dubcek had become a national hero. . . .

Secret Communications

In late May 1968, a Plenum of the Central Committee of the Czechoslovak Communist Party decided to convene an Extraordinary Congress of the Party, in order to endorse democratic reforms under way and to make changes at the top. At the same time, Soviet political and military leaders began working out a plan for military intervention in Czechoslovakia. Under the pretext of summer maneuvers, troops began to concentrate on the western border of the USSR.

On May 23, 1968 the first confidential meeting took place between Ukrainian leader Pyotr Shelest and Czech hardliner Vasil Bilak. It was held at night in a small village on the Slovak-Ukrainian border. Shelest not only listened attentively to Bilak, but also tape-recorded the conversation. Bilak requested that the two establish permanent communications and that the USSR "help" the "healthy forces." Shelest passed the tapes on to Brezhnev and [KGB chief Yuri] Andropov—the latter was charged with ensuring continuation of the contacts.

In July 1968, Shelest invited Bilak to spend a holiday in the Crimea [a Russian province] but the latter was afraid of open relations and insisted on a secret meeting. Brezhnev was informed about Bilak's desire to meet with Shelest as a plenipotentiary representative of the Soviet Politburo [Soviet executive committee]. Shelest would write of the meeting in his diary:

> Shelest took a secret flight on a military cargo plane, accompanied by KGB [Soviet secret police] technicians toting special recording devices. The plane landed at a military airport near Budapest [in Hungary]. Shelest's meeting with [Hungarian Communist party leader Janos] Kadar was in secret and lasted for more than two hours. Shelest arrived by 10 P.M. at Kadar's dacha [villa] on Lake Balaton. Bilak was informed about Shelest's arrival, but refused to meet at the dacha; he asked Shelest to meet him on the lake shore at a specially agreed upon location. The leaders of two republics—Ukraine and Slovakia—were behaving like secret agents. "I stepped out on the embankment," Shelest wrote in his memoirs. "I was in the dark. I could hear the waves, the wind, it was hard to recognize someone even at close quarters, let alone to hear somebody's voice. The time fixed for the meeting was running out and Bilak was still nowhere to be seen . . . Yet, some time later Vasil would show up. I called him, he replied. That was how we met."

It was impossible to record the discussion on the noisy lakeshore, so Shelest convinced Bilak to come to the dacha. They talked until 5 A.M. Bilak asked for help, demanding resolute action. Shelest replied that Moscow was ready for the toughest actions, but, on the other hand, the "healthy forces" also should not just wait and see.

"Why aren't you more active?" Shelest asked.

Bilak thought and then replied, "We are afraid of being accused of high treason. We are ready to support you with every means, but we don't know what to do."

"We need a letter from you which would relay your plea for help," Shelest said. "We will fully guarantee that the letter will not be made public and its authors will not be known." Bilak promised to come up with such a letter as soon as possible.

However, there was still not a unified, coherent position

in Moscow as to what to do about Czechoslovakia. It was decided to hold yet another meeting with Czechoslovak leaders (and hopefully split them). The full Soviet Politburo and the Presidium [Government Administration Committee] of the Czechoslovak Central Committee of the Czechoslovak Communist Party were to meet on the border between Czechoslovakia and the Soviet Union, in the little village of Cierna nad Tisou. . . .

The Letter

The meeting in Czierna lasted for five days, from July 28 to August 1. According to the official communique, it was held "in an atmosphere of full openness and mutual understanding and was aimed at finding ways of further development and reinforcement of traditional friendly relations between our peoples and parties." In fact, the negotiations were held in an atmosphere of polemics and threats. One of the sessions had to be interrupted when Shelest engaged in rude attacks on the Czechoslovak leaders, accusing them of betraying communist ideals and solidarity. As a sign of protest, the Czechoslovak delegation left Czierna, returning only after the Soviet delegation presented apologies.

On August 1, at the final meeting between Dubcek and Brezhnev, it was decided to continue talks, but with the participation of other socialist countries too. Bratislava was chosen as the meeting place.

Dubcek and his comrades-in-arms felt that Brezhnev sincerely wanted to solve the conflict peacefully. Western analysts and US intelligence came to the same conclusion. Yet, in fact, there was no accord whatsoever, and, on some hot issues, disagreements were even accentuated. At the time, many felt military intervention was predetermined. Dubcek too, was considering such an outcome, but he believed the odds for the intervention were not very high [he would say in 1989 that he did not expect intervention at the time].

Soviet leaders arrived in Bratislava on August 2. Shelest reminded Bilak of the letter the latter had promised to hand over. A day later the coveted letter from the "healthy forces" was in Shelest's hands. His diary records the event:

On August 3, 1968, I met in the evening with Bilak. We agreed that, before 8 P.M., he would pop into a public toilet and so would I, and that he would pass me the letter via KGB operative Savchenko. That's how it all happened. We met "by chance" in the toilet, and Savchenko discreetly passed to me, from hand-to-hand, the envelope with the long-awaited letter. The letter relayed the situation within the Czechoslovak Communist Party and in the country, the wave of right extremism; the letter also mentioned the political and moral terror unleashed against the communists which hold the right positions. The conquests of socialism were in jeopardy. . . . The letter contained a request to us that we intervene if needed to stop the counter-revolution and avoid a civil war and bloodshed. The letter was signed by: Indra, Bilak, Kolder, Barbirek, Kapek, Piller, Shvestka, Hoffman, Lenart, Strougal [Shelest likely erred in this listing of names]. When the letter was later revealed, the signatures of Barbirak, Piller, Hoffman, Lenart and Strougal were not on it.

The letter identified "an antiCommunist and anti-Soviet psychosis" in the country and urged the USSR to intervene to quash "the imminent danger of counterrevolution." Shelest passed the letter on to Brezhnev. "Thank you, Petro," Brezhnev said. "We will not forget this."

So it is that one of the major events in the history of the USSR and the world communist movement began in the public toilet of the Intourist hotel in a Bratislava suburb. Indeed, only a step separates a great deed from a farce.

The letter written by Bilak, et al to the Russian Politburo decided the issue of Warsaw Pact [alliance of European Communist nations] troop intervention. From that point forward, no negotiations or contacts could have changed the outcome. Interestingly, however, the letter carried no legal force. The signatories were not the leaders of the country or the party. But this was not a major sticking point for the Soviet leaders. But for the signatories, their participation was crucial; those who signed the letter would lead Czechoslovakia after the invasion. Indra was marked for the post of First Secretary of the Central Committee of the Czechoslovak

Communist Party, Bilak was to head the Czechoslovak government and Kolder the Popular Front. Ludwig Svoboda was to keep the post of president.

Soviet Invasion

It is commonly thought that the Czechoslovak leaders knew nothing about the Soviet invasion before it began. This is wrong. The USSR sought to exclude the possibility of resistance by the Czechoslovak army and border guards. Therefore, USSR Defense Minister Andrei Grechko personally warned his Czechoslovak counterpart, General Martin Dzur, about the upcoming invasion of Soviet, German, Polish and Hungarian units. Grechko bluntly told Dzur that he would come to regret it if a single shot were fired by the Czechoslovak army. Dzur obeyed and obviously gave orders to this effect.

On the eve of the invasion, Brezhnev also called Czechoslovak President Ludvik Svoboda, requesting that he accept the coming action in a manner that would not provoke NATO [North Atlantic Treaty Organization, a western alliance] interference.

Some high-ranking Czechoslovak security officers were also in the loop, as they created groups supportive of the action. . . .

The invasion of the Warsaw Pact army began at 11 P.M., August 20, 1968 (Czechoslovak time). The troops were ordered to eliminate all hotbeds of resistance and the cannons were in the ready positions. And yet, there was no resistance anywhere, except for a few gunshots which could have been be either a desperate act or just a provocation. The Czech population watched their allied troops march down the roads with amazement and ire. The Soviets, who came here in 1945 as liberators, were now "unwelcome guests." The Czechoslovaks refrained from any contact with the soldiers. Signs marking street names and house numbers disappeared, making troops' navigation difficult. Czech border guards did not interfere with the invasion and the Czechoslovak army was on the alert but stayed in their barracks.

On the afternoon of the 20th, a session of the Presidium of the Czechoslovak Communist Party had opened in

Prague, in the building of the Central Committee of the Czechoslovak Communist Party. Many expected the invasion, but Dubcek, citing Brezhnev's assurances, hoped for a

Soviet Dominion

Since 1956, the Soviet Union had experienced continued resistance from its satellite nations as they fought for greater freedom, independence, and democracy. Hungary witnessed rebellion in 1956, and Czechoslovakia in 1968. Soviet domination in Czechoslovakia was reestablished when Soviet forces invaded Prague in that year. In a 1972 article for The Nation, *George Charney points out that the Soviet intervention into Czechoslovakia quelled that rebellion but increased dissent and tension throughout the Soviet bloc.*

The crisis of communism precipitated by the 20th Congress of the CPSU [Communist Party of the Soviet Union] in 1956 continues in ever sharper form. The Soviet Union, despite its great power, has not been able to contain the resistance to its hegemony [political domination] and the movement for independence and democratic reform within the Communist world.

Underlying the conflict has been the growing realization that socialism, defined as membership in the Soviet bloc, has not led to independence; that independence is the precondition for genuine social progress. The aspiration for national sovereignty has been accompanied by an irresistible demand for freedom not only from Soviet tutelage but from Soviet dogmas that have warped cultures as well as economies. The Czechoslovak program and national spirit sparked a renascent mood throughout European communism. The Soviets countered with force and moved tanks into Prague to crush dissent—everywhere.

Three years have elapsed. Soviet hegemony has been reestablished at the cost of aggravating tensions and antagonisms. The intervention in Czechoslovakia was followed by the greatest protest and opposition in the history of the Communist movement.

George Charney, "Tremors After Prague," *The Nation*, May 15, 1972.

miracle. Information about the invasion was coming from different directions; but everyone understood what the roar of military cargo planes over the city meant. The leadership of the Czechoslovak Communist Party approved an Address to the People and the Party. Dubcek agreed to convene an Extraordinarily Urgent Party Congress, whose delegates were already elected from all over the country.

Yet, by 4:30 A.M. the building of the Central Committee was encircled by Soviet soldiers, armored vehicles and tanks. A squad of paratroopers entered the building, the phones went silent and the leaders of the Czechoslovak Communist Party were held at gun point. For several hours nobody knew what to do next. A huge crowd gathered on the square; people sang the Czechoslovak national anthem and shouted Dubcek's name. One Czechoslovak was killed, several were wounded.

It was not until 9 A.M. on the 21st that a group of Czechoslovak security officers entered Dubcek's office to announce that Dubcek, Smrkovsky, Frantisek Kriegel and Josef Shpachek were arrested in the name of the "revolutionary tribunal," headed by Alois Indra. Security officers led away the prisoners. A few hours before, Premier Cernik had been arrested in his government office; he had left the party central committee building. The rest of the attendees of the Party Congress were allowed to depart.

From a strictly military point of view, as Western experts later noted, the occupation of Czechoslovakia was a well-organized, fast and efficient operation, even though some 700,000 personnel (22 military divisions) participated in the action. But the operation was to be stymied by non-violent resistance.

On August 21, 1968, Brezhnev, Kosygin, Andropov and Grechko were receiving contradictory information from Czechoslovakia. Not only in Prague, but also in Bratislava, Brno and other cities, seas of indignant protesters surrounded Soviet and Warsaw Pact tanks and soldiers. The troops had no right or pretext to disperse the mass demonstrations—after all, they had come to help friends.

Special issues of the press and special radio broadcasts urged the people to keep the peace and not to erect barricades or leave their homes unless there was a special need. Soviet paratroopers in Prague were in complete isolation, surrounded by a hostile but not aggressive crowd. In some cases, young Prague dwellers dove under tanks. It was 30 [degrees] celcius in Prague those August days, and the city's residents put the pressure on, not giving any water to soldiers, and not letting them use their toilets. Radio amateurs jammed military radio broadcasts.

Politburo member and Soviet Vice-Premier Kirill Mazurov arrived in Prague with the Soviet troops. He used the name "General Trofimov," but he wore the uniform of a lieutenant-colonel. He had full authority and maintained permanent communication with Kosygin and Brezhnev. But Mazurov was at a loss; the situation in the country and in Prague was somewhat different from what Moscow-made plans called for. The "healthy forces" went into hiding; some even joined protest demonstrations. On the night of August 21–22, Indra tried to create a new "government of workers and peasants of Czechoslovakia," first headquartered in the Soviet embassy and then in a Prague hotel. These attempts fell through. It became obvious that the people would not accept an anti-Dubcek government created in the Soviet embassy.

The 22 Czechoslovak ministers who remained free, headed by Deputy Premier Lubomir Strougal, announced that they were taking power in their hands. Even though Strougal had secretly lobbied for the intervention, no one knew of this, and Strougal refused any contacts with his old allies. On August 22, in a Prague suburb, at one of the city's largest factories, the Extraordinary Congress of the Czechoslovak Communist Party was convened, protected by a people's militia. The Congress passed a number of decisions, gave its assessment of the situation in the country and elected a new Central Committee.

Army General Ivan Pavlovsky, commander of the Soviet Army, was at the head of the military action conducted on August 20–21. On August 22, Pavlovsky ordered the Warsaw Pact troops to evacuate small cities and villages, to stop the blockade of governmental buildings and to concentrate in parks and squares of the big cities. The Soviet generals demanded that the Politburo immediately make a political decision. But the Politburo was at a loss. Shelest would write in his diary:

> August 22, 1968. The situation is disastrous. Our troops are in Czechoslovakia but it is the rightist, anti-Soviet elements who call the tune there. The Central Committee, the government, the National Assembly are against us and demand the troops be immediately withdrawn from the country. To crush everything by force is dangerous, for it may trigger a civil war in the country, and a NATO interference is not excluded. To remain passive would mean to doom oneself to shame, disrespect, and would show our impotence . . . This is all the result of laxity and ill-organized actions, and the fault lies with Brezhnev in the first place. Leaflets supporting Czechoslovakia are spread in Kiev. Rumors about Brezhnev's dismissal are being spread.

On August 22, Brezhnev finally took a decision. He ordered the KGB to secretly transport Dubcek and his comrades to Ukraine (they had been flown to Poland from Prague on the evening of 21 August).

The Soviets Concede

The chairman of the Ukrainian branch of the KGB received Andropov's order to isolate the subjects but to not put them in jail, to provide guards, security and good food. The Czechoslovak leaders were taken to the town of Uzhgorod, on the Ukrainian-Slovakian border. From there, one by one, they were taken in armored carriers to the small village of Kamenets, where they were housed in special, secret dachas. According to the reports of those who accompanied them, Dubcek and Cernik were very nervous, demanding to know what was in store for them, at times weeping. Smrkovsky and Kriegel were very daring and issued protests. Shpacek and Shimon looked indifferent but behaved with dignity. Their isolation lasted only one day.

On August 23, the President of Czechoslovakia flew to Moscow. Kosygin met Svoboda at Vnukovo airport. Husak, Bilak, Dzur and Indra had accompanied Svoboda. In the

Kremlin, Svoboda refused to hold negotiations, demanding Dubcek's immediate liberation and their inclusion in the Czechoslovak delegation. Svoboda said he could not return to his country without its legitimate leaders. Otherwise, as an officer, he allegedly said he would be left with only one option—to shoot himself in his Moscow residence.

Brezhnev had to make concessions. All "political hostages" were taken to Moscow. Negotiations began in the Kremlin on August 24. The delegations' composition were almost identical to Cierna nad Tissa, but the situation and the mood were different. The negotiations were protracted and painful and lasted for several days. Brezhnev and Suslov behaved rudely but shortly changed the tone. The Soviets' political setback was all too obvious; they were negotiating only over the scale of concessions. . . .

Velvet Revolution

Dubcek and his supporters sought to consolidate the successes of the Prague Spring and keep building "socialism with a human face." Yet the Soviet leadership, by way of intricate political maneuvers, KGB intrigues and pressure, moved to dethrone the reformers. Soviet hard-liners sought a "centrist" group of leaders who could adopt the Soviet program of "normalization." This group became led by Slovak leader Gustav Husak, who united around him all of Dubcek's opponents and many of his original supporters.

In April 1969, Dubcek was unseated as party leader by Husak, who would also secure the post of Czechoslovak President several years later (following the model of the USSR's aging Brezhnev). Dubcek became Czechoslovak ambassador to Turkey, but one year later was stripped of his party membership and later would become a forester in one of the Slovak regions where he had fought as a partisan during the war.

Russia would pay clearly over the next two decades for its support of a regime which had no popularity in Czechoslovakia (and for Brezhnev's subsequent declaration that the USSR was duty bound to intervene wherever socialism was threatened by "the restoration of capitalism"). In October

1991, after perestroika [era of Soviet Reform] was in full swing in the USSR—a process very much in tune with the Prague Spring Alexander Dubcek visited Moscow. This was two years after one of the most "velvet" of all revolutions in Eastern Europe triumphed in Czechoslovakia, a revolution clearly inspired by the ideals of Prague Spring. Dubcek was received at top levels and got favorable exposure in the press—a just, though belated redress for past humiliations.

Tito's Independence

Bertram D. Wolfe

Josip Broz, known by the monicker Tito, was admired internationally as a powerful leader in post–World War II Europe. His Yugoslavia was seen as a model of communism. Tito's appeal to the people of Yugoslavia was his sense of nationalism and patriotism mixed with his egalitarian spirit. His brand of Communism was quite unlike that of the Soviets, and eventually Titoism was at odds with the imperialistic practices of Tito's mentor Joseph Stalin.

Author Bertram D. Wolfe explains in the following essay that the break between Tito and Soviet leader Stalin was the result of Soviet policy toward Yugoslavia. The Soviet Union viewed Yugoslavia as an agrarian nation, and they refused to help it industrialize despite similar aid being given to other Soviet satellite countries. Tito was disturbed that Yugoslavia was treated as a subordinate to the other nations in the Soviet Bloc and fought to free Yugoslavia from Soviet control. Wolfe enumerates the reasons that Tito was successful in gaining Yugoslavian independence from Soviet domination. His creation of a strong nation outside of Soviet hardline policies allowed Tito to become a national hero, and yet his defiance did not stop him from being a staunch Communist.

Bertram D. Wolfe is a prominent historian who wrote the American Communist Party's Manifesto in 1919. By the 1970s, however, he was a supporter of Reagan's anti-Communist policies and an expert on the failure of communism.

How shall we interpret the break between Tito and Stalin? We interpret it first in emotional terms and say that Stalinism underrates the everlasting determination of peoples to be themselves. The twentieth century's chief lesson thus far, I should say, is that national independence is one of the few things for which men are willing to fight and die.

Second, we can interpret it in historical terms—people with different experiences, different traditions, different cultures, inevitably have differing values. Even a world state would never be able to bleach out all the varied national colors from life.

Third, we can interpret it in terms of national interest and national traditions. The Yugoslavs have a tradition of resistance to outside tyrants—a tradition formed in the struggle against the Turks, strengthened in the struggle against Hitler, and now given fresh life and meaning in the struggle against Stalin.

Fourth, we can interpret it in terms of a special Balkan political tradition. Every Balkan Communist, every Balkan Socialist, every Balkan Democrat, every Balkan Liberal, has been brought up in the tradition of the need for a Federation of Balkan Republics. When we speak of "the Balkanization of Europe" we have in mind the same thing which has been the curse of life in the Balkans. The Balkan peninsula has been the playground of Great Powers—France, Austria-Hungary, Germany, Russia—and Balkan patriots have long felt that the only way their lands could cease to be a playground of the Great Powers was for them to federate and form a genuine federated power of their own. So it was almost automatic for Communists in Bulgaria, Yugoslavia, and Rumania—as it would have been automatic for Socialists or for Republicans and Democrats, the moment they came to power in all those countries and felt a kinship with each other—it was automatic to propose a Balkan Federation. But, at that moment there was only one great power that was still to be kept out of the Balkans by a Balkan Federation: namely, the Soviet Union. And Stalin reacted angrily to the proposal of a powerful Balkan Federation which might have stood up against him.

Fifth, we can interpret the Tito break in terms of personal conflict, and this is the more instructive because Tito is a kind of "pocket" Stalin. Of all the disciples of Stalin, the one that learned most from him and was closest to him was Joseph Broz, known as Tito. Now Stalinism is a jealous "ism." It is a kind of ersatz religion in which Stalin has become the infallible, the omniscient, the omnipotent leader and father of the peoples. The *vozhd* is a jealous *vozhd* and beside him there is no other *vozhd*. He may have disciples—twelve, or twelve times twelve, or any number—but he may not have partners, associates, or second-string leaders. The disciple who challenges this becomes by definition a "Judas Iscariot."

Sixth, we might interpret Titoism in ideological terms. We might bear in mind that orthodoxies tend to breed heresies; dogmas, challenge; commands, disobedience. Then the heresies, in turn, will claim to be orthodoxies, even as so many heresies in the Christian churches appeal to "primitive Christianity." So Titoism has appealed to "primitive Leninism," against Stalin's modifications or "betrayals" of what Tito claims to be orthodox Leninism. It is within this closed circle that Titoism has developed, and only now—reluctantly, hesitatingly, dubiously—some of Tito's ideologues are beginning to question certain tenets of Leninism itself.

Tito's Appeal

Having made this multiple interpretation of the development of Titoism, I want to suggest something of the multiple appeal of Titoism. It appeals to national patriotism against treason to one's country; yes, and even to the class that a Communist professes to represent. Wherever you have to put the interests of the Soviet government above the interests of your own country, your own people, and against your own working class—then you are faced with the problem of treason. Reluctance to commit these forms of treason is one of the appeals that Titoism makes to the Communist in other countries.

Second, it appeals to "primitive Leninism" as a return to purity of doctrine and true egalitarian internationalism.

Third, it appeals to fellow travelers "out on a limb" and anxious to climb down without any loss of revolutionary posture. . . . The cold war having created an intolerable situation for people out on that limb, the problem was how they could climb down, yet still appear faithful to some kind of revolutionary doctrine. . . .

Fourth, Titoism has an appeal to its neighbors still needing a Balkan Federation to defend themselves—to Italy and to Greece.

Fifth, it is of especial interest to the Atlantic Pact nations, for it represents the crack in the armor, the breach in the walls. I have every sympathy for the plight of the Yugoslav people who are still under the heel of a totalitarian dictatorship; from their standpoint it would certainly be much better if Tito were a Democrat and not a totalitarian Communist dictator. But from the standpoint of our interest at the present phase of the cold war, I can't help thinking that Tito is more useful to us as a Communist than he would be as a Democrat.

Now I turn to the genesis of the Tito break. The first aspect that we must consider is the special circumstances under which Titoist Yugoslavia was born. Like Poland, Yugoslavia resisted German invasion from the outset [of World War II]. There is this difference, however—Poland resisted both Hitler and Stalin while Titoist Yugoslavia resisted Hitler only when Stalin and Hitler broke.

Second, Yugoslavia is an ideal terrain for guerrilla warfare and although its main armies were easily smashed by the Wehrmacht [the German army], yet in the mountains of Yugoslavia guerrilla warfare was never abandoned.

Third, the Tito forces participated in the final liberation of Yugoslavia and functioned as a kind of junior ally to the Soviet Army.

Fourth, their mountains were never fully occupied by Hitler as their country was never occupied by Stalin. It was the only East European state to escape [Soviet] Red Army occupation, therefore theoretically self-liberated.

Fifth, geographically, Yugoslavia is farthest from Russia of the so-called People's Democracies. It has no contiguous border with the Soviet Union. It has direct contact with the non-Communist world—with Italy, with Greece and with the open sea along the shores of the Adriatic. These, then, are the special circumstances which made possible the rise of Titoism.

Yugoslavia Ignored

Now I should like to examine some of the differences—
muted, but stubborn—that developed between Tito and
Stalin long before either of them recognized that these differences were leading to a break. On March 5, 1942,
Moscow sent a cable to Tito, criticizing him for being too
pro-Soviet and too openly Communist in his conduct of the
struggle inside Yugoslavia. I quote a few sentences from the
Moscow cable:

> With some justification the followers of England and the
> Yugoslav government believe that the partisan movement is
> assuming a Communist character and that it intends to sovi-
> etize Yugoslavia. The basic and immediate task consists now
> in the unification of all anti-Hitler elements in order to
> crush the occupier and achieve national liberation. Is it really
> true that besides the Communists and their followers there
> are no other Yugoslav patriots with whom you could fight
> against the enemy?

Now this is an instruction—not to cease to plan for a Soviet Yugoslavia, but to slow up and dissimulate the tempo of
progress in that direction. We thus find that Tito is more
Communist and more openly pro-Soviet than Stalin wishes
him to be at that moment. A similar instruction went to
[Chinese Communist leader] Mao and, as you know, Mao
Tse-tung accepted the instruction and continued to collabo-
rate with [his rival, Chinese nationalist leader] Chiang Kai-
shek, but Tito stepped up his campaign against [his rival,
Serbian general] Mihailovich after receiving this cable. The
Soviet Union continued to maintain a "hands-off" appear-
ance until very late.

There was no Soviet mission in Yugoslavia until February
1944, although there was a military mission from Britain
from May 1942 on. In 1944 a Yugoslav brigade, trained in
Russia, came equipped with uniforms with royal Yugoslav
emblems, and only after Tito protested were the emblems
removed. In 1943, while Stalin was still uncertain whether
Mihailovich or Tito would come out on top and still wished
to avoid alarming the Western powers, he gave no direct

help to Tito. Tito was puzzled, angered, and the only answer he could find was to step up his offensive and campaign of propaganda against Mihailovich. Only when the Americans and the British showed no unfavorable reaction and when all sorts of people in America and in Britain began to echo Tito's propaganda that Mihailovich was a Nazi collaborator—only then did Stalin conclude that his cautions and fears were exaggerated and only then did he begin openly to give help to Tito. . . .

Next, it is well to remember that the party which Tito now leads is truly a Titoist party. A bit of biography will help. Tito was born Joseph Broz in 1892 in Hapsburg, Croatia. He was a war prisoner of the Russians in World War I. There he was indoctrinated by the Bolsheviks [radical Communist party], joined the Red Army, and got his first military training in the civil war that followed in Russia after World War I. Sent back to Yugoslavia, he became secretary of the Metalworkers' Union of Zagreb. In 1928 he did a tour of duty of five years in jail, where he met Mosa Pijade, who was a fellow inmate, and their close friendship and collaboration began. When he got out of jail, he took a postgraduate course in the Lenin School in Moscow.

From the Lenin School he was sent to Paris to carry on some important Comintern [headquarters of international communism] duties in connection with the Spanish Civil War. In Paris he steeped his hands in the blood of "The Purges" when the Blood Purges were carried into Spain and served to demoralize the Republican side in the Spanish Civil War. By this participation in the purge, Tito rose from an obscure second-rank figure in the Yugoslav Communist party to the chief of that party. Those earlier leaders who had stood in his way and were his superiors largely disappeared in "The Purges."

In 1941 the Yugoslav party numbered 12,000 members. Less than 3,000 of them survived at the end of World War II, but by 1948 those 3,000 had swelled to 470,000—most of whom never knew any leader but Tito.

Now a glance at the Balkan Federation question: [Bulgarian workers' movement leader] Dimitrov visited Tito at Bled in the summer of 1947. Their principal subject of conversation was the setting up of a Balkan Federation. Dimitrov for Bulgaria and Tito for Yugoslavia issued a joint communique about the immediate steps for the setting up of a Federation of Balkan People's Democratic Republics. Stalin reacted instantly with anger. Dimitrov was forced to retract and disclaim their joint initiative in articles which were published in *Pravda* and *Izvestia* [Soviet newspapers]. But Tito did not publish a disclaimer. This, therefore, is a key point in the break.

Nevertheless, in the autumn of 1947 (when the Cominform [Communist propaganda organization] was established as a public body with the primary aim of fighting the Marshall Plan [U.S. plan for European postwar recovery] and a secondary aim of setting up a federation of satellites in the Balkans under Soviet domination, which would be just the opposite of a Balkan Federation such as Dimitrov and Tito had envisioned)—at that point Tito was still the shining example and his country the most advanced of all the People's Democracies that had been created during World War II. The Cominform headquarters were in Belgrade. Tito was regarded as the most outstanding of the Balkan leaders. Everyone admired him for his power, for his having attained that power independently, and for his general manifestation of independence. Yugoslavia was being used throughout the world by Communists and fellow travelers as the model Communist state of those that had been newly born. Only after the open fight between Stalin and Tito were headquarters of the Cominform switched from Belgrade to Bucharest.

Puppet State

Now let us examine the relations between Stalin and Tito during the critical period. Tito visited Moscow in April 1945. He came back with a twenty-year treaty of friendship and mutual aid, with a military mission to run his army, an economic mission to integrate his industry into the Soviet economic plan. And he learned, to his dismay, that that plan viewed Yugoslavia as a kind of second-class agricultural, raw-material, metal-producing land, subordinate in rank to Czechoslovakia, to Poland, and to Hungary (for Czechoslovakia, Poland, and Hungary were slated for a greater degree of industrialization). I do not have to tell you that Czechoslovakia, Poland, and Hungary possessed a greater degree of industrialization at the time when they were taken over by the Communists.

At that interview Tito was, moreover, urged into open battle with his own people. One way in which Stalin keeps puppets as puppets is to get them thus into open struggle with their own people. He was urged to go head-on into forced collectivization of Yugoslav agriculture. He recognized that his army was to be reduced to an auxiliary troop of the Soviet army and that the whole scheme reduced Yugoslavia to a subordinate part in a detailed blueprint from Moscow to all her satellites. He recognized, too, that far from "withering away," this form of state domination was destined to grow stronger and the Soviet empire would be ever more unified, and the Balkan portions of it ever more subjected and coordinated into the Soviet empire. He was faced with the dilemma that Yugoslavia was to remain as before—poor, backward, weak, dependent, and subject to the will of greater powers, in this case the Soviet Union.

He paid a second visit to Stalin in May and June 1946. Here they went into more detail on the same matters. He learned that the USSR was going to reorganize the Yugoslav army with modern tactics and modern equipment. There was to be no national manual of arms in this thoroughly national guerrilla army, but it was to take the Soviet manual of arms, just as, a little later, Hungary was ordered to teach its soldiers to take commands in Russian as well as in Hungarian. There was to be no national arms industry—generous equipment with weapons but if at any time they wore out or at any time Tito needed new munitions for them, he would have to come "hat in hand" to the Soviet Union once more. There was a Soviet mission to go to Yugoslavia and take virtual command of the Yugoslav army, just as the Yugoslavs were permitted to send a mission to Albania to take virtual command of the Albanian army.

The Soviet intelligence was to teach the Yugoslav intelligence how to operate and was to have such plenary powers that it could easily bypass the Yugoslav intelligence and act as an espionage system on Tito and his fellow Communists. The Soviet technicians were to get notably higher salaries and, like the Soviet army officers, were to get plenary powers and be in key spots.

Tito Stands Up to Moscow

Tito left Moscow crestfallen and conferred with his Balkan confederates for closer cooperation to create counterpressure so that the Communists of the Balkans would be treated with more wisdom (as he thought) and more dignity than had thus far been the case. For the moment all the leaders of the other Balkan countries looked to Tito for leadership, not realizing how far things would go. There followed a period of maneuver. The Comintern, or Cominform, was ordering a sudden drastic turn to the "Left," in connection with the stepping up of its "cold war.". . . Tito, as a good Stalinist, recognized the symptoms and made a sudden ultra-Left swing himself—went way to the "Left" of the orders which he expected would come from Moscow any day, and announced that he was determined to "liquidate immediately all remnants of Capitalism in trade and in industry and agriculture." This drastic turn to the Left is something for which Yugoslav economy and Yugoslav agriculture are still paying the penalty at present, as each day's news indicates.

Stalin was as smart as Tito, and when he saw Tito taking this Left turn on his own so that he could not be criticized as an "opportunist," he recognized that this meant "fight." And so the Politburo [executive council] of the Communist party of the Soviet Union began secret consultations with selected members of other Central Committees concerning Tito's "errors" and Tito's "excessive independence." And the Cominform (which had been set up for the fight on the Marshall Plan) now sharpened its offensive instruments for a major war on Tito and Titoism.

In late 1947 the Cominform met in Belgrade—on September 27—and Tito was still a leader among the Cominform leaders. He criticized heads of other Communist parties for their timidity. He was shown sympathy by Dimitrov, by Gomulka [of Poland], by Gheorghiu-Dej of Rumania. Even Thorez [of France] and Togliatti [of Italy], who were present, were hesitant and showed some admiration for the courage and the independence that Tito was showing. Zhdanov, representing the Soviet Union, was also friendly to Tito, but he was in the beginning of his eclipse in the Soviet Union and died in 1948. His people were rapidly removed from places of power.

At the beginning of March 1948, the vice premier of Yugoslavia, Kardelj, went to Moscow in a vain effort to persuade Moscow to send more machinery for the purpose of the industrialization of Yugoslavia. He came back emptyhanded. On March 18, the Soviet government secretly withdrew all military advisers and instructors from Tito's army, charging that they were "surrounded by hostility." On March 19 they withdrew all civilian missions, charging "a lack of hospitality and a lack of confidence." On March 20, Tito demanded an explanation.

He wrote to [Soviet foreign minister] Molotov, "We are amazed. We cannot understand. We are deeply hurt. Openly inform us what the trouble is.". . .

This brings us to the notion of Kremlin imperialism, which Tito's break has made so clear. The subordination of the Yugoslav economy into the overall plans and profits of Soviet industry; the attempt by the Soviet Union to get proconsul's rights and extraterritorial status for its agents; its ambassador to be entitled to interfere in Yugoslav internal affairs; its agents to have the right to access to state secrets; its right to organize its own intelligence service to spy on the Yugoslav leaders, to be exempt from Yugoslav espionage and to recruit Yugoslav citizens as Soviet spies; its insistence that Soviet officers should get three or four times as much salary from Yugoslavia as the Yugoslav generals and to have overriding powers; its insistence on the rights of the Communist party of the Soviet Union to interfere in the affairs of the Communist party of Yugoslavia and of the Yugoslav state.

Now Soviet imperialism combines all the imperialisms that have ever been invented in the long history of man: from the most ancient direct pillage and plunder and kidnapping of populations and extermination of elites to leave peoples leaderless, and the sowing of waste lands for strategic purposes, to the early twentieth-century form of economic penetration, and then it has super-added its own forms of expansion of the total state through terror, concentration camps, deportations, police systems, and the like.

Let us examine for a moment what we might call "classic economic imperialism." The Soviet Union had set up (as Tito has now made clear by publishing the documents) mixed companies, *juspad* and *justa*—shipping and aviation. Theoretically, the stock is owned fifty-fifty by the Soviet government and the Yugoslav government, but the Soviet government paid in only 9.83 percent of its share during the period in which the Yugoslav government had paid in 76.25 percent of its share. The managing director in Yugoslavia was a Soviet appointee; his assistant was a Yugoslav who was, for all practical purposes, ignored. Soviet planes were allowed to fly into Yugoslavia, but Yugoslav planes were not allowed to fly into the Soviet Union. Yugoslavia paid 52 percent more for her freight shipment on the Danube than the Soviet Union did and 30 percent more (for reasons that are not clear to me) than any other satellite did. In other words, here was a system of direct economic exploitation thinly disguised as an equal partnership.

Similarly, to keep it in subjection, the army equipment of Yugoslavia was left without replacement parts. Yugoslavia sent metals (principally iron) to Czechoslovakia and asked in return for machinery in order to manufacture trucks. Czechoslovakia under Soviet orders sent not machinery to manufacture trucks, but trucks, meaning "you will never manufacture your own trucks." Yugoslavia found that all its molybdenum was being monopolized by the Soviet government. Its cost of production was fantastically high—500,000 dinars per ton according to the Yugoslavia White Book; but the Soviet monopoly paid only the world price—instead of 500,000 dinars, 45,000 dinars—so that Yugoslavia lost 455,000 dinars on every ton that was delivered; the more it delivered, the more it lost.

Finally, in this relation of metropolis to colony there was

an ill-concealed basic contempt. One example will suffice: In one of the notes of the Soviet government to the Yugoslav government, dated August 30, 1949, you will find this sentence: "The puppy is feeling so good that it barks at the elephant." Nevertheless, the puppy has so far checked the elephant. We must now examine how the puppy managed to hold the elephant at bay. . . .

Tito on the Offensive

In the chess game which now ensued both Tito and Stalin played by the same book. Tito was able to anticipate each move. Every time Stalin touched a piece, he envisaged the entire alteration of configuration of the game—for he was playing the same game. He was invited to Moscow to parley—he politely declined the invitation. He was invited to Bucharest [the capital of Rumania] to parley at the Second Cominform session—he stayed away. Attempts were made to assassinate him—he protected himself well, though not as cautiously as Stalin did.

But there is an invisible wall which helps to protect him. There is danger in assassinating him before he has been discredited, before he has gone through the process of acknowledging his errors, discrediting himself, spitting in his own face, crawling, apologizing, and doing all the other things that Cominform leaders have to learn to do at certain stages in their careers. Only then could he be safely exterminated, confessed, "purged," or assassinated. But to assassinate him before this has happened is to make a banner and a martyr of him. This, too, protects him. A coup d'etat [sudden, violent overthrow] was tried against him, but he comes from a land where people, as they say in Mexico, "learn to get up early"; that is, he drew first.

In April 1948, before the open break, he threw [Serbian political rivals] Hebrang and Zujovic in jail, recognizing that they were secretly organizing a Stalinist faction in his party. . . . When General Arso Jovanovic, who was trained in Moscow and returned to serve in his army, packed his bags one night and made for the frontier, Tito seemed to get the jump again and Jovanovic was shot trying to escape.

A "revolution" in Yugoslavia has been called for, and called for, and called for—but the calls fall on deaf ears. Tito, who had enormous opposition in his own country, undoubtedly has less opposition today than he had when Stalin attacked him, rather than more opposition. With his internal opposition, every knock from Stalin is a kind of boost. He was gradually moved over into the position of a national hero. Without ceasing to be a Communist he is also in the position of a national hero, defending Yugoslavia's independence against a great, bullying power. Therefore, Stalin's committees in exile have been branded as "puppets," "traitors," and Tito himself is a hero even with the people who resent his total state regime.

Charging Tito with ingratitude and lack of discipline has not proved effective, so Stalin has tried more complex ideological attacks. But an ideological attack permits an ideological defense. The Cominform has said that Yugoslavia has a police regime, terror, no party democracy, holds no party congresses. Tito answers, "You have a police regime; you have terror; you also, have no party democracy; you hold no party congresses."

So every article of the indictment has become a fortiori [all the more] an article of the indictment of the Stalin regime itself, and this is the most distressing thing that has happened to Stalin since he came to power. Gradually Tito has stepped up his defensive until it has become an offensive, and he has done it with rare tactical skill. Today the Soviet regime is truly on the defensive against this tiny, ridiculous "puppy who is barking at the elephant"; on the defensive because from inside the Communist camp come the clear words of truth about Soviet imperialism and Soviet terror and Soviet ruthlessness which, when they come from non-Communists, have less effectiveness. This is the true crack in the Kremlin wall of infallibility. Therefore Stalin cannot tolerate it and refuses to tolerate it, but he tries expedient after expedient, move after move—and every time Tito, playing by the same book, having gone through the same hard school, and having a somewhat better moral case, outguesses Stalin and blocks each move on his part.

There are only two possible moves which might bring results. One of them is to drive all his neighbor states into an attack—an open war upon him. This is too dangerous. Danger No. 1: that the armies of the Balkan neighbor states are themselves infected with some admiration for this assertion of independence of a Balkan power; Danger No. 2: Tito has (on a Balkan scale) a mighty good army and may not be overthrown without the intervention of the Soviet Union; Danger No. 3 (and largest of all): during the period when Stalin wants neither total peace nor total war he cannot risk an open attack upon Tito, for out of a local war too easily can come a total war. . . .

Now according to the inner nature of the Stalin regime the direct opposite procedure is taken—to tighten the bonds. Given both the ruthless total state that the Soviet Union is and the kind of man Stalin is, he can think of nothing but to squeeze tighter; to coordinate the countries more rapidly into his machine; to hasten the conflict between rulers and ruled; to remove those who have any roots in their own country and put in their places puppets who are completely dependent upon him; to let loose a hail of blood purges, executions of faithful and devoted Communists like Laszlo Rajk, Traicho Kostov, Clementis, Gomulka, and like loyal collaborators such as Foreign Minister Jan Masaryk of Czechoslovakia. There has been a hail of accusations of Titoism, and one by one the men who have national roots in their own country, in their own Communist parties and in their own laboring classes—these men have been executed in advance of the possibility that they might some day commit the crime of considering the interests of their country as different from the interests of the Soviet empire.

However, there is also a danger in that method of solving the problem of Titoism. When you draw the bonds tighter and tighter you augment the potential discontent. Thus the Soviet empire appears to grow tighter and stronger with its more ruthless coordination of all of its parts, but at the same time that strategy introduces fresh elements of weakness into every one of the lands that Stalin dominates.

Appendix of Documents

Document 1: On Communism and the Proletariat

Friedrich Engels was a German socialist writer and philosopher from England. He collaborated with his friend and colleague Karl Marx in issuing the Communist Manifesto. *The manifesto called for the overthrow of the capitalist system in the hope that the workers of the world would unite to form a worldwide socialist revolution. Here, in his* Principles of Communism, *issued the year before the* Communist Manifesto, *Engels discusses the rise of the proletariat after the industrial revolution that took place in England in the second half of the eighteenth century.*

Question 1: What is Communism?

Answer: Communism is the doctrine of the conditions of the liberation of the proletariat [working class].

Question 2: What is the proletariat?

Answer: The proletariat is that class in society which draws its means of livelihood wholly and solely from the sale of its labour and not from the profit from any kind of capital; whose weal and woe, whose life and death, whose whole existence depends on the demand for labour, hence, on the alternations of good times and bad in business, on the vagaries of unbridled competition. The proletariat, or class of proletarians, is, in a word, the working class of the nineteenth century.

Question 3: Proletarians, then, have not always existed?

Answer: No. Poor folk and working classes have always existed, and the working classes have mostly been poor. But there have not always been workers and poor people living under the conditions just stated; in other words, there have not always been proletarians any more than there has always been free and unbridled competition.

Question 4: How did the proletariat originate?

Answer: The proletariat originated in the industrial revolution which took place in England in the second half of the last [eighteenth] century and which has since then been repeated in all the civilized countries of the world. This industrial revolution was brought about by the invention of the steam-engine, various spinning machines, the power loom, and a whole series of other mechanical devices. These machines which were very expensive and hence could be bought only by big capitalists, altered the whole previous mode of production and ousted the former workers because machines turned out cheaper and better commodities than could the workers with their inefficient spinning-wheels and hand-looms. These machines delivered industry wholly into the hands of the big capitalists and rendered the workers' meagre property (tools, hand-looms, etc.) entirely worthless, so that the capitalists soon had everything in their hands and nothing remained to the workers. This marked the introduction of the factory system into the textile industry.

Once the impulse to the introduction of machinery and the factory system had been given, this system spread quickly to all other branches of industry, especially cloth- and book-printing, pottery, and the metalware industry. Labour was more and more divided among the individual workers, so that the worker who formerly had done a complete piece of work, now did only part of that piece. This division of labour made it possible to supply products faster and therefore more cheaply. It reduced the activity of the individual worker to a very simple, constantly repeated mechanical motion which could be performed not only as well but much better by a machine. In this way, all these industries fell one after another under the dominance of steam, machinery, and the factory system, just as spinning and weaving had already done. But at the same time they also fell into the hands of the big capitalists, and there too the workers were deprived of the last shred of independence. Gradually, not only did manufacture proper come increasingly under the dominance of the factory system, but the handicrafts, too, did so as big capitalists ousted the small masters more and more by setting up large workshops which saved many expenses and permitted an elaborate division of labour. This is how it has come about that in the civilized countries almost all kinds of labour are performed in factories, and that in almost all branches handicraft and manufacture have been superseded by large-scale industry. This process has to an ever greater degree ruined the old middle class, especially the small handicraftsmen; it has entirely transformed the condition of the workers; and two new classes have come into being which are gradually swallowing up all others, namely:

I. The class of big capitalists, who in all civilized countries are already in almost exclusive possession of all the means of subsistence and of the raw materials and instruments (machines, factories) necessary for the production of the means of subsistence. This is the bourgeois class, or the bourgeoisie.

II. The class of the wholly propertyless, who are obliged to sell their labour to the bourgeoisie in order to get in exchange the means of subsistence necessary for their support. This class is called the class of proletarians, or the proletariat.

Friedrich Engels, *Principles of Communism*. Peking, China: Foreign Languages Press, 1977.

Document 2: Class Struggle

Karl Marx and his associate Friedrich Engels published the Communist Manifesto *in 1848. They wanted to spark a worldwide social and economic revolution. In this excerpt, Karl Marx asserts that the history of man is a constant cycle of class struggle and revolution.*

The history of all hitherto existing society is the history of class struggles.

Freeman and slave, patrician [noble] and plebeian [commoner], lord and serf, guild-master and journeyman, in a word, oppressor and oppressed, stood in constant opposition to one another, carried on uninterrupted, now hidden, now open fight, a fight that each time ended, either in a revolutionary re-constitution of society at large, or in the common ruin of the contending classes.

In the earlier epochs of history we find almost everywhere a complicated arrangement of society into various orders, a manifold gradation of social rank. In ancient Rome we have patricians, knights, plebeians, slaves; in the middle ages, feudal lords, vassals [servants], guild-masters, journeymen, apprentices, serfs; in almost all of these classes, again, subordinate gradations.

Karl Marx, *Manifesto of the Communist Party*, 1848. Gale Group History Resource Center. http://galenet.galegroup.com/servlet/HistRC.

Document 3: Revolution and Counterrevolution in Germany

The Address of the Central Committtee to the Communist League, *written in March 1850 by Karl Marx and Friedrich Engels, was a plea to German workers to strengthen the league to its former prominence in Germany and for the workers to overcome the bourgeois counterrevolution there. The pamphlet was distributed to progressive German ex-patriots living abroad and reveals how violent class revolutions were expected to be.*

Brothers!

In the two revolutionary years 1848–49 the League proved itself in two ways: first, in that its members energetically took part in the movement in all places, that in the press, on the barricades and on the battlefields, they stood in the front ranks of the only decidedly revolutionary class, the proletariat. The League further proved itself in that its conception of the movement as laid down in the circulars of the congresses and of the Central Committee of 1847 as well as in *The Communist Manifesto* has turned out to be the only correct one, that the expectations expressed in those documents have been completely fulfilled and the conception of present-day social conditions, previously propagated only in secret by the League, is now on everyone's lips and is openly preached in the market places. At the same time the formerly firm organization of the League has been considerably slackened. A large part of the members who directly participated in the revolutionary movement believed the time for secret societies to have gone by and public activities alone sufficient. The individual circles and communities allowed their connections with the Central Committee to become loose and gradually dormant. Consequently, while the democratic party, the party of the petty bourgeoisie [middle class], organized itself more and more in Germany, the workers' party lost its only firm foothold, remained organized at the most in individual localities for local purposes and in the general movement thus came completely under the domination and leadership of the petty-bourgeois democrats. An end must be put to this state of affairs; the independence of the workers must be restored. The Central Committee realized this necessity and therefore already in the winter of 1848–49 it sent an emissary, Joseph Moll, to Germany for the reorganization of the League. Moll's mission, however, failed to produce any lasting effect, partly because the German workers at that time had not acquired sufficient experience and partly because it was interrupted by the insurrection in May last year. Moll himself took up the musket, entered the Baden-Palatinate army and fell on June 29 in the battle of the River Murg. The League lost in him one of its oldest, most active and most trustworthy members, one who had been active in all the congresses and Central Committees and even prior to this had carried out a series of missions with great success. After the defeat of the revolutionary parties of Germany and France in July 1849, almost all the members of the Central Committee came together again in London, replenished their numbers with new revolutionary forces and set about reorganizing the League with renewed zeal.

This reorganization can only be carried out by an emissary, and the Central Committee considers it extremely important that the emissary should leave precisely at this moment when a new revolution is impending, when the workers' party, therefore, must act in the most organized, most unanimous and most independent fashion possible if it is not to be exploited and taken in tow again by the bourgeoisie as in 1848.

Brothers! We told you as early as 1848 that the German liberal bourgeois would soon come to power and would immediately turn their newly acquired power against the workers. You have seen how this forecast came true. Indeed it was the bourgeois who, immediately after the March movement of 1848, took possession of the state power and at once used this power to force back the workers, their allies in the struggle, into their former oppressed position. Though the bourgeoisie was not able to accomplish this without uniting with the feudal party, which had been disposed of in March, without finally even surrendering power once again to this feudal absolutist party, still it has secured conditions for itself which, in the long run, owing to the financial difficulties of the government, would place power in its hands and would safeguard all its interests, if it were possible for the revolutionary movement to assume already a so-called peaceful development. In order to safeguard its rule, the bourgeoisie would not even need to make itself odious by taking violent measures against the people, since all such violent steps have already been taken by the feudal counterrevolution. Developments, however, will not take this peaceful course. On the contrary, the revolution, which will accelerate this development, is near at hand, whether it will be called forth by an independent uprising of the French proletariat or by an invasion of the Holy Alliance against the revolutionary Babylon.

Karl Marx and Friedrich Engels, *Address of the Central Committee to the Communist League.* Peking, China: Foreign Languages Press, 1977.

Document 4: Class Warfare in Prerevolution Russia

In this excerpt written in 1906, the infamous dictator Joseph Stalin discusses the complex nature of society and its motley mix of classes and class origins. He points out that a clear division between the proletariat class and the capitalist class has emerged out of this complexity in the early twentieth century. He then describes how the two classes in Russia, which once lived together in relative peace, are organizing and mobilizing for a major confrontation.

Present-day society is extremely complex! It is a motley patchwork of classes and groups—the big, middle and petty bourgeoisie; the big, middle and petty feudal landlords; journeymen, unskilled labourers and skilled factory workers; the higher, middle and lower clergy; the higher, middle and minor bureaucracy; a heterogeneous intelligentsia, and other groups of a similar kind. Such is the motley picture our society presents!

But it is also obvious that the further society develops the more clearly two main trends stand out in this complexity, and the more sharply this complex society divides up into two opposite camps—the capitalist camp and the proletarian [working class] camp. The January economic strikes (1905) clearly showed that Russia is indeed divided into two camps. The November strikes in St. Petersburg (1905) and the June–July strikes all over Russia (1906), brought the leaders of the two camps into collision and thereby fully exposed the present-day class antagonisms. Since then the capitalist camp has been wide awake. In that camp feverish and ceaseless preparation is going on; local associations of capitalists are being formed, the local associations combine to form regional associations and the regional associations combine in all Russian associations; funds and newspapers are being started, and all-Russian congresses and conferences of capitalists are being convened. . . .

Thus, the capitalists are organising in a separate class with the object of curbing the proletariat.

On the other hand, the proletarian camp is wide awake too. Here, too, feverish preparations for the impending struggle are being made. In spite of persecution by the reaction, here, too, local trade unions are being formed, the local unions combine to form regional unions, trade union funds are being started, the trade union press is growing, and all-Russian congresses and conferences of workers' unions are being held. . . .

It is evident that the proletarians are also organising in a separate class with the object of curbing exploitation.

There was a time when "peace and quiet" reigned in society. At that time there was no sign of these classes and their class organisations. A struggle went on at that time too, of course, but that struggle bore a local and not a general class character; the capitalists had no associations of their own, and each capitalist was obliged to deal with "his" workers by himself. Nor did the workers have any unions and, consequently, the workers in each factory were obliged to rely only on their own strength. True, local Social-Democratic organisations led the workers' economic struggle, but everybody will agree that this leadership was weak and casual; the Social-Democratic organisations could scarcely cope with their own Party affairs.

The January economic strikes, however, marked a turning point. The capitalists got busy and began to organise local associations. The capitalist associations in St. Petersburg, Moscow, Warsaw, Riga and other towns were brought into being by the January strikes. As regards the capitalists in the oil, manganese, coal and sugar industries, they converted their old, "peaceful" associations into "fighting" associations, and began to fortify their positions. But the capitalists were not content with this. They decided to form an all-Russian association, and so, in March 1905, on the initiative of Morozov, they gathered at a general congress in Moscow. That was the first all-Russian congress of capitalists. Here they concluded an agreement, by which they pledged themselves not to make any concessions to the workers without previous arrangement among themselves and, in "extreme" cases—to declare a *lockout* [an employers' strike]. That was the starting point of a fierce struggle between the capitalists and the proletarians. It marked the opening of a series of big lockouts in Russia. To conduct a big struggle a strong association is needed, and so the capitalists decided to meet once again to form a still more closely-knit association. Thus, three months after the first congress (in July 1905), the second all-Russian congress of capitalists was convened in Moscow. Here they reaffirmed the resolutions of the first congress, reaffirmed the necessity of lockouts, and elected a committee to draft the rules and to arrange for the convocation of another congress.

J.V. Stalin, *The Class Struggle*. Moscow, USSR: Foreign Languages Publishing House, 1954.

Document 5: The True Workers' Revolution in Russia

In this excerpt from the November 6 and 9, 1918, issues of the Soviet newspaper Pravda, *Joseph Stalin explains how the February Revolution of 1917, although won by the workers, peasants, and soldiers, was co-opted by the bourgeois property owners and the Kerensky-led provisional government. This kept the Russian people locked into an imperialistic war (World War I) and an ongoing famine. It wasn't until the October uprising that the workers took back the revolution.*

The February Revolution harboured irreconcilable inner contradictions. The revolution was accomplished by the efforts of the workers and the peasants (soldiers), but as a result of the revolution power passed not to the workers and peasants, but to the bourgeoisie [middle class]. In making the revolution the workers and peasants wanted to put an end to the war and to secure peace. But the bourgeoisie, on coming to power, strove to use the revolutionary ardour of the masses for a continuation of the war and against peace. The economic disruption of the country and the food crisis demanded the expropriation of capital and industrial establishments for the benefit of the workers, and the confiscation of the landlords' land for the benefit of the peasants, but the bourgeois Milyukov-Kerensky Government stood guard over the interests of the landlords and capitalists, resolutely protecting them against all encroachments on the part of the workers and peasants. It was a bourgeois revolution, accomplished by the agency of the workers and peasants for the benefit of the exploiters.

Meanwhile, the country continued to groan under the burden of the imperialist war, economic disintegration and the breakdown of the food supply. The [war] front was falling to pieces and melting away. Factories and mills were coming to a standstill. Famine was spreading through the country. The February Revolution, with its inner contradictions, was obviously not enough for "the salvation of the country." The Milyukov-Kerensky Government was obviously incapable of solving the basic problems of the revolution.

A new, *socialist* revolution was required to lead the country out of the blind alley of imperialist war and economic disintegration.

That revolution came as a result of the October uprising.

By overthrowing the power of the landlords and the bourgeoisie and replacing it by a government of workers and peasants, the October Revolution resolved the contradictions of the February Revolution at one stroke. The abolition of the omnipotence of the landlords and kulaks [merchants] and the handing over of the land for the use of the labouring masses of the countryside; the expropriation of the mills and factories and their transfer to control by the workers; the break with imperialism and the ending of the predatory war; the publication of the secret treaties and the exposure of the policy of annexations; lastly, the proclamation of self-determination for the labouring masses of the oppressed peoples and the recognition of the independence of Finland—such were the basic measures carried into effect by the Soviet power in the early period of the Soviet revolution.

That was a genuinely *socialist* revolution.

The revolution, which started in the centre, could not long be confined to that narrow territory. Once having triumphed in the centre, it was bound to spread to the border regions. And, indeed, from the very first days of the revolution, the revolutionary tide spread from the North all over Russia, sweeping one border region after another. But here it encountered a dam in the shape of the "National Councils" and regional "governments" (Don, Kuban, Siberia) which had been formed prior to the October Revolution. The point is that these "national governments" would not hear of a socialist revolution. Bourgeois by nature, they had not the slightest wish to destroy the old, bourgeois order; on the contrary, they considered it their duty to preserve and consolidate it by every means in their power. Essentially imperialist, they had not the slightest wish to break with imperialism; on the contrary, they had never been averse to seizing and subjugating bits and morsels of the territory of "foreign" nationalities whenever opportunity offered. No wonder that the "national governments" in the border regions declared war on the socialist government in the centre. And, once they had declared war, they naturally became hotbeds of reaction, which attracted all that was counter-revolutionary in Russia. Everyone knows that all the counter-revolutionaries thrown out of Russia rushed to these hotbeds, and there, around them, formed themselves into whiteguard "national" regiments.

But, in addition to "national governments," there are in the border regions national workers and peasants. Organized even before the October Revolution in their revolutionary Soviets patterned on the Soviets in the centre of Russia, they had never severed connections with their brothers in the North. They too were striving to defeat the bourgeoisie; they too were fighting for the triumph of socialism. No wonder that their conflict with "their own" national governments grew daily more acute. The October Revolution only strengthened the alliance between the workers and peasants of the border regions and the workers and peasants of Russia, and inspired them with faith in the triumph of socialism. And the war of the "national governments" against the Soviet power brought the conflict of the national masses with these "governments" to the point of a complete rupture, to open rebellion against them.

Thus was formed a socialist alliance of the workers and peasants of all Russia against the counter-revolutionary alliance of the bourgeois national "governments" of the border regions of Russia.

J.V. Stalin, *Works*. Moscow, USSR: Foreign Languages Publishing House, 1953.

Document 6: The Russian Army Defects

Journalist John Reed documents the days leading up to the fall of the provisional government and the rise of the Bolsheviks. Reed was a famous American journalist who witnessed the Russian Revolution firsthand. In this excerpt from his book, Reed recounts his meeting with revolution leader Leon Trotsky, who tells of the Russian army's defection to the Bolshevik cause. Reed holds the distinction of being the only American to be buried in the Soviet Kremlin in Moscow.

On October 17 (actually October 30),[1] by appointment, I went up to a small, bare room in the attic of Smolny to talk with Trotsky. In the middle of the room he sat on a rough chair at a bare table. Few questions from me were necessary; he talked rapidly and steadily for more than an hour. The substance of his talk, in his own words, I give here:

"The Provisional Government is absolutely powerless. The bourgeoisie [middle class] is in control, but this control is masked by a fictitious coalition with the *oborontsi* [moderate] parties. Now, during the Revolution, one sees revolts of peasants who are tired of waiting for their promised land; and all over the country, in all the toiling classes, the same disgust is evident. This domination by the bourgeoisie is only possible by means of civil war. The Kornilov method [i.e., by military force] is the only way by which the bourgeoisie can control. But it is force which the bourgeoisie lacks. . . . The Army is with us. The conciliators and pacifists, Socialist Revolutionaries and Mensheviks [socialist majority party], have lost all authority—because the struggle between the peasants and the landlords, between the workers and the employers, between the soldiers and the officers, has become more bitter, more irreconcilable than ever. Only by the concerted action of the popular mass, only by the victory of proletarian [working class] dictatorship, can the Revolution be achieved and the people saved. . . .

"The Soviets [workers' councils] are the most perfect representatives of the people—perfect in their revolutionary experience, in their ideas and objects. Based directly upon the army in the trenches, the workers in the factories, and the peasants in the fields, they are the backbone of the Revolution.

"There has been an attempt to create a power without the Soviets—and only powerlessness has been created. Counter-revolutionary schemes of all sorts are now being hatched in the corridors of the Council of the Russian Republic. The Cadet party represents the counter-revolution militant. On the other side, the Soviets represent the cause of the people. Between the two camps there are no groups of serious importance. . . . It is the *lutte finale* [end]. The bourgeois counter-revolution organizes all its forces and waits for the moment to attack us. Our answer will be decisive. We will complete the work scarcely begun in March, and advanced during the Kornilov affair. . . ."

He went on to speak of the new Government's foreign policy:

1. Russia followed a different calendar.

"Our first act will be to call for an immediate armistice on all fronts, and a conference of peoples to discuss democratic peace terms [to pull out of World War I]. The quantity of democracy we get in the peace settlement depends on the quantity of revolutionary response there is in Europe. If we create here a Government of the Soviets, that will be a powerful factor for immediate peace in Europe; for this Government will address itself directly and immediately to all peoples, over the heads of their Governments, proposing an armistice. At the moment of the conclusion of peace the pressure of the Russian Revolution will be in the direction of 'no annexations, no indemnities, the right of self-determination of peoples,' and a *Federated Republic of Europe*. . . .

"At the end of this war I see Europe re-created, not by the diplomats, but by the proletariat. The Federated Republic of Europe— the United States of Europe—that is what must be. National autonomy no longer suffices. Economic evolution demands the abolition of national frontiers. If Europe is to remain split into national groups, then Imperialism will recommence its work. Only a Federated Republic of Europe can give peace to the world." He smiled— that fine, faintly ironical smile of his. "But without the action of the European masses, these ends cannot be realized—now. . . ."

Now while everybody was waiting for the Bolsheviks [radical socialist minority party] to appear suddenly on the streets one morning and begin to shoot down people with white collars on, the real insurrection took its way quite naturally and openly.

The Provisional Government planned to send the Petrograd garrison to the front.

The Petrograd garrison numbered about sixty thousand men, who had taken a prominent part in the Revolution [i.e., the overthrow of the czar in February]. It was they who had turned the tide in the great days of March, created the Soviets of Soldiers' Deputies, and hurled back [General] Kornilov from the gates of Petrograd.

Now a large part of them were Bolsheviks. When the Provisional Government talked of evacuating the city, it was the Petrograd garrison which answered, "If you are not capable of defending the capital, conclude peace; if you cannot conclude peace, go away and make room for a People's Government which can do both. . . ."

It was evident that any attempt at insurrection depended upon the attitude of the Petrograd garrison. The Government's plan was to replace the garrison regiments with "dependable" troops—Cossacks, Death Battalions. The Army Committees, the "moderate" Socialists and the TsIK [Central Executive Committee] supported the Government. A widespread agitation was carried on at the Front and in Petrograd, emphasizing the fact that for eight months the Petrograd garrison had been leading an easy life in the barracks of the capital, while their exhausted comrades in the trenches starved and died.

Naturally there was some truth in the accusation that the garrison regiments were reluctant to exchange their comparative comfort for the hardships of a winter campaign. But there were other reasons why they refused to go. The Petrograd Soviet feared the Government's intentions, and from the Front came hundreds of delegates, chosen by the common soldiers, crying, "It is true we need reinforcements, but more important, we must know that Petrograd and the Revolution are well-guarded. . . . Do you hold the rear, comrades, and we will hold the front!"

On October 12 (actually October 25), behind closed doors, the Central Committee of the Petrograd Soviet discussed the formation of a special Military Committee to decide the whole question. The next day a meeting of the Soldiers' Section of the Petrograd Soviet elected a Committee, which immediately proclaimed a boycott of the bourgeois newspapers, and condemned the TsIK for opposing the Congress of Soviets. On October 16 (29), in open session of the Petrograd Soviet, Trotsky proposed that the Soviet formally sanction the Military Revolutionary Committee. "We ought," he said, "to create our special organization to march to battle, and if necessary to die. . . ." It was decided to send to the front two delegations, one from the Soviet and one from the garrison, to confer with the Soldiers' Committees and the General Staff.

At Pskov, the Soviet delegates were met by General Tcheremissov, commander of the Northern Front, with the curt declaration that he had ordered the Petrograd garrison to the trenches, and that was all. The garrison committee was not allowed to leave Petrograd. . . .

A delegation of the Soldiers' Section of the Petrograd Soviet asked that a representative be admitted to the Staff of the Petrograd District. Refused. The Petrograd Soviet demanded that no orders be issued without the approval of the Soldiers' Section. Refused. The delegates were roughly told, "We only recognize the TsIK. We do not recognize you; if you break any laws, we shall arrest you."

On October 17 (30) a meeting of representatives of all the Petrograd regiments passed a resolution: "*The Petrograd garrison no longer recognizes the Provisional Government. The Petrograd Soviet is our Government. We will obey only the orders of the Petrograd Soviet, through the Military Revolutionary Committee.*" The local military units were ordered to wait for instructions from the Soldiers' Section of the Petrograd Soviet.

John Reed, *Ten Days That Shook the World*. Franklin, TN: Tantallon Press, 2002.

Document 7: Victory Over Capitalism

In this excerpt from a pamphlet circulated in Moscow in July 1919, Lenin praises the heroism, sacrifice, and discipline displayed by the Red Army and the workers during the Russian civil war waged against the landowners and capitalists. Lenin acknowledges that the overthrow of the bourgeoisie and the establishment of communism was a daunting undertaking, but that this victory in Russia is a harbinger of a greater revolution to come.

The press reports many instances of the heroism of the Red Army men. In the fight against Kolchak, Denikin and other forces of the landowners and capitalists, the workers and peasants very often display miracles of bravery and endurance, defending the gains of the socialist revolution. The guerrilla spirit, weariness and indiscipline are being overcome; it is a slow and difficult process, but it is making headway in spite of everything. The heroism of the working people making voluntary sacrifices for the victory of socialism—this is the foundation of the new, comradely discipline in the Red Army, the foundation on which that army is regenerating, gaining strength and growing.

The heroism of the workers in the rear is no less worthy of attention. In this connection, the *communist subbotniks* [a soviet volunteer workday] organised by the workers on their own initiative are really of enormous significance. Evidently, this is only a beginning, but it is a beginning of exceptionally great importance. It is the beginning of a revolution that is more difficult, more tangible, more radical and more decisive than the overthrow of the bourgeoisie [middle class], for it is a victory over our own conservatism, indiscipline, petty-bourgeois egoism, a victory over the habits left as a heritage to the worker and peasant by accursed capitalism. Only when *this* victory is consolidated will the new social discipline, socialist discipline, be created; then and only then will a reversion to capitalism become impossible, will communism become really invincible.

V.I. Lenin, *Collected Works*. 4th English Edition. Moscow, USSR: Progress Publishers, 1965.

Document 8: China's Mighty Peasant Storm

Of all of the Chinese revolutionaries, it was only Mao Tse-tung who saw the potential of the peasants in overthrowing the imperialist regime. He predicted that the peasants would "rise like a mighty storm, like a hurricane, a force so swift and violent that no power, however great, will be able to hold it back." The following letter of March 1927 was written in response to the criticism Mao and the peasant movement were receiving from the Communist Party in China. The party never saw the potential in the peasant forces; instead it believed in the Soviet model built upon the will of the urban working class.

During my recent visit to Hunan I made a first-hand investigation of conditions in the five counties of Hsiangtan, Hsianghsiang, Hengshan, Liling and Changsha. In the thirty-two days from January 4 to February 5, I called together fact-finding conferences in villages and county towns, which were attended by experienced peasants and by comrades working in the peasant movement, and I listened attentively to their reports and collected a great deal of material. Many of the hows and whys of the peasant movement were the exact opposite of what the gentry in Hankow and Changsha are saying. I saw and heard of many strange things of which I had hitherto been unaware. I believe the same is true of many other places, too. All talk directed against the peasant movement must be speedily set right. All the wrong measures taken by the revolutionary authorities concerning the peasant movement must be speedily changed. Only thus can the future of the revolution be benefited. For the present upsurge of the peasant movement is a colossal event. In a very short time, in China's central, southern and northern provinces, several hundred million peasants will rise like a mighty storm, like a hurricane, a force so swift and violent that no power, however great, will be able to hold it back. They will smash all the trammels that bind them and rush forward along the road to liberation. They will sweep all the imperialists, warlords, corrupt officials, local tyrants and evil gentry into their graves. Every revolutionary party and every revolutionary comrade will be put to the test, to be accepted or rejected as they decide. There are three alternatives. To march at their head and lead them? To trail behind them, gesticulating and criticizing? Or to stand in their way and oppose them? Every Chinese is free to choose, but events will force you to make the choice quickly.

GET ORGANIZED!

The development of the peasant movement in Hunan may be divided roughly into two periods with respect to the counties in the province's central and southern parts where the movement has already made much headway. The first, from January to September of last year, was one of organization. In this period, January to June was a time of underground activity, and July to September, when the revolutionary army was driving out Chao Heng-ti, one of open activity. During this period, the membership of the peasant associations did not exceed 300,000–400,000, the masses directly under their leadership numbered little more than a million, there was as yet hardly any struggle in the rural areas, and consequently there was very little criticism of the associations in other circles. Since its members served as guides, scouts and carriers of the Northern Expeditionary Army, even some of the officers had a good word to say for the peasant associations. The second period, from last October to January of this year, was one of revolutionary action. The membership of the associations jumped to two million and the masses directly under their leadership increased to ten million. Since the peasants generally enter only one name for the whole family on joining a peasant association, a membership of two million means a mass following of about ten million. Almost half the peasants in Hunan are now organized. In counties like Hsiangtan, Hsianghsiang, Liuyang, Changsha, Liling, Ninghsiang, Pingkiang, Hsiangyin, Hengshan, Hengyang, Leiyang, Chenhsien and Anhua, nearly all the peasants have combined in the peasant associations or have come under their leadership. It was on the strength of their extensive organization that the peasants went into action and within four months brought about a great revolution in the countryside, a revolution without parallel in history.

Mao Tse-tung, *Selected Works of Mao Tse-tung.* Peking, China: Foreign Languages Press, 1967.

Document 9: Mao's Plan for an Independent Regime

By 1928 China's Red Army and the Chinese Communists had carved out their own small sovereign territory in the midst of Kuomintang (Nationalist) controlled land. On November 25, 1928, Mao Tse-tung sent the following report to the Central Committee of the Communist Party of China in an attempt to explain how this independent regime of workers, peasants, and Red Army guerrillas could continue to grow and prosper despite the efforts of the Nationalists to crush communism.

China is the only country in the world today where one or more small areas under Red political power have emerged in the midst of a White [Nationalist] regime which encircles them. We find on analysis that one reason for this phenomenon lies in the incessant splits and wars within China's comprador and landlord classes. So long as these splits and wars continue, it is possible for an armed independent regime of workers and peasants to survive and grow. In addition, its survival and growth require the following conditions: (1) a sound mass base, (2) a sound Party organization, (3) a fairly strong Red Army, (4) terrain favourable to military operations, and (5) economic resources sufficient for sustenance.

An independent regime must vary its strategy against the encircling ruling classes, adopting one strategy when the ruling class regime is temporarily stable and another when it is split up. In a period when the ruling classes are split up, as during the wars between Li Tsung-jen and Tang Sheng-chih in Hunan and Hupeh Provinces and between Chang Fa-kuei and Li Chi-shen in Kwangtung Province, our strategy can be comparatively adventurous and the area carved out by military operations can be comparatively large. However, we must take care to lay a solid foundation in the central districts so that we shall have something secure to rely on when the White terror strikes. In a period when the regime of the ruling classes is comparatively stable, as it was in the southern provinces after April this year, our strategy must be one of gradual advance. In such a period, the worst thing in military affairs is to divide our forces for an adventurous advance, and the worst thing in local work (distributing land, establishing political power, expanding the Party and organizing local armed forces) is to scatter our personnel and neglect to lay a solid foundation in the central districts. The defeats which many small Red areas have suffered have been due either to the absence of the requisite objective conditions or to subjective mistakes in tactics. Mistakes in tactics have been made solely because of failure to distinguish clearly between the two kinds of period, that in which the regime of the ruling classes is temporarily stable and that in which it is split up. In a period of temporary stability, some comrades advocated dividing our forces for an adventurous advance and even proposed leaving the defence of extensive areas to the Red Guards alone, as though oblivious of the fact that the enemy could attack not merely with the landlords' levies but even in concentrated operations with regular troops. In local work, they utterly neglected to lay a solid foundation in the central districts and attempted unrestricted expansion regardless of whether it was within our capacity. If anyone advocated a policy of gradual advance in military operations or a policy of concentrating our effort in local work on laying a solid foundation in the central districts so as to secure an invincible position, they dubbed him a "conservative". Their wrong ideas were the root cause of the defeats sustained last August by the Hunan-Kiangsi border area and by the Fourth Red Army in southern Hunan.

Our work in the Hunan-Kiangsi border area began in October last year. At the start, all our Party organizations in the counties were defunct. The local armed forces consisted only of the two units under [Red generals] Yuan Wen-tsai and Wang Tso in the vicinity of the Chingkang Mountains, each unit having sixty rifles in bad repair, while the peasant self-defence corps in the counties of Yunghsin, Lienhua, Chaling and Linghsien had been totally disarmed by the landlord class and the revolutionary ardour of the masses had been stifled. By February this year Ningkang, Yunghsin, Chaling and Suichuan had county Party committees, Linghsien had a special district Party committee, and in Lienhua a Party organization was beginning to function and establish connections with the Wanan County Committee. All the counties except Linghsien had a few local armed units.

Mao Tse-tung, *The Selected Works of Mao Tse-tung.* Peking, China: Foreign Languages Press, 1965.

Document 10: Ascertaining Yugoslavia's Socialism

Josip Broz (Tito) became Communist Yugoslavia's premiere in 1945. By 1948, a split had developed between Yugoslavia and Joseph Stalin's Soviet Union. Tito had asserted independence from the Soviet Union and advocated his brand of communism that placed national patriotic interests and economic well-being over international socialist goals. Tito's communism did not sit well with Moscow. The Communist Party of the Soviet Union (CPSU) drafted an open letter in 1963, asking how the Comintern [Communist International Organization, whose purpose was to spread communism worldwide] should view Yugoslavia. The Chinese Communist Party wrote the following answer in September.

Is Yugoslavia a socialist country?

This is not only a question of ascertaining the nature of the Yugoslav state, but it also involves the question of which road the socialist countries should follow: whether they should follow the road of the October Revolution and carry the socialist revolution through to the end or follow the road of Yugoslavia and restore capitalism. In addition, it involves the question of how to appraise the Tito clique: whether it is a fraternal Party and a force against imperialism or a renegade from the international communist movement and a lackey of imperialism.

On this question there are fundamental differences of opinion between the leaders of the CPSU, on the one hand, and ourselves and all other Marxist-Leninists, on the other.

All Marxist-Leninists hold that Yugoslavia is not a socialist country. The leading clique of the League of Communists of Yugoslavia has betrayed Marxism-Leninism and the Yugoslav people and consists of renegades from the international communist movement and lackeys of imperialism.

The leaders of the CPSU, on the other hand, hold that Yugoslavia is a socialist country and that the League of Communists of Yugoslavia bases itself on Marxism-Leninism and is a fraternal Party and a force against imperialism.

In its Open Letter of *July 14* the Central Committee of the CPSU declares that Yugoslavia is a "socialist country" and that the Tito clique is a "fraternal Party" that "stands at the helm of the ship of state".

Recently Comrade [Nikita] Khrushchev [Soviet leader from 1953–1964] paid a visit to Yugoslavia and in a number of speeches he revealed the real standpoint of the leaders of the CPSU still more clearly, and completely discarded the fig-leaf with which they had been covering themselves on this question.

In Khrushchev's opinion, Yugoslavia is not only a socialist country but an "advanced" socialist country. There, one finds not "idle talk about revolution" but "actual construction of socialism", and the development of Yugoslavia is "a concrete contribution to the general world revolutionary workers' movement", which Khrushchev rather envies and wishes to emulate.

In Khrushchev's opinion, the leaders of the CPSU and the Titoites are "not only class brothers" but "brothers tied together . . . by the singleness of aims confronting us". The leadership of the CPSU is a "reliable and faithful ally" of the Tito clique.

Khrushchev believes he has discovered genuine Marxism-Leninism in the Tito clique. The Central Committee of the CPSU was merely pretending when it asserted in its Open Letter that "differences on a number of fundamental ideological questions still remain between the CPSU and the Yugoslav League of Communists". Now Khrushchev has told the Tito clique that "we belong to one and the same idea and are guided by the same theory", and that both stand on the basis of Marxism-Leninism.

The Polemic on the General Line of the International Communist Movement. Peking, China: Foreign Languages Press, 1965.

Document 11: Cult of Personality

In the following speech, Soviet leader Nikita Khrushchev acknowledges that the cult of Joseph Stalin had grown considerably after his death in

1953. According to Khrushchev, the conservative Soviet leadership began to venerate Stalin as a god, and, in his opinion, this sort of hero worship is not consistent with Marxist-Leninist principles. Khrushchev, of course, wanted to move the Soviet Union out from under the shadow of Stalin's oppressive reign and solidify his own control over the superpower. The speech was released in the United States in 1956.

COMRADES! In the report of the Central Committee of the Party at the XXth Congress, in a number of speeches by delegates to the Congress, as also formerly during the plenary CC/CPSU sessions, quite a lot has been said about the cult of the individual and about its harmful consequences.

After Stalin's death the Central Committee of the Party began to implement a policy of explaining concisely and consistently that it is impermissible and foreign to the spirit of Marxism-Leninism to elevate one person, to transform him into a superman possessing supernatural characteristics akin to those of a god. Such a man supposedly knows everything, sees everything, thinks for everyone, can do anything, is infallible in his behavior. Such a belief about a man, and specifically about Stalin, was cultivated among us for many years.

The objective of the present report is not a thorough evaluation of Stalin's life and activity. Concerning Stalin's merits, an entirely sufficient number of books, pamphlets and studies had already been written in his lifetime. The role of Stalin in the preparation and execution of the Socialist Revolution, in the Civil War, and in the fight for the construction of Socialism in our country is universally known. Everyone knows this well. At the present we are concerned with a question which has immense importance for the Party now and for the future—[we are concerned] with how the cult of the person of Stalin has been gradually growing, the cult which became at a certain specific stage the source of a whole series of exceedingly serious and grave perversions of Party principles, of Party democracy, of revolutionary legality.

Nikita Khrushchev, *Khrushchev Remembers*. Trans. by Strobe Talbot. Boston: Little, Brown and Co., 1970.

Document 12: The Individual and Socialism

In the following editorial letter from 1965, Cuban socialist and revolutionary Che Guevara expresses his belief that the only way individuals can assist in the building of socialism is to alter their consciousness through re-education. Guevara sees this as a daunting task, as the individual has been deeply influenced by his or her past as well as imperialist society.

I shall now attempt to define the individual, the actor in this strange and moving drama that is the building of socialism, in his twofold existence as a unique being and a member of the community.

I believe that the simplest approach is to recognize his unmade quality. He is an unfinished product. The flaws of the past are translated into the present in the individual consciousness, and constant efforts must be made to eradicate them. The process is twofold: On the one hand, society acts on the individual by means of direct and indirect education, while on the other hand, the individual undergoes a conscious phase of self-education.

The new society in process of formation has to compete very hard with the past. This makes itself not only in the individual consciousness, weighed down by the residues of an education and an upbringing systematically oriented toward the isolation of the individual, but also by the very nature of this transition period, with the persistence of commodity relations. The commodity is the economic cell of capitalist society: As long as it exists, its effects will make themselves felt in the organization of production and therefore in man's consciousness.

[Karl] Marx's scheme conceived of the transition period as the result of the explosive transformation of the capitalist system torn apart by its inner contradictions: Subsequent reality has shown how some countries, the weak limbs, detach themselves from the imperialist tree, a phenomenon foreseen by [Vladimir] Lenin. In those countries, capitalism has developed sufficiently to make its effects felt on the people in one way or another, but it is not its own inner contradictions that explode the system after exhausting all of its possibilities. The struggle for liberation against an external oppressor, the misery that has its origin in foreign causes such as war, whose consequences make the privileged classes fall upon the exploited, the liberation movements aimed at overthrowing neocolonial regimes, are the customary factors in this process. Conscious action does the rest.

In these countries, there still has not been achieved a complete education for the work of society, and wealth is far from being within the reach of the masses through the simple process of appropriation. Underdevelopment and the customary flight of capital to "civilized" countries make impossible a rapid change without sacrifices. There still remains a long stretch to be covered in the building of the economic base, and the temptation to follow the beaten paths of material interest as the lever of speedy development is very great.

There is a danger of not seeing the forest because of the trees. Pursuing the chimera of achieving socialism with the aid of the blunted weapons left to us by capitalism (the commodity as the economic cell, profitability, and individual material interest as levers, etc.), it is possible to come to a blind alley. And the arrival there comes about after covering a long distance where there are many crossroads and where it is difficult to realize just when the wrong turn was taken. Meanwhile, the adapted economic base has undermined the development of consciousness. To build communism, a new man must be created simultaneously with the material base.

That is why it is so important to choose correctly the instrument of mass mobilization. That instrument must be fundamentally of a moral character, without forgetting the correct use of material incentives, especially those of a social nature.

As I already said, in moments of extreme danger it is easy to activate moral incentives: To maintain their effectiveness, it is necessary to develop a consciousness in which values acquire new categories. Society as a whole must become a huge school. . . .

Bertram Silverman, ed., *Man and Socialism in Cuba: The Great Debate.* New York: Scribner, 1971.

Document 13: Deviations from Socialism

In the Brezhnev Doctrine, delivered on November 12, 1968, Soviet premier Leonid Brezhnev expresses the Soviet policy toward other socialist nations. He points out that each individual socialist sovereignty has its own unique way of achieving and developing socialism. Brezhnev stresses that while minor deviations are not seen as a threat to international socialism, major deviations will be considered counterrevolutionary and a blight on the socialist worldview.

The experience of struggle and a realistic appraisal of the situation that has taken shape in the world also attest very clearly to the fact that it is vitally necessary that the Communists of socialist countries raise high the banner of socialist internationalism and constantly strengthen the unity and solidarity of the socialist countries. . . . The C.P.S.U. [Communist Party of the Soviet Union] has always advocated that each socialist country determine the concrete forms of its development along the path of socialism by taking into account the specific nature of their national conditions. But it is well known, comrades, that there are common natural laws of socialist construction, deviation from which could lead to deviation from socialism as such. And when external and internal forces hostile to socialism try to turn the development of a given socialist country in the direction of restoration of the capitalist system, when a threat arises to the cause of socialism in that country—a threat to the security of the socialist commonwealth as a whole—this is no longer merely a problem for that country's people, but a common problem, the concern of all socialist countries.

Leonid Brezhnev, *Brezhnev Doctrine*, November 12, 1968. Gale Group History Resource Center. http://galenet.galegroup.com/servlet/HistRC.

Document 14: Revolution Then and Now

The following excerpt is taken from a speech given by Fidel Castro in Santiago de Cuba on January 1, 1999. The speech was part of the celebration of the fortieth anniversary of the victory of the Cuban Revolution. Castro waxes nostalgically about the feelings of victory he experienced as Baptista and his oppressive regime were ousted from Cuba on December 18, 1956, and victory belonged to Castro and his rebel army. He then notes that future revolutionaries will witness the inevitable fall of capitalism, the force that has underpinned most oppression in the world.

I am trying to recall that night of January 1, 1959; I am reliving and perceiving impressions and details as if everything were occurring at this very moment. It seems unreal that destiny has given us the rare privilege of once more speaking to the people of Santiago de Cuba from this very same place, 40 years later.

Before dawn on that day, with the arrival of the news that the dictator and the main figures of his opprobrious regime had fled in the face of the irrepressible advance of our forces, for a few seconds I felt a strange sensation of emptiness. How was that incredible victory possible in just over 24 months, starting from that moment on December 18, 1956, when—after the extremely severe setback which virtually annihilated our detachment—we managed to gather together seven rifles to resume the battle against a combination of military forces which totaled 800,000 armed men, thousands of trained officers, high morale, attractive privileges, a totally unquestioned myth of invincibility, infallible advising and guaranteed supplies from the United States? Just ideas which a valiant people claimed as their own worked a military and political victory. Subsequent vain and ridiculous attempts to salvage what remained of that exploiting and oppressive system were swept away by the Rebel Army, the workers and the rest of the people in 24 hours.

Our fleeting sadness at the moment of victory was nostalgia for the experiences we had lived through, the vivid memory of the comrades who fell throughout the struggle, a full awareness that those exceptionally difficult and adverse years obliged us to be better than we were, and to transform them into the most fruitful and creative ones of our lives. . . .

The yesterday's people, illiterate and semi-illiterate, and with really only a minimal political awareness, were capable of making the Revolution, of defending the nation, of subsequently achieving an exceptional political consciousness and initiating a revolutionary process that is unparalleled in this hemisphere and in the world. I do not say that out of any ridiculous chauvinistic spirit, or with the absurd pretension of believing ourselves better than others; I am saying it because as a result of fate or destiny, the Revolution that was born on that January 1 has been subjected to the hardest trial faced by any revolutionary process in the world.

With the participation of three generations, our heroic people of yesterday and today, our eternal people, have resisted 40 years of aggression, blockade, and economic, political and ideological warfare waged by the strongest and richest imperialist power that has ever existed in the history of the world. The most extraordinary page of glory, and of patriotic and revolutionary determination has been written during these years of the special period, when we were left absolutely alone in the middle of the West, 90 miles from the United States, and we decided to carry on. . . .

The economic order which dominates the planet will inevitably fall. Even a child in school who knows how to add, subtract, multiply and divide well enough to pass an arithmetic test can understand that.

The current system is unsustainable because it is based on blind and chaotic laws which are ruinous and destructive to society and nature.

The very theoreticians of neoliberal globalization, that system's best academics, spokespersons and defenders are unsure, hesitant, contradictory. There are a thousand questions which cannot be answered. It is hypocritical to state that human freedom and the absolute freedom of the market are inseparable concepts, as if laws of this kind, which have emerged from the most selfish, unequal and merciless systems ever known, were compatible with freedom for human beings, who the system has turned into mere commodities. . . .

The tens of millions of children in the world who are forced to work, to prostitute themselves, to supply organs, to sell drugs in order to survive; the hundreds of millions of unemployed, critical poverty, the trafficking of drugs, of immigrants, of human organs, like the colonialism of the past and its dramatic legacy of underdevelopment today, and all of the social calamities in the world today, have arisen from systems based on these laws. It is impossible to forget that the struggle for markets led to the horrific butchery of the two world wars of this century.

We cannot ignore the fact that the principles of the market are an inseparable part of the historic development of humanity, but any rational person would have every right to reject the presumed perpetuation of such social principles as the foundation for the subsequent development of the human species.

Fidel Castro, speech given at the main ceremony for the fortieth anniversary of the triumph of the revolution, on January 1, 1999.

Document 15: French Colonialism and Vietnamese Independence

In Vietnam's Declaration of Independence, set forth on September 2, 1945, Ho Chi Minh criticizes the oppressive and inhumane colonialism practiced by the French in Vietnam. He also emphasizes the determination of the Vietnamese people to fight French domination at all costs.

All men are created equal; they are endowed by their Creator with certain inalienable Rights; among these are Life, Liberty, and the pursuit of Happiness.

This immortal statement was made in the Declaration of Independence of the United States of America in 1776. In a broader sense, this means: All the peoples on the earth are equal from birth, all the peoples have a right to live, to be happy and free.

The Declaration of the French Revolution made in 1791 on the Rights of Man and the Citizen also states: "All men are born free and with equal rights, and must always remain free and have equal rights."

Those are undeniable truths.

Nevertheless, for more than eighty years, the French imperialists, abusing the standard of Liberty, Equality, and Fraternity, have violated our Fatherland and oppressed our fellow citizens. They have acted contrary to the ideals of humanity and justice.

In the field of politics, they have deprived our people of every democratic liberty.

They have enforced inhuman laws; they have set up three distinct political regimes in the North, the Center, and the South of Viet-Nam in order to wreck our national unity and prevent our people from being united.

They have built more prisons than schools. They have mercilessly slain our patriots; they have drowned our uprisings in rivers of blood.

They have fettered public opinion; they have practiced obscurantism against our people.

To weaken our race they have forced us to use opium and alcohol.

In the field of economics, they have fleeced us to the backbone, impoverished our people and devastated our land.

They have robbed us of our rice fields, our mines, our forests, and our raw materials. They have monopolized the issuing of bank notes and the export trade.

They have invented numerous unjustifiable taxes and reduced our people, especially our peasantry, to a state of extreme poverty.

They have hampered the prospering of our national bourgeoisie; they have mercilessly exploited our workers.

In the autumn of 1940, when the Japanese fascists violated Indochina's territory to establish new bases in their fight against the Allies, the French imperialists went down on their bended knees and handed over our country to them.

Thus, from that date, our people were subjected to the double yoke of the French and the Japanese. Their sufferings and miseries increased. The result was that, from the end of last year to the beginning of this year, from Quang Tri Province to the North of Viet-Nam, more than two million of our fellow citizens died from starvation. On March 9 [1945], the French troops were disarmed by the Japanese. The French colonialists either fled or surrendered, showing that not only were they incapable of "protecting" us, but that, in the span of five years, they had twice sold our country to the Japanese.

On several occasions before March 9, the Viet Minh League [independence organization] urged the French to ally themselves with it against the Japanese. Instead of agreeing to this proposal, the French colonialists so intensified their terrorist activities against the Viet Minh members that before fleeing they massacred a great number of our political prisoners detained at Yen Bay and Cao Bang.

Notwithstanding all this, our fellow citizens have always manifested toward the French a tolerant and humane attitude. Even after the Japanese Putsch [uprising] of March, 1945, the Viet Minh League helped many Frenchmen to cross the frontier, rescued some of them from Japanese jails, and protected French lives and property.

From the autumn of 1940, our country had in fact ceased to be a

French colony and had become a Japanese possession. After the Japanese had surrendered to the Allies, our whole people rose to regain our national sovereignty and to found the Democratic Republic of Viet-Nam. The truth is that we have wrested our independence from the Japanese and not from the French. The French have fled, the Japanese have capitulated, Emperor Bao Dai has abdicated. Our people have broken the chains which for nearly a century have fettered them and have won independence for the Fatherland. Our people at the same time have overthrown the monarchic regime that has reigned supreme for dozens of centuries. In its place has been established the present Democratic Republic.

For these reasons, we, members of the Provisional Government, representing the whole Vietnamese people, declare that from now on we break off all relations of a colonial character with France; we repeal all the international obligation that France has so far subscribed to on behalf of Viet-Nam, and we abolish all the special rights the French have unlawfully acquired in our Fatherland.

The whole Vietnamese people, animated by a common purpose, are determined to fight to the bitter end against any attempt by the French colonialists to reconquer their country. We are convinced that the Allied nations, which at Teheran and San Francisco have acknowledged the principles of self-determination and equality of nations, will not refuse to acknowledge the independence of Viet-Nam.

A people who have courageously opposed French domination for more than eighty years, a people who have fought side by side with the Allies against the fascists during these last years, such a people must be free and independent.

For these reasons, we, members of the Provisional Government of the Democratic Republic of Viet-Nam, solemnly declare to the world that Viet-Nam has the right to be a free and independent country—and in fact it is so already. The entire Vietnamese people are determined to mobilize all their physical and mental strength, to sacrifice their lives and property in order to safeguard their independence and liberty.

Ho Chi Minh, "Declaration of Independence of the Democratic Republic of Vietnam," September 2, 1945.

Chronology

1848
Karl Marx and his associate Friedrich Engels present their Communist Manifesto to the world; the document urges the proletarian workers to unite and establish a worldwide socialist revolution; it describes the class struggles and the exploitation of the worker that are characteristic of capitalist society.

1914
World War I begins. Russia will join the Allies to fight the Central Powers (Germany, Austria-Hungary, and Turkey).

1917
February: The Russian Revolution is born amid mass worker demonstrations, a military mutiny, and social chaos in the capital city of Petrograd; a provisional government is put together, the Petrograd Soviet is established, and Czar Nicholas II abdicates.
October: The Bolsheviks seize power with little resistance from counterrevolutionary forces or competing revolutionary organizations, establishing the first socialist state in the history of mankind; the Soviets take control of the government and immediately issue a series of social reforms.

1918
March: The Bolsheviks reluctantly sign the Treaty of Brest-Litovsk; the treaty concedes large areas of land to the Central Powers, but allows Russia to back out of a long and protracted war.
June 26: The founding Congress of the Korean Socialist Party commences in Khabarovsk, Russia, under the direction of Yi Tong-hwi.

1919
The Comintern is established by Soviet leader Vladimir Ilich Lenin; the purpose of the organization is to spread communism throughout the world.
March 1: Mass demonstrations are sparked as Korean intellectuals seek independence from Japan.
June: Ho Chi Minh arrives at Versailles, France, with a a paper documenting the abuses of colonialism, and, more specifically, the way in which France is exploiting the Vietnamese people. President Woodrow Wilson is there to sign a treaty to end World War I; Wilson pays little attention to Ho's document.

1922

May: Lenin begins to suffer from serious health problems and is forced to hand over his political responsibilities; he informs the Central Committee that he is firmly against Joseph Stalin as a possible successor.

1923

March: Lenin suffers a severe stroke; he dies eight months later.
June: Ho Chi Minh leaves France for Moscow, where he comes into contact with major Soviet leaders such as Joseph Stalin and Leon Trotsky.

1925

The Korean Communist Party is founded in Seoul.

1927

Mao Tse-tung publishes a paper titled "Report on an Investigation of the Agrarian Movement in Hunan."
April: Chinese Nationalist leader Chiang Kai-shek exterminates hundreds of Communists and purges them from the Kuomintang.

1929

Joseph Stalin takes over as the new leader of Russia.
June: Ho Chi Minh establishes the Vietnamese Communist Party at a soccer stadium in Hong Kong; the party calls for a proletarian dictatorship and independence from France.

1934

November: The Chinese Soviet Republic is declared; Mao is announced as its chairman.

1935

October: Chiang Kai-shek and his Kuomintang army forge an all out offensive upon the Communists in hopes of exterminating them completely; Mao and his dwindling guerrilla army flee across the hinterlands of China on the "Long March."

1936

Stalin begins purging the Soviet Union of all dissidents; millions are exiled, imprisoned, or killed.

1939

World War II begins; the Soviet Union again joins the Allies against the Axis powers (Germany, Italy, and Japan).

1941

Ho Chi Minh establishes the Viet Minh (Vietnam Independence League).

1945

August 14: World War II comes to an end; Stalin's forces move into Eastern Europe, overtaking Poland, Hungary, Czechoslovakia, Bulgaria, East Germany, Romania, and Albania.

1946

January: Kim Il Sung becomes leader of the Communist Party of North Korea.

1948

Stalin expels Yugoslavia from the international socialist movement.

1949

October 1: Mao Tse-tung and the Chinese Communists declare victory over the Kuomintang Nationalist Army; the Peoples Republic of China is officially declared.

1953

Stalin dies; Khrushchev becomes first secretary of the Communist Party.

January: Mao Tse-tung establishes the initial "Five Year Plan" to jump-start China's economy.

1954

Vietnamese Communist forces defeat the French; Ho Chi Minh becomes president of North Vietnam.

1956

November: Fidel Castro, Che Guevara, and their small guerrilla army set sail from Mexico toward Cuba in an attempt to overthrow the oppressive Batista regime; the campaign ends in a bloody defeat at the hands of Batista's army; the guerrilla forces retreat into the rural Sierra Maestra.

1958

July: Mao Tse-tung begins the Great Leap Forward—an attempt to reach a higher plane of communism than the Soviets; the program eventually fails and results in famine and violence.

1959

January 1: Castro and his followers take over as the leaders of Cuba after a two-year guerrilla campaign in which they defeat Batista's army; it is the first socialist state ever established in the Americas.

For Further Research

Books

Robert J. Alexander, *Communism in Latin America*. New Brunswick, NJ: Rutgers University Press, 1957.

Fernando Claudin, *The Communist Movement: From Comintern to Cominform*. Part 1. New York: Monthly Review, 1975.

G.D.H. Cole, *What Marx Really Meant*. Westport, CT: Greenwood, 1970.

Olivia Coolidge, *Makers of the Red Revolution*. Boston: Houghton Mifflin, 1963.

F.W. Deakin, H. Shukman, and H.T. Willets, *A History of World Communism*. New York: Barnes and Noble, 1975.

Arif Dirlik, *Paths to the Future: Communist Organization and Marxist Ideology*. New York: Oxford University Press, 1998.

Ben Fowkes, *Karl Marx, Capital: A Critique of Political Economy*. New York: Penguin, 1992.

G.F. Hudson, *Fifty Years of Communism, Theory and Practice, 1917–1967*. New York: Basic Books, 1968.

Richard Lowenthal, *World Communism, the Disintegration of a Secular Faith*. New York: Oxford University Press, 1964.

Mao Tse-tung, *Quotations from Mao Tse-tung*. New York: Praeger, 1968.

Karl Marx and Friedrich Engels, *The Communist Manifesto*. New York: Norton, 1988.

James O'Connor, *The Origins of Socialism in Cuba*. Ithaca, NY: Cornell University Press, 1970.

Douglas Pike, *History of Vietnamese Communism, 1925–1976*. Stanford, CA: Hoover Institute, 1978.

Richard Pipes, *A Concise History of the Russian Revolution*. New York: Alfred A. Knopf, 1995.

John Reed, *Ten Days that Shook the World*. Franklin, TN: Tantallon, 2002.

Amaury de Riencourt, *The Soul of China*. New York: Harper and Row, 1965.

Stuart Schram, *Mao Tse-tung*. New York: Penguin, 1974.

Donald R. Shanor, *Soviet Europe*. New York: Harper and Row, 1975.

Dae Sock Suh, *The Korean Communist Movement, 1918–1948*. Princeton, NJ: Princeton University Press, 1967.

Robert F. Turner, *Vietnamese Communism, Its Origins and Development*. Stanford, CA: Hoover Institute, 1975.

Bertram D. Wolfe, *Revolution and Reality*. Chapel Hill: University of North Carolina Press, 1981.

Periodicals

Tony Ashworth, "Soldiers Not Peasants: The Moral Basis of the February Revolution of 1917," *Sociology*, August 1992.

Ernesto F. Betancourt, "Castro's Legacy," *Society*, July/August 1994.

George Charney, "Tremors After Prague," *Nation*, May 8, 1972.

Brian Crozier, "Ferment in Eastern Europe," *National Review*, March 8, 1985.

Graham Darby, "The October Revolution," *History Review*, September 1997.

Peter Goldman, "What Vietnam Did to Us," *Newsweek*, December 14, 1981.

Louis O. Kelso, "Karl Marx: The Almost Capitalist," *American Bar Association Journal*, March 1957.

Theodore von Laue, "A Perspective on History: The Soviet System Reconsidered," *Historian*, Winter 1999.

Gordon H. McCormick, "Che Guevara: The Legacy of a Revolutionary Man," *World Policy Journal*, Winter 1997.

Roy Medvedev, "A Very Hot Summer in Prague," *Russian Life*, August/September 1998.

Constantine Poulos, "Revolution in Eastern Europe," *Nation*, June 21, 1947.

James C. Thompson Jr., "How Could Vietnam Happen," *Atlantic Monthly*, April 1968.

U.S. News and World Report, "Bigger War for the U.S. in Asia?" August 17, 1964.

———, "One Continent Where Reds Are Busier Than Ever," November 2, 1959.

Websites

Communism Online, www.acerj.com/CommOnline. This privately run site offers a short history of the Soviet Union as well as a time line and biography section. Links to other sites on communism are provided.

History of China, www.chaos.umd.edu/history/toc.html. A privately run site offering a condensed history of China. Several pages deal with the People's Republic.

Manifesto of the Communist Party, www.anu.edu.au. The full text of *The Communist Manifesto* can be found at this site.

Marxist.org Internet Archive, www.marxists.org. A comprehensive site dealing with the origins and application of Marxist theory. Archival subjects range from art to women and Marxism.

Time 100: Leaders and Revolutionaries, www.time.com/time/time100. An online catalog that contains biographies and time lines of some of the most important Communist leaders of the twentieth century. The site is part of *Time* magazine online.

Index